Cost Management Guidebook

Fourth Edition

Steven M. Bragg

AccountingTools®

For more information about AccountingTools® products, visit our Web site at www.accountingtools.com.

ISBN-13: 978-1-64221-052-1

Printed in the United States of America

Table of Contents

Preface

One of the primary responsibilities of management is to ensure that costs are appropriately managed. This means that costs are focused on the primary needs of a business, and that controls are in place to keep other expenditures from taking place. In the *Cost Management Guidebook*, we explore how these analysis and control requirements can be achieved, while also including several hundred suggestions that are targeted at cost reductions throughout a business.

The *Cost Management Guidebook* gives you the tools to decide which costs are essential and which can be pared away, while also addressing the following topics:

- How can I use direct costing to analyze expenditure decisions?
- How can target costing be used to reduce the cost of a product?
- Why do certain cost objects accumulate more costs than others?
- How can I improve profitability by analyzing constraints?
- What specific strategies can I use to reduce costs?
- How can I put a lid on the costs of compensation and benefits?
- What are the techniques for enhancing the effectiveness of sales and marketing?
- What is the best process flow to reduce the total cost of procurement?
- How can I reduce the cost of company financing arrangements?
- What decision path should I follow when making capital budgeting decisions?
- Which reports and measurements can be used to support a system of cost management?

The *Cost Management Guidebook* is designed for both professional accountants and students, since both can benefit from its detailed approach to overhauling the entire system of corporate cost management. The book also provides enough specific cost reduction tips that you may spend years using them to drive down costs. As such, it may earn a place on your book shelf as a reference tool for years to come.

Centennial, Colorado
September 2020

About the Author

Steven Bragg, CPA, has been the chief financial officer or controller of four companies, as well as a consulting manager at Ernst & Young. He received a master's degree in finance from Bentley College, an MBA from Babson College, and a Bachelor's degree in Economics from the University of Maine. He has been a two-time president of the Colorado Mountain Club, and is an avid alpine skier, mountain biker, and certified master diver. Mr. Bragg resides in Centennial, Colorado. He has written more than 200 books and courses, including *New Controller Guidebook*, *GAAP Guidebook*, and *Payroll Management*.

Steven maintains the accountingtools.com web site, which contains continuing professional education courses, the Accounting Best Practices podcast, and thousands of articles on accounting subjects.

Buy Additional AccountingTools Courses

AccountingTools offers more than 1,200 hours of CPE courses, with concentrations in accounting, auditing, finance, taxation, and ethics. Related courses that you might like include:

- Activity-Based Costing
- Activity-Based Management
- Budgeting
- Capital Budgeting
- Cost Accounting Fundamentals
- Revenue Management

Go to accountingtools.com/cpe to view these additional courses.

AccountingTools®

Chapter 1
Overview of Cost Management

Introduction

The management of costs is an enormously important aspect of running a business, and yet is one that few companies pursue in an organized manner. In this chapter, we present the strongest possible case for cost management, including a discussion of how it impacts profits and a multitude of other advantages. We also note the ways in which control over costs can slip away from the management team, the environment needed to bring costs back under control, and several related topics.

The Economics of Cost Management

Close attention to managing costs is always worthwhile, because it can have a startling impact on profitability. However, the typical organization is far more oriented toward where its next sale will come from, rather than how to keep from incurring a few pennies of cost within the organization. While increasing sales is always a laudable goal, consider the impact of cost management on profitability. One dollar of sales may translate into 10% of before-tax profits, or perhaps much less. Let us assume that the average business is doing fairly well, and is earning 10% before income taxes. What if management decides to double profits? Either it has to double sales or remove 10 cents in costs. While removing the 10 cents in costs may not be easy, doing so is entirely under the control of the company. Conversely, doubling sales requires the agreement of customers, which may not be forthcoming. In short, it is usually easier to improve profits through cost reduction than through sales expansion.

It is useful to understand the formula for the equivalent amount of sales that must be generated to create an additional dollar of profit, since doing so creates a strong argument in favor of cost management. The formula is:

$$1 \div \text{Profit percentage} = \text{Equivalent sales volume}$$

EXAMPLE

Excalibur Shaving Company, maker of the world's sharpest razor blades, is under pressure from its investors to increase its dividend. The board of directors is concerned that the business cannot do so on a long-term basis without cutting into its cash reserves, and so asks the CFO to look into ways to increase profits that will help the company meet the demands of investors.

The company's before-tax profit margins are currently 15%, but total before-tax profits must double in order to provide the dividends demanded by investors, who require an extra

$1,000,000 of cash per year. One approach would be to double sales. However, the razor blade market is no longer growing, so doubling sales would require a radical drop in prices to lure customers away from competitors, thereby leaving no additional margin. The only alternative is to chop expenses throughout the organization.

If the CFO can find $1,000,000 of cost savings within the business, the amount of additional revenues that the company will not have to generate is $6,666,667, which is calculated as follows:

$$(1 \div 15\% \text{ Profit margin}) \times \$1,000,000 \text{ Required profit increase} = \$6,666,667$$

As an example of the multiplier effect associated with generating additional profits, a company that earns five cents on the dollar can earn an additional five cents either by saving that amount of cost, or by generating 20 times that amount in revenues. Or, to take the case of a *very* profitable organization, a business that earns 25 cents on the dollar can earn an additional amount either by saving 25 cents or by generating four times that amount in revenues. Thus, the multiplier effect makes it much easier to increase profits through proper cost management than through revenue improvements.

In short, increasing profits always presents management with a choice of either reducing costs or increasing revenues by a much larger amount.

How Costs Increase

There are many ways in which a company can gradually lose control over its costs. In the following bullet points, we note several of the more common ways in which costs can expand over time:

- *Differentiation strategy.* Management may decide that it will pursue a differentiation strategy, where it provides high-end goods or services to customers. Since this strategy inherently involves high prices, management can make the mistake of assuming that the underlying cost structure can also be quite high. This is not the case. Those aspects of the business that support the customer relationship will certainly require additional expenditures, but all other aspects of the business must still be subjected to a detailed and ongoing cost review. Companies pursuing differentiation strategies frequently ignore costs, which eventually causes trouble when their bloated cost structures interfere with their performance.
- *Fast growth.* A common reason for the failure of cost management is when management sees an opportunity to expand, and so spends all of its time focusing on revenue growth, rather than cost control. This situation is especially common when additional company locations are added and the new managers of these locations are insufficiently trained in controlling costs.

- *Management by example.* If a business goes through a period of earning unusually large profits, there will be a tendency by management to indulge in the excess cash flow to spend more than would normally be considered prudent. By the time profits eventually decline back to the industry norm (or below), management's example of excessive spending will have likely spread throughout the organization.
- *Natural cost inflation.* Unless acted upon vigorously, costs always increase due to inflation. This is particularly true for compensation costs, where there is an expectation among employees that some sort of pay raise will be granted every year, both to offset the effects of inflation and to reward them for their increased level of experience with the business.
- *Old systems.* The systems that a company initially installs must be upgraded over time to accommodate the growth of the business. If not, holes will appear in the system of controls and archaic systems will still be used to run major processes, resulting in inordinately high expenditures.
- *System complexity.* The systems used by a business will increase in complexity over time. For example, a company gradually expands its product line, which calls for better inventory tracking, enhanced production scheduling, and expanded marketing. As another example, a company starts off by only accepting cash payments, but later grants credit, which calls for a credit granting function and the ability to monitor the amount of available credit remaining. Whenever complexity increases, so too does the amount of staff required to manage the system, along with more specialized positions (such as a credit manager, for the second example just described).
- *Traditional expenditures.* Once a cost is incurred, employees become accustomed to it and begin to consider it an essential part of the business, which makes it more difficult to eradicate at a later date. For example, covered parking is probably not necessary, but is viewed by employees as a useful benefit. Similarly, a Friday afternoon staff party may become a fixture of the company culture, but is not actually necessary.
- *Unconsolidated acquisitions.* When a business buys another company, it is also acquiring all of the different procedures, processes, computer systems, forms and traditions of the acquiree – all of which are different from those of the acquirer. Unless the acquirer actively works on standardizing all of these items, it is likely that the combined entity will have a higher level of complexity when viewed as a combined entity. After a few of these unconsolidated acquisitions, the business as a whole may become so complex that it is essentially unmanageable.

The main takeaway from the preceding list is how easy it is to experience a runaway cost situation. But if you can find a way to take control of this cost train wreck, the advantages noted in the next section can yield a very favorable operating environment.

Advantages of Cost Management

When management first signs on to a program of cost management, the intent is usually just to increase profits. However, there are additional advantages that such a program can realize, because of the continuing examination of how the business operates. Also, the extra cash generated by the program can be re-employed within the business. Consider the following positive effects:

- *Adaptability.* When a business pays close attention to its costs, this means it is also paying close attention to its systems. Consequently, it is more capable of adapting to changing circumstances by altering those systems. For example, a business that experiences a sudden collapse in a key market is more likely to survive the experience through a rapid changeover in those costs and systems that it knows so well.
- *Complexity reduction.* A natural outcome of cost management is the realization that less complex systems are less expensive. Thus, the ongoing analysis of costs will likely yield a reduction in the complexity of products, product lines, production facilities, processes, and various administrative activities. Also, unrelated business units are more likely to be spun off or shut down. Further, less complexity requires fewer analysts to manage the complexity. The end result of complexity reduction should be a business that is easier to manage and is more tightly focused.
- *Funding buffer.* Active cost management gives a business extra cash in comparison to its competitors. This means that each sale generates more margin, and that overhead expenditures are reduced, resulting in a larger balance in the corporate bank account. This extra cash gives the business a buffer in the event of a downturn in sales, and more time with which to roll out new products. In short, the resulting funding buffer can yield a serious competitive advantage.
- *Pricing pressure.* In some industries, there is constant pressure from competitors to reduce the price points for products, especially in the consumer goods arena. If this is the case, a strong cost management program can ensure that profits are not whittled away by ongoing rounds of price reductions. Severe pricing pressure is a particular problem in those industries where the cost structure is primarily fixed; in this situation, competitors are more willing to drive down prices in order to fill their unused capacity.
- *Reinvestment.* With the extra cash generated by a cost management system, it is easier to find funding for a number of activities that can contribute to the long-term competitiveness of the business and the cohesion of its workforce. For example, fixed assets can be replaced in a timely manner, equipment maintenance is always performed on time, targeted training can be assigned to employees, and an adequate research and development process can be maintained.

- *Strategic view of costs*. A business that attends to its costs knows when to incur or avoid overhead costs. Though it may seem that overhead is to be avoided at all times, this is not really the case. The corporate strategy may call for a large expenditure in a particular area, such as a chain of distribution warehouses, or an advanced product design center. When management has a full understanding of company costs, it knows when to make these key expenditures, and to keep piling on funding in the future in order to maintain its strategic advantage.

Cost management tends to be a process of small gains, compounded over time. There may initially be a few cases where large amounts of unnecessary costs are peeled away, but the instances of these "low hanging fruit" items will dwindle over time. Instead, the real victories in cost management are a multitude of minor improvements. The gains may initially appear small – perhaps a 1% reduction in costs in a year, or the avoidance of a 1% gain in costs over a year. But consider the effect in comparison to a competitor that does not engage in this detailed level of cost management. Over time, the company opens up a sizeable cost advantage over its competitor, which can be used in a variety of ways. For example, the company may be able to afford a price reduction for a key product, allowing it to take market share away from the competitor. Or, the resulting increased cash flow allows the company to acquire the competitor. In short, a long-term focus on cash management gives a business a notable competitive advantage.

The Cost Management Environment

It is not sufficient to simply march into the office one day and declare that the company will now engage in cost management. A great deal more is needed to ensure that cost management becomes a key focus of the business. Consider the following improvements that must be made:

- *Managers as role models*. Employees model their behavior on what their bosses do. If they observe that managers talk about cost management but continue to pay for lavish travel and entertainment lifestyles, chances are good that employees will ignore the cost management speeches. Only by practicing what they preach and being parsimonious spenders will managers find that employees show an interest in cost management.
- *Qualified managers*. It is particularly important that the business have a cost-oriented CFO, controller, and cost accountant that can continually maintain pressure on the organization to review costs. This includes an ongoing series of cost investigations that they bring to the attention of the senior management team, as well as feedback loops to inform every one of their progress toward cost management goals.
- *Consistent enforcement*. There should be no pockets of free spending within the company. Instead, management should ensure that costs are examined with great care in all departments. This approach even applies to

those areas where additional expenditures are considered a strategic necessity. In this latter case, it is still possible to be prudent in making expenditures, even while addressing a strategic necessity. For example, if a strategic imperative requires that a new distribution warehouse be installed in a new sales region, this does not prevent a prudent company from acquiring the property on the best possible terms and investigating the purchase of second-hand storage racks for the warehouse.

- *Persistent enforcement.* Cost management never ends, so a great deal of effort is required to ensure that the organization maintains its focus on this topic. This means not being diverted by "flavor of the month" initiatives. Instead, the entire workforce must be intent on the less-glamorous grind of examining every cost, over and over again.

- *Strong controls.* A set of carefully-selected control points, such as requiring a department manager's approval on a purchase requisition, can be of assistance in reducing the number of egregious and unnecessary expenditures. However, the number of cost controls should be limited to those locations where they can provide the most assistance, since an excessive number of controls interfere with the smooth flow of operations.

- *Cost responsibility.* Someone should be held accountable for every cost. This does not just mean that each department manager is responsible for the costs incurred by his or her department. Instead, the concept extends deeper into the organization, potentially encompassing every employee.

- *Reporting.* The reporting system should be a tool for cost management. This means that a complete set of reports should be generated that identifies expenditures, as well as a report distribution system that pushes this information out into the organization. See the Responsibility Reporting section in the *Cost Management Reports* chapter for more information.

- *Immediate feedback.* There should be a culture of setting short-term cost management goals on an ongoing basis, which is reinforced by continual feedback from the reporting system that was just mentioned. Otherwise, cost management becomes an ephemeral long-term goal that people only talk about as part of the annual budgeting process, and which is therefore not pursued with any vigor.

All of the preceding items are general principles to be followed in a high-performance cost management environment. In addition, we must point out an enormous cost trap, which is acquisitions and strategic partnerships. The attention of the management team can be seriously diverted by an acquisition for months or even years, which means that it is not attending to cost management of the original business. Further, the majority of acquisitions and partnerships have been proven to lose money. Consequently, unless there is a strong strategic imperative to engage in these activities, do not do so. Or, stated differently, do not engage in casual acquisitions and strategic partnerships.

The Customer Service Conundrum

One of the largest unintended effects of cost management is that some changes may impact customers in a negative manner. Cost management can have all of the following negative effects on customers:

- Slower customer service response times
- Reduced product quality
- Slower delivery of orders
- Slower field service

In some situations, management can plan around these effects by only imposing them on the least profitable customers. Thus, a highly-profitable customer may be assigned a specific customer service contact person who is always available, while a marginal customer may have to call a general customer service line and listen to an automated voice response system. However, these effects should be intentional and well-planned, rather than unintended.

There are several ways to keep cost management from interfering with the customer experience. For example, a customer experience manager could be appointed who must review all changes that impact customers. Alternatively, senior management could mandate that all other areas besides customer-centric functions be addressed first in a cost management program. Another possibility is to link a benchmarking study with any proposed cost reductions that affect customers, to ensure that the impact will still place the company above the median in customer service issues. Yet another alternative is to enroll several key customers in a review panel that states its opinion on cost reductions before they are implemented.

Another view of cost management is from the ethical perspective. Under no circumstances should certain costs ever be cut back to the point where customers are endangered. For example, purchasing lower-quality parts could cause a baby stroller to collapse, injuring an infant. Or using a less expensive but also less qualified maintenance company could cause a plane to crash. Or scrimping on hazardous waste storage could cause these wastes to pollute the areas near a factory. In these situations, the ethical issues alone should drive management to spend more, rather than less. In addition, consider the long-term impact on a business that has cut costs in these areas, and which then faces catastrophic damage claims. Perhaps the best way to deal with customer-endangerment issues is to take a proactive stance by spending *more* in these areas and then marketing the fact that the business is a leader in ensuring customer safety.

The Effects of Cutting Too Deep

It is easy for an overly enthusiastic management team to cut too deeply into a business to save every last shred of excess cost. By doing so, the following negative effects may arise:

- *Loss of knowledge.* When pursuing cost reductions, a common outcome is that the more expensive employees are laid off. However, the reason these employees are more expensive is that they have accumulated more knowledge about the company, its processes, products, and customers than their lower-cost replacements. Consequently, a business may suffer a gradual erosion in its abilities over time, resulting in the loss of its competitive advantage. Further, the laid-off employees are likely to be hired by competitors, thereby transferring the company's knowledge base to the competition.
- *Loss of capacity.* If there is excess capacity in a business, a likely outcome of a cost management system is that this capacity will be gradually reduced. Eventually, the company may find that it is unable to respond to any surges in customer demand unless it embarks on an expensive and time-consuming reacquisition of capacity. A loss of capacity is particularly damaging in a growth industry where the market itself is expanding in size, and where merely generating the same sales from period to period means that a business is losing market share.
- *Loss of quality.* Product quality may decline, since costs are being stripped out of products and the quality of raw materials may be reduced. Similarly, the quality of services may decline if lower-cost employees are hired who have less experience, or if they are provided with less training. This problem can have a direct impact on customer satisfaction, and therefore on customer retention.

These issues will inevitably reduce the competitiveness of a business, leading to its eventual decline. Consequently, as you proceed through the remainder of this book, be aware of the negative effects of pursuing certain types of cost reductions.

A Note of Caution

In this chapter, we have noted a number of reasons why a firm should pay close attention to its costs. However, this does not mean that a company should necessarily use an ongoing program of cost reduction as the basis for a low-price strategy. According to an article published in the April 2013 edition of the *Harvard Business Review*, those companies performing at the most superior levels consistently do so by competing based on such differentiators as durability, convenience, or functionality, rather than having the lowest prices. For example, a plumbing firm that is willing to show up late at night can charge a massive price for doing so, while a lower-cost firm that only operates during normal hours will not receive the business at all. Because of the competitive positions taken by these firms, they can charge unusually high prices, which translate into a high gross margin percentage. In these cases, profits are so high that they can afford to incur higher costs than anyone else in their industries. In short, it can make sense to deliberately incur higher costs in order to establish a competitive position that allows a business to charge higher prices, thereby garnering higher profits.

Summary

This chapter has addressed why cost management is so vital to the success of a business, while also presenting the dangers of cutting costs too deeply. Having presented an overview of cost management, we move in the next chapters to a discussion of the types of costs in a business, as well as a number of cost analysis tools. After that, we address the major cost areas – compensation, benefits, sales and marketing, production, procurement, administration, and more. By the end of this book, you should have a good idea of which costs are most easily managed, and how to prudently reduce them while still maintaining the strategic direction of your business.

Chapter 2
Types of Costs

Introduction

Before delving into the many tools available for managing the cost structure of a business, it is useful to first understand the types of costs that a business can incur. By doing so, you can gain an understanding of which costs can be included in a decision model, the time periods over which costs change, how costs react to changes in activity, and similar issues. In this chapter, we describe the types and characteristics of several types of costs. While reviewing this material, keep in mind that some costs may have characteristics of *several* of the general cost types described below.

Fixed Costs

A fixed cost is a cost that does not vary in the short term, irrespective of changes in production or sales levels. Here are several examples of fixed costs:

- Amortization
- Depreciation
- Insurance
- Interest expense
- Property taxes
- Rent
- Salaries

Over the long term, few (if any) costs are truly fixed. For example, a thirty-year lease can be eliminated after the thirtieth year, so the expense is actually variable if viewed over a 31-year time period.

Companies with a high proportion of fixed costs (such as an oil refinery) have a high breakeven point, above which they earn outsized profits, but below which they may incur large losses. Companies with a low proportion of fixed costs have a low breakeven point, above which they earn more modest profits, and below which their risk of loss is reduced.

Companies with high fixed costs have a greater incentive to engage in price wars to gain some additional incremental revenue, because they can recognize the bulk of these additional revenues as profit.

EXAMPLE

Gatekeeper Corporation has constructed a toll road, for which it charges a fee of $1.00 per vehicle. The cost to operate the toll road is almost entirely fixed, at $200,000 per month. If 200,000 drivers use the road, the company breaks even. In August, a massive flu outbreak reduces driver volume to just 80,000 trips, so the business loses $120,000. In the next month, the flu outbreak is over and driver volume returns to a higher level of 240,000 trips, so the company earns a profit of $40,000.

Variable Costs

A variable cost is a cost that varies in relation to production volume, the amount of services provided, or some other activity measure. In the absence of any type of activity, there should be no variable costs. Here are several examples of variable costs, mostly related to a production environment:

- Direct materials
- Piece rate labor
- Production supplies
- Billable staff wages
- Commissions
- Credit card fees
- Freight out

To calculate total variable costs, the formula is:

Total quantity of units produced × Variable cost per unit = Total variable cost

Direct materials are considered a variable cost. Direct labor may not be a variable cost if labor is not added to or subtracted from the production process as production volumes change. Most types of overhead are not considered a variable cost.

If a business has a large proportion of variable costs in its cost structure, then most of its expenses will vary in direct proportion to revenues, so it can weather a business downturn better than a company that has a high proportion of fixed costs.

EXAMPLE

Laid Back Corporation manufactures business chairs. The cost of the direct materials used to manufacture its Executive Sweet chair is $320. There is also a piece rate payment to the production staff of $15 for every chair that is produced without defects, and a 3% commission on the sale of each unit sold, for which the net retail price is $1,000. Based on this information, the variable cost of the chair is $365 (calculated as $320 of materials, $15 of labor, and $30 of commissions).

11

Another cost related to the production of this chair is $200 of factory overhead. However, since the total pool of factory overhead costs does not vary within the likely range of production volumes, it is not considered a variable cost.

Mixed Costs

A mixed cost is a cost that contains both a fixed and variable component. It is of some importance to understand the mix of these elements of a cost, in order to predict how costs will change with different levels of activity. Typically, a portion of a mixed cost may be present in the absence of all activity, in addition to which the cost may also vary in proportion to changes in some type of activity.

As the level of usage of a mixed cost item increases, the fixed component will not change, while the variable component will increase. The formula for this relationship is:

$$Y = a + bx$$

Y = Total cost
a = Total fixed cost
b = Variable cost per unit of activity
x = Number of units of activity

EXAMPLE

Nefarious Industries owns a building, for which the total cost incurred is a mixed cost. The depreciation associated with the asset is a fixed cost, since it does not vary from year to year, while the utilities expense varies depending on usage of the building. The fixed cost of the building is $100,000 per year, while the variable cost of utilities is $250 per occupant. If the building contains 100 occupants, the mixed cost calculation is:

$100,000 Fixed cost + ($250/occupant × 100 occupants) = $125,000

EXAMPLE

Oberlin Acoustics has a broadband contract with the local cable company, which it pays $500 per month for the first 500 gigabytes of usage per month, after which the price increases by $1 per gigabyte used. The following table shows the mixed cost nature of the situation, where there is a baseline fixed cost, above which the cost increases at the same pace as usage:

Gigabytes	Variable Cost	Fixed Cost	Total Cost
500	$0	$500	$500
600	100	500	600
700	200	500	700
800	300	500	800
900	400	500	900

Mixed costs are common in a corporation, since many departments require a certain amount of baseline fixed costs in order to support any activities at all, and also incur variable costs to provide different quantities of service above the baseline level of support.

The *high-low method* can be used to separate out the fixed and variable portions of a mixed cost. The essential concept is to collect the cost at a high activity level and again at a low activity level, and then extract the fixed and variable components from this information.

EXAMPLE

Billabong Machining Company produces 10,000 green widgets in June at a cost of $50,000, and 5,000 green widgets in July at a cost of $35,000. There was an incremental change between the two periods of $15,000 and 5,000 units, so the variable cost per unit during July must be $15,000 divided by 5,000 units, or $3 per unit.

The high-low method is subject to several problems that tend to yield inaccurate results. The problems are:

- *Outlier data.* Either the high or low point information (or both) used for the calculation might not be representative of the costs normally incurred at those volume levels, due to outlier costs that are higher or lower than would normally be incurred. This problem can be mitigated by collecting information at other activity levels and affirming the fixed and variable relationships at these other levels.
- *Step costs.* Some costs are only incurred at specific volume points and not below those volumes. If a step cost occurred at a volume level between the high and low points used for the calculation, costs would rise because of

the step cost, and be incorrectly considered variable costs when the increase is really due to an increased fixed cost.

- *Estimate only*. There are too many variables that can impact both the costs and unit volumes required for the calculation. For example, the unit volume may be lower than usual because a batch of product was scrapped, or the cost may be higher because overtime costs were incurred to run a production line longer than usual.

Because of these issues, the high-low method does not yield overly precise results.

Step Costs

A step cost is a cost that does not change steadily with changes in activity volume, but rather at discrete points. A step cost is a fixed cost within certain boundaries, outside of which it will change. When stated on a graph, step costs appear to be incurred in a stair step pattern, with no change over a certain volume range, then a sudden increase, then no change over the next (and higher) volume range, then another sudden increase, and so on. The same pattern applies in reverse when the volume of activity declines.

For example, a facility cost will remain steady until additional floor space is constructed, at which point the cost will increase to a new and higher level as the entity incurs new costs to maintain the additional floor space, to heat and air condition it, and so forth.

As another example, a company can produce 10,000 widgets during one eight-hour shift. If the company receives additional customer orders for more widgets, then it must add another shift, which requires the services of an additional shift supervisor. Thus, the cost of the shift supervisor is a step cost that occurs when the company reaches a production requirement of 10,001 widgets. This new level of step costs will continue until yet another shift must be added, at which point the company will incur another step cost for the shift supervisor for the night shift.

Step costing is extremely important to be aware of when a company is about to reach a new and higher activity level, since a large new cost may be incurred. In some cases, incurring the extra amount of a step cost may eliminate profits that management had been expecting to accompany an increase in volume. If the increase in volume is relatively minor, but still calls for incurring a step cost, it is possible that profits will actually *decline*; a close examination of this issue may result in a business turning away sales in order to maintain its profitability.

Conversely, a company should be aware of step costs when its activity level declines, so that it can reduce costs in an appropriate manner to maintain profitability. This may require an examination of the costs of terminating staff, selling off equipment, or tearing down structures.

The point at which a step cost will be incurred can be delayed by implementing production efficiencies, which increase the number of units that can be produced with the existing production configuration.

Marginal Costs

Marginal cost is the cost of one additional unit of output. Marginal costing is used to determine the optimum production quantity for a company, where it costs the least amount to produce additional units. If a company operates within this "sweet spot," it can maximize its profits.

For example, a production line currently creates 10,000 widgets at a cost of $30,000, so that the average cost per unit is $3.00. However, if the production line creates 10,001 units, the total cost is $30,002, so the marginal cost of the one additional unit is only $2. This is a common effect, because there is rarely any additional overhead cost associated with a single unit of output, resulting in a lower marginal cost.

In some cases, step costs may take effect (see the preceding Step Costs section), so that the marginal cost is actually much higher than the average cost for a unit. To use the same example, what if the company must start up a new production line on a second shift in order to create unit number 10,001? If so, the marginal cost of this additional unit might be vastly higher than $2 – it may be thousands of dollars, because the business has to start up an extra production line to create that single unit.

A more common situation lying between the preceding two alternatives is when a production facility operating near capacity simply pays overtime to its employees for them to work somewhat longer to create that one additional unit. If so, the marginal cost will increase to include the cost of overtime, but not to the extent caused by a step cost.

The marginal cost of customized goods tends to be quite high, whereas it is very low for highly standardized products that are manufactured in bulk.

Differential Costs

Differential cost is the difference between the cost of two alternative decisions, or of a change in output levels. The concept is used to reach decisions about which alternatives to pursue, and which to drop. The concept can be particularly useful in step costing situations, where producing one additional unit of output may require a substantial additional cost. Here are two examples:

- *Alternative decisions.* There is a choice between running a fully-automated operation that produces 100,000 widgets per year at a cost of $1,200,000, or of using direct labor to manually produce the same number of widgets for $1,400,000. The differential cost between the two alternatives is $200,000.
- *Change in output.* A work center can produce 10,000 widgets for $29,000 or 15,000 widgets for $40,000. The differential cost of the additional 5,000 widgets is $11,000.

In essence, the revenues and expenses from one decision can be lined up next to similar information for the alternative decision, and the difference between all line items in the two columns is the differential cost.

A differential cost can be a variable cost, a fixed cost, or a mixed cost. The concept does not focus on the nature of a cost, but rather on the gross difference between the costs of the alternatives or changes in output.

Discretionary Costs

A discretionary cost is a cost or capital expenditure that can be curtailed or even eliminated in the short term without having an immediate impact on short-term output. Management may reduce discretionary costs when there are cash flow difficulties, or when it wants to present enhanced short-term earnings. However, a prolonged period of reduction in discretionary costs gradually reduces the quality of a company's product pipeline, reduces awareness by customers, increases machine downtime, and may also decrease product quality and increase employee turnover. Examples of discretionary costs are:

- Advertising
- Employee training
- Equipment maintenance
- Research and development

Committed Costs

A committed cost is an investment that a business entity has already made and cannot recover by any means, as well as obligations already made that the business cannot get out of. Be aware of which costs are committed costs when reviewing a company's expenditures for possible cutbacks or asset sales.

For example, if a company buys a machine for $40,000 and also issues a purchase order to pay for a maintenance contract for $2,000 in each of the next three years, all $46,000 is a committed cost, because the company has already bought the machine and has a legal obligation to pay for the maintenance. A multi-year property lease agreement is also a committed cost for the full term of the lease, since it is extremely difficult to terminate a lease agreement.

Sunk Costs

A sunk cost is a cost that an entity has incurred, and which it can no longer recover by any means. Sunk costs should not be considered when making the decision to continue investing in an ongoing project, since the cost cannot be recovered. However, many managers continue investing in projects because of the sheer size of the amounts already invested in the past. They do not want to "lose the investment" by curtailing a project that is proving to not be profitable, so they continue pouring more cash into it. Rationally, they should consider earlier investments to be sunk costs, and therefore exclude them from consideration when deciding whether to continue with further investments.

EXAMPLE

Kelvin Corporation spends $50,000 on a marketing study to see if its new water-based thermometer will succeed in the marketplace. The study concludes that the device will not be profitable. At this point, the $50,000 is a sunk cost. Kelvin should not continue with further expenditures for the project, despite the amount of its earlier investment.

Summary

Several types of costs were outlined in this chapter, which we will refer to in a variety of discussions later in this book. When reference is made to any of these costs, please note that a specific cost rarely can be considered a pure cost type. That is, a cost that can be considered entirely fixed or variable is rather uncommon. Instead, costs are likely to contain elements of several types of costs. For example, a credit card fee might initially appear to be an entirely variable cost, until you consider that the fee contains a small minimum charge that represents a fixed cost. Further, the credit card fee may decline after a certain amount of charging volume is reached, which is a reverse step cost. Consequently, the treatment of a cost cannot be in accordance with a black-and-white concept. Instead, each cost tends to incorporate a unique set of features that places it within the boundaries of several types of costs at once.

Chapter 3
Direct Costing as an Analysis Tool

Introduction

Direct costing is a specialized form of cost analysis that only uses variable costs to make decisions. It is extremely useful for short-term decisions, but can lead to harmful results if used for long-term decision making. In this chapter, we will describe the concept, as well as those situations in which it is most useful, and the scenarios where it can lead to incorrect conclusions.

Overview of Direct Costing

In brief, direct costing is the analysis of incremental costs. Direct costs are most easily illustrated through examples, such as:

- The costs actually consumed when a product is manufactured
- The incremental increase in costs when production is ramped up
- The costs that disappear when a production line is shut down
- The costs that disappear when an entire subsidiary is shut down

The examples show that direct costs can vary based upon the level of analysis. For example, when reviewing the direct cost of a single product, the only direct cost may be the materials used in its construction. However, if you are contemplating shutting down an entire company, then the direct costs are *all* costs incurred by that company – including all of its production and administrative costs. The main point to remember is that a direct cost is any cost that changes as the result of either a decision or a change in volume.

Direct costs do not necessarily align with the way in which costs are accumulated in an accounting system, which calls for some selective cost extraction from various sources to arrive at the proper set of direct costs.

EXAMPLE

The management of Dude Skis wants to know how much it will cost to increase production of its Drag Knuckle Skis from 5,000 units to 8,000 units, so that it can sell the additional 3,000 skis for a wholesale price (in aggregate) of $900,000. The most obvious direct cost is the cost of the wood core and graphite laminate used in the skis, at a cost of $150 per pair of skis. In addition, the company will require three additional staff whose labor cost will be $25 per pair of skis. Finally, the company must lease a lamination machine for $30,000, which it can then return to the lessor after the production run is complete.

For the purposes of this specific production-increase decision, then, the associated direct costs are:

Incremental revenue	$900,000
Cost of materials ($150 × 3,000 units)	450,000
Cost of labor ($25 × 3,000 units)	75,000
Cost of lamination machine	30,000
Total of all direct costs	555,000
Contribution margin	$355,000

Note in the preceding example that the financial analyst could probably obtain the cost of materials from the existing bill of materials for the Drag Knuckle ski, but would have to obtain the labor cost from the production manager, and the lamination machine's lease cost from the industrial engineering manager. Thus, it is clear that much of the information needed for a direct costing analysis does not come from the accounting database; in addition, it may involve nothing more than estimated costs, since the analysis involves an action that has not yet taken place, and for which there is no exact cost information.

A key issue with direct costing is the large variety of costs that are ignored. In the preceding example, note the absence of any costs related to the management of the production facility, or an administrative charge, or machine setup labor by the engineering staff. The reason these costs are not included is that the costs are the same, whether or not the company elects to increase its ski production. Only costs exhibiting incremental changes as a result of the decision are included in a direct costing analysis.

Contribution Margin versus Gross Margin

The typical direct costing question may simply be "how much money do I *save* if..." but it may also be, "how much money do I *make* if..." In the latter case, the answer requires giving management not only a listing of direct costs, but also the projected amount of earnings. Doing so usually involves the *contribution margin*, which is calculated as revenues minus all direct costs. This measurement varies from the more common gross margin, which also includes a deduction for allocated overhead costs. Since overhead costs are almost never categorized as direct costs, use the contribution margin.

EXAMPLE

Dude Skis wants to create an entirely new line of skis that can be used separately to ski uphill, and then lock together into a single monoski for downhill use. It is called the Chump Ski. The company projects incremental revenues from the new line of skis of $1,000,000, as well as incremental labor costs of $200,000, incremental material costs of $400,000, overhead that is directly traceable to the new product of $120,000, and a general manufacturing overhead allocation of $80,000. The existing production equipment can accommodate the new product with no changes. The calculation of the margin on the Chump Ski line is:

	Contribution Margin Calculation	Gross Margin Calculation
Revenue	$800,000	$800,000
Expenses		
Materials	400,000	400,000
Labor	200,000	200,000
Traceable overhead	120,000	120,000
General overhead	--	80,000
Total expenses	720,000	800,000
Margin	$80,000	$0
Margin percentage	10%	0%

The contribution margin reveals a positive outcome of $80,000, while the gross margin calculation (which includes the general overhead allocation) shows no profit at all. If management only saw the gross margin calculation, it might elect to avoid rolling out the Chump Ski line, whereas the contribution margin might be sufficiently positive to encourage an alternative course of action.

Direct Costing as an Analysis Tool

Direct costing is of great use as an analysis tool. The following decisions all involve the use of direct costs as inputs to decision models. What is immediately noticeable in the examples accompanying these decision models is the simplicity and clarity of the direct costing format, because it deals with only a small subset of total costs – those that are impacted by the decision. All other costs are irrelevant for the purposes of the decision being addressed, and so can be excluded from the model. In particular, they contain no allocations of overhead, which are irrelevant for many short-term decisions.

Automation Investments

A common scenario is for a company to invest in automated production equipment in order to reduce the amount it pays to its direct labor staff. Under direct costing, the key information to collect is the incremental labor cost of any employees who will be terminated, as well as the new period costs to be incurred as part of the equipment purchase, such as the depreciation on the equipment and maintenance costs.

EXAMPLE

Dude Skis plans to acquire an automated graphics lamination machine, which it will use to laminate graphics onto its high-end skis. It plans to eliminate three direct labor positions and add one maintenance technician as a result of this change. The lamination machine costs $100,000 and will be depreciated over five years. The fully burdened cost of all three direct labor positions is $90,000, while the fully burdened cost of the new maintenance technician is $55,000. Dude's financial analyst constructs the following table to summarize the situation:

Direct cost additions	
Annual machine depreciation	+$20,000
Maintenance technician	+55,000
Direct cost deductions	
Direct labor positions	-90,000
Net change in direct costs	-$15,000

The table reveals that Dude should install the machine, since there will be a net decline in direct costs. Additional factors to consider might be any history of machine breakdowns that could lead to the rehire of the laid off workers, as well as the risk that the machine's manufacturer will go out of business and can therefore no longer support the machine. These are qualitative risk factors.

Cost Reporting

Direct costing is very useful for controlling variable costs, because a variance analysis report can be created that compares the actual variable cost to what the variable cost per unit should have been. Fixed costs are not included in this analysis, since they are associated with the period in which they are incurred, and so are not direct costs. A simple reporting format follows, which focuses the attention of management solely on direct costs.

EXAMPLE

Dude Skis closely tracks the direct cost of its skis, and does so by comparing actual variable costs per unit to budgeted costs. The following report shows its direct cost analysis for January production of its low-cost line of children's introductory skis.

Actual unit production = 2,703 ski pairs			
Variable Cost Item	Actual Cost per Unit	Budgeted Cost per Unit	Variance per Unit
Wood core	$42.50	$41.75	-$0.75
Fiberglas wrap	38.84	37.52	-1.32
Edging	4.11	4.03	-0.08
Tip and tail caps	0.39	0.42	+0.03
Lamination	4.72	4.73	+0.01
Totals	$90.56	$88.45	-$2.11

The report does not include direct labor, since Dude's management does not feel that labor costs vary sufficiently with production volumes to warrant being included in the report.

The example only showed direct costs. Management will likely want to also track its ability to control fixed costs, so it can use a separate report for those items that itemizes total period costs by expense type, as compared to budgeted amounts. An example appears in the following exhibit.

Fixed Cost Control Report

Fixed Cost Item	Actual Cost	Budgeted Cost	Variance
Accounting and legal	$12,500	$12,000	-$500
Insurance	7,400	7,200	-200
Salaries, administration	29,000	27,400	-1,600
Rent	18,000	18,000	0
Utilities	4,700	4,000	-700
Totals	$71,600	$68,600	-$3,000

Note that the direct cost variance analysis report was designed for costs at the individual unit level, while the fixed cost variance analysis report was designed for total costs in a period. It is easier for management to take remedial action by using these differing formats for different types of costs.

Customer Profitability

Some customers require a great deal of support, but also place such large orders that a company still earns a large profit from the relationship. If there are such resource-intensive situations, it makes sense to occasionally calculate how much money the company really earns from each customer. This analysis may reveal that the company would be better off eliminating some of its customers, even if this results in a noticeable revenue decline.

EXAMPLE

Dude Skis sells to Stuffy Skis, which is a high-end retailer of the most expensive all-mountain skis, as well as Warehouse Sports, which retails the lowest-cost skis through many outlets to beginner skiers. The skis that Dude sells to Stuffy have the highest margins, and Stuffy requires little administrative support. Warehouse buys in massive volume, but only buys low-margin items, and returns 20% of its purchases under various pretexts in order to clear out its inventory at the end of the season. Dude's management wants to know how much it earns from each customer, and whether it should drop either one. Dude's financial analyst constructs the following table:

	Stuffy Customer	Warehouse Customer
Revenue	$520,000	$2,780,000
Direct costs		
Materials	210,000	1,390,000
Direct labor	100,000	550,000
Customer service cost	0	130,000
Sales returns cost	0	600,000
Total direct costs	310,000	2,670,000
Contribution margin ($)	$210,000	$110,000
Contribution margin (%)	40%	4%

In the table, there is no customer service cost at all for Stuffy Skis, since no customer service positions would be eliminated if Dude were to drop Stuffy as a customer. On the other hand, there are four customer service employees assigned to the Warehouse Sports account who would be laid off if Dude were to drop that account.

The analysis reveals that Stuffy Skis produces far more contribution margin than Warehouse Sports, despite much lower revenues. However, this does not mean that Dude should eliminate Warehouse as a customer, since it still produces $110,000 of contribution margin. If Dude has a large amount of overhead to cover, it may be quite necessary to continue dealing with Warehouse Sports in order to retain the associated amount of contribution margin.

The preceding format can be expanded to include not just a single customer, but also sales for an entire region or product line.

Profit-Volume Relationship

Direct costing is useful for plotting changes in profit levels as sales volumes change. It is relatively simple to create a direct costing table, such as the one in the following example, which points out the volume levels at which additional direct costs will be incurred, so that management can estimate the amount of profit at different levels of corporate activity.

EXAMPLE

Dude Skis is conducting its annual budgeting process, and the financial analyst is called upon to create a profit-volume table that shows the amount of profit before taxes that Dude is likely to earn at different unit volume sales levels. The company currently produces 50,000 pairs of skis per year, and this figure is unlikely to decline. He learns that the company can produce an additional 10,000 pairs of skis without incurring any additional overhead costs. However, if the company expands production by an additional 20,000 pairs, it will incur an additional $750,000 in annual overhead expenses, and will likely also have to reduce its prices by 10% in order to achieve that volume level. Based on this information, he constructs the following table:

	Number of Skis Sold		
Number of ski pairs	50,000	60,000	70,000
Direct cost per pair of skis	$210	$210	$210
Net sales price per pair sold	380	380	342
Total revenue	19,000,000	22,800,000	23,940,000
Total direct cost	10,500,000	12,600,000	14,700,000
Total period cost	8,000,000	8,000,000	8,750,000
Profit	$500,000	$2,200,000	$490,000
Profit %	3%	10%	2%

The analysis reveals that Dude should certainly make every effort to increase its sales by an additional 10,000 units, since this will result in a significant improvement in its profitability. However, expanding by yet another 10,000 units may be a bad idea, since the company must accept lower per-unit prices as well as more overhead. In fact, the additional growth by 20,000 units, when coupled with an increased need for working capital and reduced profitability, may put the company in serious operating difficulties.

As just noted in the preceding example, include a working capital analysis with any profit-volume analysis, so that management can see the cost of expansion in terms of the increased investment in accounts receivable, payable, and inventory.

EXAMPLE

To continue with the preceding example, the management of Dude Skis is concerned about the working capital impact of expanding the business by 20,000 pairs of skis, and so it asks the financial analyst for a revised analysis that includes projected working capital costs for the base-line scenario of 50,000 units, and for the highest-volume scenario of 70,000 units. The following table presents this information:

	Number of Skis Sold	
Number of ski pairs	50,000	70,000
Total revenue	$19,000,000	$23,940,000
Profit	500,000	490,000
Working capital components		
+ Accounts receivable	+$1,600,000	+$2,400,000
+ Inventory	+3,200,000	+4,000,000
- Accounts payable	-1,100,000	-1,300,000
Total working capital	$3,700,000	$5,100,000

The working capital assumptions in the table are that the same proportions of inventory and accounts payable will carry forward from the 50,000 unit activity level to the 70,000 unit activity level. However, the accounts receivable investment is assumed to increase, since the company will be making many of the incremental sales to a new group of retailers who are assumed to pay slower than the current group of retailers.

The working capital analysis reveals that Dude Skis would have to invest an extra $1,400,000 in its business in order to grow to a 70,000 unit level, while earning a somewhat lower profit. Clearly, the company should avoid this expansion, though the 60,000 unit sales level noted in the preceding example has a much better payoff, and should be considered.

Outsourcing

Direct costing is useful for deciding whether to manufacture an item in-house or maintain a capability in-house, or whether to outsource it. If the decision involves manufacturing in-house or elsewhere, it is crucial to determine how many staff and which machines will actually be eliminated; in many cases, these resources are simply shifted elsewhere within the company, so there is no net profit improvement by shifting production to a supplier.

EXAMPLE

Dude Skis currently has a small plastic injection molding operation in-house, from which it molds the tip and tail guards for its skis. A local plastic injection molding firm visits Dude Skis and offers to produce these items for $0.41 per set. Management asks the financial analyst to determine whether this will result in improved profits for the company, using the assumption that the company would sell its injection molding machine if the supplier's offer is accepted.

According to Dude's cost records, the cost of a set of tip and tail guards is $0.56, which is comprised of the following items:

Cost Items	Direct Costs	Overhead
Resin	$0.25	
Color	0.02	
Scrap	0.01	
Injection molder depreciation	0.03	
Injection molder maintenance	0.02	
Injection molding labor	0.05	
Injection molding labor benefits	0.01	
Manufacturing overhead		$0.12
Administrative overhead		0.5
Total	$0.39	$0.17

In the preceding table, the injection molder depreciation cost of $0.03 per unit would not have been included if the company had chosen to keep the machine. However, since it plans to sell the machine if it accepts the supplier's offer, the depreciation is directly related to the decision, and so is a direct cost.

The costs comprising the overhead allocations will not decline if the company outsources this component, so the overhead is not a direct cost.

The table reveals that the direct costs associated with the analysis are lower than the supplier's offered price, so the company should reject the outsourcing option and continue to produce the tip and tail guards in-house. This decision is also reasonable from a risk management perspective, since Dude Skis would otherwise be permanently eliminating its capability to produce the part in-house, which could potentially leave it at the mercy of any price increases later imposed by the supplier.

Direct Costing Pitfalls

Direct costing is an analysis tool, but it is only usable for certain types of analysis. In some situations, it can provide incorrect results. This section describes the key issues with direct costing to be aware of.

Increasing Costs

Direct costing is sometimes targeted at whether to increase production by a specific amount in order to accept an additional customer order. For the purposes of this specific decision, the analyst usually assumes that the direct cost of the decision will be the same as the historical cost. However, the cost may actually increase. For example, if a machine is already running at 80% of capacity and a proposed decision will increase its use to 90%, this incremental difference may very well result in a disproportionate increase in the maintenance cost of the machine. Thus, be aware that a specific direct costing scenario may contain costs that are only relevant within a narrow range; outside of that range, costs may be substantially different.

EXAMPLE

Dude Skis has received an inquiry from a Japanese ski manufacturer that wants to outsource a production run of 5,000 skis. The total revenue from the proposed deal is $1,000,000 and Dude's direct cost is projected to be $800,000, which is based on the $700,000 of materials and $100,000 of labor required to manufacture the skis. Initially, it therefore appears that Dude can earn $200,000 on the deal.

However, Dude's production equipment is fully utilized during its single shift of operation, so this order will require employing a second shift that is paid a 10% shift differential, as well as an on-site supervisor and maintenance technician. There will also be an assumed 10% scrap rate caused by having a less well-trained work force on that shift. These additional costs are:

Cost Item	Amount
Overtime	$10,000
Scrap	70,000
Supervisor	65,000
Maintenance technician	45,000
Total	$190,000

Given that these additional costs leave a paltry $10,000 profit, Dude should either reject the inquiry or negotiate a higher price. The increased costs caused by the production being outside of Dude's normal operating range caused the deal (as proposed) to fail.

Indirect Costs

Direct costing does not account for indirect costs, because it is designed for short-term decisions where indirect costs are not expected to change. However, all costs change over the long term, which means that a decision that can impact a company over a long period of time should address long-term changes in indirect costs. Consequently, if a company uses an ongoing series of direct cost analyses to drive its pricing decisions, it may end up with an overall pricing structure that is too low to pay for its overhead costs. This is an especially pernicious problem for companies with a very high proportion of overhead costs, such as information technology companies that invest heavily in new products.

EXAMPLE

Dude Skis has a new software development group that has created a downloadable software product that allows skiers to track which runs they have skied each day, when tied into the global positioning chips on their smart phones. Under a direct costing analysis, the only cost to the company when a sale is made is a 2% credit card fee. However, Dude's programming team costs $200,000 per year, and charging a vanishingly small fee for the product will never pay for the overhead cost.

Instead, Dude's marketing manager conducts a survey of the market, learns that there is a potential market of 50,000 users at a price point of $10 per download, and accordingly prices the product at $10. This approach comfortably generates enough cash to pay for the related amount of overhead, also creates an additional profit, and is not based in any way on the direct cost of the product.

Relevant Range

A direct costing analysis is usually only valid within the constraints of the current capacity level. It requires a more sophisticated form of direct costing analysis to account for changes in costs as sales volumes or production volumes change. This shortcoming can be overcome by consulting with the industrial engineering staff to determine additional capacity costs.

EXAMPLE

Dude Skis is considering an expansion of a prototype skiing platform for disabled skiers. It constructed 100 units as a pilot project, and sold them easily at a price of $2,000 and a direct cost of $750 each. Initial forecasts indicate that Dude could sell 5,000 units per year. Thus, the initial analysis indicates that Dude could earn a contribution margin of $6,250,000 on this new opportunity.

The trouble is that the direct costing analysis is based on the costs incurred during a pilot project. Launching a fully-equipped and properly managed product line will introduce an additional $1,000,000 per year of depreciation costs, as well as $4,000,000 of overhead costs that are directly related to the product. Consequently, the new product will be more likely to earn $1,250,000 per year than the $6,250,000 that was initially indicated.

Summary

Direct costing is an excellent analysis tool for cost management. It is almost always used to create a model to answer a question about what actions management should take. It is most useful for short-term decisions, and least useful when a longer-term time frame is involved - especially in situations where a company must generate sufficient margins to pay for a large amount of overhead. Though useful, direct costing information is problematic in situations where incremental costs may change significantly, or where indirect costs may be pertinent to the decision.

Chapter 4
Cost-Volume-Profit Analysis

Introduction

We have thus far defined a number of cost types and the uses to which direct costing analysis can be put. In this chapter, we integrate fixed and variable costs into several additional tools that can be used for cost management. The concept of contribution margin is examined first, as well as how it can be employed in a different income statement format. We then use contribution margin to derive the breakeven point of a business, and discuss the uses to which breakeven analysis can be put. The breakeven concept is then extended to calculate the margin of safety. These issues are all components of cost-volume-profit analysis, for which we provide a number of examples. Finally, we address sales mix, which impacts the results of a cost-volume-profit analysis. In total, this chapter is intended to provide the reader with a view of how sales volumes interact with the cost structure of a business to achieve profitability.

Contribution Margin

The contribution margin is a product's price minus its variable costs, resulting in the incremental profit earned for each unit sold. The total contribution margin generated by an entity represents the total earnings available to pay for fixed expenses and generate a profit. The contribution margin concept can be applied throughout a business, for individual products, product lines, profit centers, subsidiaries, and for an entire organization.

The measure is useful for determining whether to allow a lower price in special pricing situations. If the contribution margin is excessively low or negative, it would be unwise to continue selling a product at that price point. It is also useful for determining the profits that will arise from various sales levels (see the next example). Further, the concept can be used to decide which of several products to sell if they use a common bottleneck resource, so that the product with the highest contribution margin is sold.

To determine the amount of contribution margin for a product, subtract all variable costs of a product from its revenues, and divide by its revenue. The calculation is:

$$\frac{\text{Product revenue} - \text{Product variable costs}}{\text{Product revenue}}$$

EXAMPLE

The Iverson Drum Company sells drum sets to high schools. In the most recent period, it sold $1,000,000 of drum sets that had related variable costs of $400,000. Iverson had $660,000 of fixed costs during the period, resulting in a loss of $60,000.

Revenue	$1,000,000
Variable expenses	400,000
Contribution margin	600,000
Fixed expenses	660,000
Net loss	-$60,000

Iverson's contribution margin is 60%, so if it wants to break even, the company needs to either reduce its fixed expenses by $60,000 or increase its sales by $100,000 (calculated as the $60,000 loss divided by the 60% contribution margin).

EXAMPLE

The president of Giro Cabinetry is examining the gross margins on the five products that his company sells. A summary of this information is:

Product	Sales Price	Variable Cost	Fixed Cost	Gross Margin	Contribution Margin
A	$100	$60	$30	10%	40%
B	200	100	60	20%	50%
C	75	25	23	36%	67%
D	400	300	120	-5%	25%
E	325	230	98	-1%	29%

Fixed costs are comprised of factory overhead, which is assigned to products based on their prices. Thus, a high-priced product will be assigned more fixed cost than a lower-priced product. However, there is no linkage between price and fixed cost, so the fixed cost allocations are artificial.

Based on the information in the table, the president might be tempted to cancel products D and E, since both have negative gross margins. However, if he were to do so, the factory overhead would still remain, and would not be allocated among the smaller number of remaining products, which would reduce their gross margins. Only by examining the contribution margin is it obvious that *all* of the products are profitable, and should be retained in order to generate sufficient profits to offset the total amount of fixed costs incurred by the company.

Contribution Margin Income Statement

A contribution margin income statement is an income statement in which all variable expenses are deducted from sales to arrive at a contribution margin, from which all fixed expenses are then subtracted to arrive at the net profit or loss for the period. Thus, the arrangement of expenses in the income statement corresponds to the nature of the expenses. This income statement format is a superior form of presentation, because the contribution margin clearly shows the amount available to cover fixed costs and generate a profit or loss. The format is particularly useful for determining the contribution margin for an entire product line or business unit, rather than for an individual product, as was described in the last section.

In essence, if there are no sales, a contribution margin income statement will have a zero contribution margin, with fixed costs clustered beneath the contribution margin line item. As sales increase, the contribution margin will increase in conjunction with sales, while fixed costs should remain approximately the same.

This form of income statement varies from a normal income statement in the following three ways:

- Fixed production costs are aggregated lower in the income statement, after the contribution margin;
- Variable selling and administrative expenses are grouped with variable production costs, so that they are a part of the calculation of the contribution margin; and
- The gross margin is replaced in the statement by the contribution margin.

The format of a contribution margin income statement appears in the following exhibit.

Contribution Margin Income Statement Layout

+	Sales
-	Variable production expenses (such as materials, supplies, and variable overhead)
-	Variable selling and administrative expenses (such as commissions)
=	Contribution margin
-	Fixed production expenses (including most overhead)
-	Fixed selling and administrative expenses (such as corporate expenses)
=	Net profit or loss

The key difference between the gross margin found in a normal income statement and the contribution margin in this format is that fixed production costs are included in the cost of goods sold to calculate the gross margin, whereas they are not included in the same calculation for contribution margin. This means that the contribution margin income statement is sorted based on the variability of the underlying cost information, rather than by the functional areas or expense categories found in a normal income statement.

It is useful to create an income statement in the contribution margin format when you want to determine that proportion of expenses that truly varies directly with revenues. In many businesses, the contribution margin will be substantially higher than the gross margin, because such a large proportion of its production costs are fixed, and few of its selling and administrative expenses are variable.

Breakeven Point

The breakeven point is the sales volume at which a business earns exactly no money, where all contribution margin earned is needed to pay for the company's fixed costs. The concept is most easily illustrated in the following chart, where fixed costs occupy a block of expense at the bottom of the table, irrespective of any sales being generated. Variable costs are incurred in concert with the sales level. Once the contribution margin on each sale cumulatively matches the total amount of fixed costs, the breakeven point has been reached. All sales above that level directly contribute to profits.

Breakeven Table

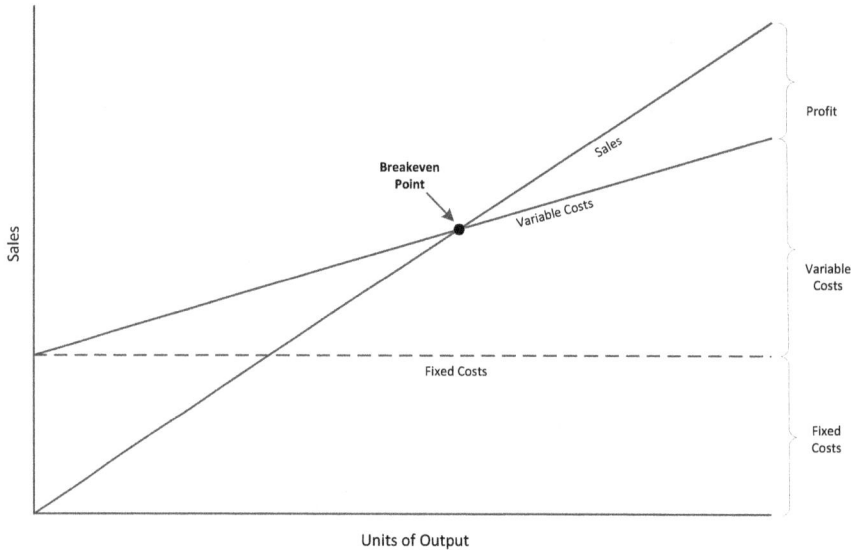

Knowledge of the breakeven point is useful for the following reasons:

- Determining the amount of remaining capacity after the breakeven point is reached, which reveals the maximum amount of profit that can be generated.
- Determining the impact on profit if automation (a fixed cost) replaces labor (a variable cost).
- Determining the change in profits if product prices are altered.

- Determining the amount of losses that could be sustained if the business suffers a sales downturn.

In addition, the breakeven concept is useful for establishing the overall ability of a company to generate a profit. When the breakeven point is near the maximum sales level of a business, this means it is nearly impossible for the company to earn a profit even under the best of circumstances.

Management should constantly monitor the breakeven point, particularly in regard to the last item noted, in order to reduce the breakeven point whenever possible. Ways to do this include:

- *Cost analysis.* Continually review all fixed costs, to see if any can be eliminated. Also review variable costs to see if they can be eliminated, since doing so increases margins and reduces the breakeven point.
- *Margin analysis.* Pay close attention to product margins, and push sales of the highest-margin items, thereby reducing the breakeven point.
- *Outsourcing.* If an activity involves a fixed cost, consider outsourcing it in order to turn it into a per-unit variable cost, which reduces the breakeven point.
- *Pricing.* Reduce or eliminate the use of coupons or other price reductions, since they increase the breakeven point.
- *Technologies.* Implement any technologies that can improve the efficiency of the business, thereby increasing capacity with no increase in cost.

To calculate the breakeven point, divide total fixed expenses by the contribution margin (which was described in an earlier section). The formula is:

$$\frac{\text{Total fixed expenses}}{\text{Contribution margin percentage}}$$

A more refined approach is to eliminate all non-cash expenses (such as depreciation) from the numerator, so that the calculation focuses on the breakeven cash flow level. The formula is:

$$\frac{\text{Total fixed expenses} - \text{Depreciation} - \text{Amortization}}{\text{Contribution margin percentage}}$$

Another variation on the formula is to focus instead on the number of units that must be sold in order to break even, rather than the sales level in dollars. This formula is:

$$\frac{\text{Total fixed expenses}}{\text{Average contribution margin per unit}}$$

EXAMPLE

The management of Ninja Cutlery is interested in buying a competitor that makes ceramic knives. The company's due diligence team wants to know if the competitor's breakeven point is too high to allow for a reasonable profit, and if there are any overhead cost opportunities that may reduce the breakeven point. The following information is available:

Maximum sales capacity	$5,000,000
Current average sales	$4,750,000
Contribution margin percentage	35%
Total operating expenses	$1,750,000
Breakeven point	$5,000,000
Operating expense reductions	$375,000
Revised breakeven level	$3,929,000
Maximum profits with revised breakeven point	$375,000

The analysis shows that the competitor has an inordinately high breakeven point that allows for little profit, if any. However, there are several operating expense reductions that can trigger a steep decline in the breakeven point. The management of Ninja Cutlery makes an offer to the owners of the competitor, based on the cash flows that can be gained from the reduced breakeven level.

A potential problem with the breakeven concept is that it assumes the contribution margin in the future will remain the same as the current level, which may not be the case. The breakeven analysis can be modeled using a range of contribution margins to gain a better understanding of possible future profits and losses at different unit sales levels. See the Sales Mix section for a discussion of variations in contribution margin.

EXAMPLE

Milford Sound sells a broad range of audio products. The CFO is concerned that the average contribution margin of these products has been slipping over the past few years, as customers have been switching to personal audio devices. The current average contribution margin is 38%, but the declining trend indicates that the margin could be 30% within two years. The CFO uses this information to construct the following breakeven analysis for the company:

	Current Case	Projected Case
Total fixed costs	$20,000,000	$20,000,000
÷ Contribution margin	38%	30%
= Breakeven sales	$52,632,000	$66,667,000

The calculation shows that the breakeven point will increase by $14 million over the next two years. Since Milford's current sales level is $58,000,000, this means that the company faces the alternatives of driving a massive sales increase, fixed cost reductions, or margin improvements in order to remain profitable.

Margin of Safety

The margin of safety is the reduction in sales that can occur before the breakeven point of a business is reached. The amount of this buffer is expressed as a percentage.

The margin of safety concept is especially useful when a significant proportion of sales are at risk of decline or elimination, as may be the case when a sales contract is coming to an end. By knowing the amount of the margin of safety, management can gain a better understanding of the risk of loss to which a business is subjected by changes in sales. The opposite situation may also arise, where the margin of safety is so large that a business is well-protected from sales variations.

To calculate the margin of safety, subtract the current breakeven point from sales, and divide the result by sales. The breakeven point is calculated by dividing the contribution margin into total fixed expenses. The formula is:

$$\frac{\text{Total current sales} - \text{Breakeven point}}{\text{Total current sales}}$$

To translate the margin of safety into the number of units sold, use the following formula instead:

$$\frac{\text{Total current sales} - \text{Breakeven point}}{\text{Selling price per unit}}$$

If the margin of safety is expressed as the number of units sold, the result works best if a company only sells one type of product. Otherwise, it can be difficult to translate the result into a range of products that have different price points and contribution margins.

EXAMPLE

Lowry Locomotion is considering the purchase of new equipment to expand the production capacity of its toy tractor product line. The addition will increase Lowry's operating costs by $100,000 per year, though sales will also be increased. Relevant information is noted in the following table:

	Before Machinery Purchase	After Machinery Purchase
Sales	$4,000,000	$4,200,000
Contribution margin percentage	48%	48%
Fixed expenses	$1,800,000	$1,900,000
Breakeven point	$3,750,000	$3,958,000
Profits	$120,000	$116,000
Margin of safety	6.3%	5.8%

The table reveals that both the margin of safety and profits worsen slightly as a result of the equipment purchase, so expanding production capacity is probably not a good idea.

Cost-Volume-Profit Analysis

Cost-volume-profit (CVP) analysis is designed to show how changes in product margins, prices, and unit volumes impact the profitability of a business. It is one of the fundamental financial analysis tools for ascertaining the underlying profitability of a business. The components of cost-volume-profit analysis are:

- *Activity level.* This is the total number of units sold in the measurement period.
- *Price per unit.* This is the average price per unit sold, including any sales discounts and allowances. The price per unit can vary substantially from period to period, based on changes in the mix of products and services, which may be caused by old product terminations, new product introductions, and the seasonality of sales.
- *Variable cost per unit.* This is the totally variable cost per unit sold, which is usually just the amount of direct materials and the sales commission associated with a unit sale. Nearly all other expenses do not vary with sales volume, and so are considered fixed costs.
- *Total fixed cost.* This is the total fixed cost of the business within the measurement period. This figure tends to be relatively steady from period to period, unless there is a step cost transition where the company has elected to incur an entirely new cost in response to a change in activity level (such as adding a production line).

These components can be mixed and matched in a variety of ways to arrive at different types of analysis. For example:

- What is the breakeven unit volume of a business? We divide the total fixed cost of the company by its contribution margin per unit. Thus, if a business has $50,000 of fixed costs per month, and the average contribution margin of a product is $50, then the necessary unit volume to reach a breakeven sales level is 1,000 units.

- What unit quantity is needed to achieve $__ in profits? We add the target profit level to the total fixed cost of the company, and divide by its contribution margin per unit. Thus, if the CEO of the business in the last example wants to earn $20,000 per month, we add that amount to the $50,000 of fixed costs, and divide by the average contribution margin of $50 to arrive at a required unit sales level of 1,400 units.

- If I add a fixed cost, what sales are needed to maintain profits of $__? We add the new fixed cost to the target profit level and original fixed cost of the business, and divide by the unit contribution margin. To continue with the last example, the company is planning to add $10,000 of fixed costs per month. We add that to the $70,000 baseline fixed costs and profit and divide by the $50 average contribution margin to arrive at a new required sales level of 1,600 units per month.

- If I cut unit prices by $__, how many additional units must be sold to maintain profit levels? To continue with the last example, the baseline fixed costs are $60,000, profits are $20,000, and the contribution margin is $50 per unit. The plan is to reduce the unit price by $10 in an attempt to increase sales. Doing so will decrease the contribution margin to $40. To calculate the total number of unit sales required, we divide the $40 contribution margin per unit into the combined fixed costs and profits to arrive at total unit sales of 2,000. Thus, if prices are cut by $10, unit sales must increase by 400 units from the last example in order to maintain profit levels.

In short, the various components of CVP analysis can be used to uncover the financial results arising from many possible scenarios.

EXAMPLE

The president of Micron Metallic is working through the annual budgeting process, and wants to know how many stamping machines the company must produce in the upcoming year in order to earn a target before-tax profit of $3,000,000. The business has $24,000,000 of fixed costs, and its contribution margin per unit is $20,000. The calculation of units to sell is:

$$\frac{\$24,000,000 \text{ Fixed costs} + \$3,000,000 \text{ Target profit}}{\$20,000 \text{ Contribution margin per unit}}$$

$$= 1,350 \text{ Units}$$

The analysis can be refined to include the impact of income taxes, so that the formula for establishing a target after-tax profit for a certain number of units sold becomes:

$$\frac{\text{Fixed costs} + (\text{Target profit} \div (1 - \text{Tax \%}))}{\text{Contribution margin per unit}}$$

EXAMPLE

To continue with the last example, the president of Micron Metallic wants to determine the number of stamping machines that must be sold in order to achieve an *after-tax* profit of $3,000,000, using the same information. The tax rate is 35%. The calculation is:

$$\frac{\$24,000,000 \text{ Fixed costs} + (\$3,000,000 \text{ Target profit} \div (1 - 35\%))}{\$20,000 \text{ Contribution margin per unit}}$$

$$= 1,431 \text{ Units}$$

We do not present a single cost-volume-profit formula, for there is no single formula that applies to all situations. Instead, the basic concept must be revised to meet the requirements of each financial analysis topic as it arises.

Sales Mix

Sales mix refers to the proportions of different products and services that comprise the total sales of a company. In most cases, each product or service that a company provides has a different contribution margin, so changes in sales mix (even if the total sales level remains the same) usually result in differing amounts of profit.

EXAMPLE

The CFO of Creekside Industrial is examining the sales and profit figures for the past two months, and is having difficulty understanding why sales were identical, but profits were radically different in the two months. He creates the following analysis of sales of the company's two types of batteries:

	January			February		
	Product A	Product B	Total	Product A	Product B	Total
Sales	$2,000,000	$3,500,000	$5,500,000	$4,000,000	$1,500,000	$5,500,000
Variable costs	1,600,000	1,400,000	3,000,000	3,200,000	600,000	3,800,000
Variable cost %	80%	40%	55%	80%	40%	69%
Contribution	400,000	2,100,000	2,500,000	800,000	900,000	1,700,000
Fixed costs			2,000,000			2,000,000
Profit (loss)			$500,000			-$300,000

Because sales have shifted between the two products, which have radically different contribution margins, the profit level is heavily impacted by the sales mix.

If a company introduces a new product that has a low profit, and which it sells aggressively, it is quite possible that profits will decline even as sales increase. Conversely, if a company elects to drop a low-profit product line and instead push sales of a higher-profit product line, total profits can increase even as total sales decline.

Tip: Sales managers must be aware of sales mix when they devise commission plans for the sales staff, since the intent should be to incentivize the sales staff to sell high-profit items. Otherwise, a poorly-constructed commission plan could push the sales staff in the direction of selling the wrong products, which alters the sales mix and results in lower profits.

A cost accounting variance called the *sales mix variance* is used to measure the difference in unit volumes in the actual sales mix from the planned sales mix. Follow these steps to calculate it at the individual product level:

1. Subtract budgeted unit volume from actual unit volume and multiply by the standard contribution margin.
2. Do the same for each of the products sold.
3. Aggregate this information to arrive at the sales mix variance for the company.

The formula is:

(Actual unit sales – Budgeted unit sales) × Budgeted contribution margin

---

EXAMPLE

Oberlin Acoustics expects to sell 100 platinum harmonicas, which have a contribution margin of $12 per unit, but actuals sells only 80 units. Also, Oberlin expects to sell 400 stainless steel harmonicas, which have a contribution margin of $6, but actually sells 500 units. The sales mix variance is:

Platinum harmonica: (80 actual units – 100 budgeted units) × $12 contribution margin = -$240

Stainless steel harmonica: (500 actual units – 400 budgeted units) × $6 contribution margin = $600

Thus, the aggregated sales mix variance is $360, which reflects a large increase in the sales volume of a product having a lower contribution margin, combined with a decline in sales for a product that has a higher contribution margin.

Summary

The interaction of unit costs, fixed costs, sales volumes, and contribution margins is critical to an understanding of cost management, since these concepts can be used to model financial results. By altering the inputs to a cost-volume-profit model, one can estimate how the results of a business will change, which affects management's decisions to invest in fixed assets, withdraw products, cut back business units, hire staff, and so forth.

A note of caution must be inserted into this discussion. Cost-volume-profit analysis assumptions are not entirely under the control of an organization. It may be possible to adhere to planned changes in costs, but unit sales and product price points may not be accepted by customers, rendering a financial model invalid. Consequently, it may be necessary to revise these models frequently in response to pilot tests in the market; alternatively, incorporate worst-case scenarios for unit sales and price points, in case customer acceptance of a new company initiative is indifferent.

Chapter 5
Target Costing

Introduction

One of the key reasons why organizations struggle to attain profitability is the low margins earned on their products. This situation typically arises from the product design process, where the engineering staff cobbles together a product without regard to the price at which the product must sell, or the features desired by customers. The result is a low product margin that no one discovers until after the product has launched. Management then engages in an after-the-fact battle to reduce the cost of products after their designs have been completed.

The primary management concept that can change this situation is *target costing*, under which a company plans in advance for the product price points, product costs, and margins that it wants to achieve. If it cannot manufacture a product at these planned levels, then it cancels the product entirely. With target costing, a management team has a powerful tool for continually monitoring products from the moment they enter the design phase and onward throughout their product life cycles. This chapter describes how target costing works.

The Basic Steps of Target Costing

Target costing has been in existence for a number of years and is used by many companies, so the primary steps in the process are well defined. They are:

1. *Conduct research.* The first step is to review the marketplace in which the company wants to sell products. The team needs to determine the set of product features that customers are most likely to buy, and the amount they will pay for those features. The team must learn about the perceived value of individual features, in case they later need to determine what impact there will be on the product price if they drop one or more of them. It may be necessary to later drop a product feature if the team decides that it cannot provide the feature while still meeting its target cost. At the end of this process, the team has a good idea of the target price at which it can sell the proposed product with a certain set of features, and how it must alter the price if it drops some features from the product.

2. *Calculate maximum cost.* The company provides the design team with a mandated gross margin that the proposed product must earn. By subtracting the mandated gross margin from the projected product price, the team can easily determine the maximum target cost that the product must achieve before it can be allowed into production.

3. *Engineer the product.* The engineers and procurement personnel on the team now take the leading role in creating the product. The procurement

staff is particularly important if the product has a high proportion of purchased parts; they must determine component pricing based on the necessary quality, delivery, and quantity levels expected for the product. They may also be involved in outsourcing parts, if this results in lower costs. The engineers must design the product to meet the cost target, which will likely include a number of design iterations to see which combination of revised features and design considerations results in the lowest cost.

4. *Ongoing activities*. Once a product design is finalized and approved, the team is reconstituted to include fewer designers and more industrial engineers. The team now enters into a new phase of reducing production costs, which continues for the life of the product. For example, cost reductions may come from waste reductions in production (known as kaizen costing), or from planned supplier cost reductions. These ongoing cost reductions yield enough additional gross margin for the company to further reduce the price of the product over time, in response to increases in the level of competition. Kaizen costing does not generate the size of cost reductions that can be achieved through initial design changes, but it can have a cumulatively significant impact over time.

EXAMPLE

SkiPS is a maker of global positioning systems (GPS) for skiers, which they use to log how many vertical feet they ski each day. SkiPS conducts a marketing survey to decide upon the features it needs to include in its next generation of GPS device, and finds that skiers want a device they can strap to their arm or leg, and which does not require recharging during a multi-day vacation.

The survey indicates that skiers are willing to pay no more than $150 for the device, while the first review of costs indicates that it will cost $160 to manufacture. At a mandated gross margin percentage of 40%, this means that the device must attain a target cost of $90 ($150 price × (1 – 40% gross margin). Thus, the design team must reduce costs from $160 to $90.

The team decides that the GPS unit requires no display screen at all, since users can plug the device into a computer to download information. This eliminates the LCD display and one computer chip. It also prolongs the battery life, since the unit no longer has to provide power to the display. The team also finds that a new microprocessor requires less power; given these reduced power requirements, the team can now use a smaller battery.

Finally, the team finds that the high-impact plastic case is over-engineered, and can withstand a hard impact with a much thinner shell. After the team incorporates all of these changes, it has reached the $90 cost target. SkiPS can now market a new device at a price point that allows it to earn a generous gross profit.

Value Engineering Considerations

The product engineering process noted above in step three involves many considerations. Here are examples of ways to reduce the cost of a product in order to meet a target cost:

- *Revise the manufacturing process.* The industrial engineering staff may be called upon to create an entirely new manufacturing process that uses less labor or less expensive machinery. It is entirely possible that multiple processes will be entirely eliminated from the production process. In particular, there may be an opportunity to eliminate various quality reviews from the process if product quality can be ensured by other means.

- *Reduce durability.* It is possible that the preliminary product design incorporates a product durability level that is actually *too* robust, thereby creating an opportunity to carefully decrease the level of product durability in order to cut costs. The typical result of this change is to completely eliminate some types of structural reinforcement from the product, or to at least downgrade to a less durable material in some parts of the product.

- *Reduce product features.* It may turn out to be quite expensive to offer certain features in a product. If so, the team needs to decide if it can delete one or more of these features while accepting a lower projected product price for which the net effect is an improved product margin. This type of value engineering must be carefully weighed against the problem of eliminating so many key features that the product will no longer be attractive to customers.

- *Reduce the number of parts.* It may be possible to simplify the design by using fewer parts, especially if doing so reduces the cost of assembling the final product. However, this concept can be taken too far, especially when many standard parts are replaced by a smaller number of customized (and therefore more expensive) parts.

- *Replace components.* It is possible that slightly different components are available at a substantially reduced cost; if so, the design engineers can modify the product to accommodate the different components. This is an especially common avenue when a product is initially designed to include components that have a high per-unit cost, and which can be replaced with components on which the company already earns significant volume discounts by using them across multiple product lines.

- *Design for easier manufacture.* To avoid time-consuming mistakes in the manufacturing process, consider designing the product so that it can only be assembled in a single way – all other attempts to assemble the product in an incorrect manner will fail. By doing so, there will be fewer product failures or recalls, which reduces the total cost of the product. It may be necessary to *increase* the cost of a product in order to create the optimum design for manufacturing, thereby reducing the total cost of the product over its full life span.

- *Ask suppliers*. Suppliers may have significant insights into how to reduce the costs of the various components they are contributing to the final product design, particularly in regard to altering material content or changing the manufacturing process. Suppliers may be willing to serve on design teams and contribute their expertise in exchange for being the sole source of selected components.

If the project team finds that it can comfortably meet the target cost without engaging in all of the preceding steps, then it should work through the activity list anyways. By doing so, it can generate sufficient room between the actual and target gross margins that management now has the option to reduce the product price below the target level, which may attract additional sales.

The Cost Reduction Program

The methods used by the design team are more sophisticated than simply saying, "folks, we need to cut $150 in costs – anyone have any ideas?" Instead, the team uses one of two approaches to more tightly focus its cost reduction efforts:

- *Tied to components*. The design team allocates the cost reduction goal among the various product components. This approach tends to result in incremental cost reductions to the same components that were used in the last iteration of the product. This approach is commonly used when a company is simply trying to refresh an existing product with a new version, and wants to retain the same underlying product structure. The cost reductions achieved through this approach tend to be relatively low, but also result in a high rate of product success, as well as a fairly short design period.
- *Tied to features*. The product team allocates the cost reduction goal among various product features, which focuses attention away from any product designs that may have been inherited from the preceding model. This approach tends to achieve more radical cost reductions (and design changes), but also requires more time to design, and also runs a greater risk of product failure or at least greater warranty costs.

Of the two methods noted here, companies are more likely to use the first approach if they are looking for a routine upgrade to an existing product, and the second approach if they want to achieve a significant cost reduction or break away from the existing design.

The Milestone Review Process

What if the project team simply cannot meet the target cost? Rather than completing the design process and creating a product with a substandard profit margin, the correct response is to stop the development process and move on to other projects instead. This does not mean that management allows its project teams to struggle on for months or years before finally giving up. Instead, they must come within a set percentage of the cost target on various milestone dates, with each successive milestone requirement coming closer to the final target cost. Milestones may occur on specific dates, or when key completion steps are reached in the design process, such as at the end of each design iteration.

EXAMPLE

Milagro Corporation is developing a new espresso machine that only works with its specially-developed strain of coffee bean. Milagro conducts market research and concludes that the product cannot sell for more than $200. At the company's required gross margin of 40%, this means that the target cost of the product is $120. Management sets a maximum design duration of six months, with milestone reviews at one-month intervals. The results of the month-end milestone reviews are:

Review Date	Cost Goal	Actual Cost Estimate	Actual Cost Variance from Goal	Allowed Variance From Cost Goal
Jan. 31	$120	$150	25%	30%
Feb. 28	120	143	19%	20%
Mar. 31	120	138	15%	15%
Apr. 30	120	134	12%	10%
May 31	120	Cancelled	--	5%
June 30	120	Cancelled	--	0%

As the table reveals, the Milagro project team was able to stay ahead of the cost target at the end of the first two months, but then was barely able to meet the allowable variance in the third month, and finally fell behind in the fourth month. Management then cancelled the project, saving itself the cost of continuing the project team for several more months when it was becoming obvious that the team would not be able to achieve the target cost.

Though management may cancel a design project that cannot meet its cost goals, this does not mean that the project will be permanently shelved. Far from it. Instead, management should review old projects at least once a year to see if the circumstances have changed sufficiently for them to possibly become viable again. A more precise review approach is to have each project team formulate a set of variables that should initiate a product review if a trigger point is reached (such as a decline in the price of a commodity that is used in the product design). If any of these trigger points are reached, the projects are immediately brought to the attention of management to see if they should be revived.

Problems with Target Costing

Target costing is difficult to initiate, because of the uncertainty surrounding the eventual release of a product. A company that allows its engineering department sole responsibility for creating products will achieve product releases on a fairly consistent schedule, even though some of the products may not be overly profitable. Under target costing, it is quite possible that a company may cancel a series of projects before they reach fruition, resulting in a frantic marketing department that sees no new products entering the pipeline. The solution is a combination of firm support by senior management and ongoing questioning of whether the target gross margin is too high to be achievable. It is entirely possible that an overly enthusiastic management team sets an excessively high gross margin standard for its new target costing process, and then sees no products survive the process. Consequently, it may take some time before management understands what gross margin levels will result in a target costing process that can churn out an acceptable number of products.

Another problem with target costing is the unwillingness of management to cancel a project. They do not want to see their investment in a project thrown away, and so they keep funding it for "just one more month," hoping that the team will find a way to achieve the target cost. The end result is a very long design process that absorbs more design costs than expected, and which still does not achieve the target cost. The only way to resolve this issue is an iron resolve to terminate projects in a timely manner.

Finally, a design team needs a strong leader to keep control of the opinions of the various departments that are represented on the team. For example, the marketing department may hold out for certain product features, while the design engineers claim that those same features introduce too many costs into the product. The best team leader is not one who unilaterally decides on the product direction, but rather one who can craft a group decision, and if necessary weed out those who are unwilling to work with the rest of the group.

The Members of a Design Team

The members of the design team are drawn from multiple disciplines, and their contributions are all essential to the success of a product launch. These positions are:

- *Design engineering.* The design engineers play the most prominent role on the team, since they must create a series of product iterations that incorporate the cost reductions needed to achieve the target cost.
- *Industrial engineering.* A significant part of a product's cost arises during the production process, so industrial engineers must become involved in order to give feedback to the design engineers regarding which design elements should be used that require the lowest production costs.
- *Cost accounting.* A cost accountant should be with the team at all times, constantly compiling the expected cost of a design as it goes through a

series of iterations. The cost accountant also compares the expected cost to the target cost, and communicates the status of the product cost situation to both the team members and management on a periodic basis.

- *Procurement*. The purchasing department is a valuable contributor to the team, since many components will likely be sourced to third parties, and an experienced procurement person can have a significant positive impact on the cost of purchased components.
- *Marketing*. The marketing department is particularly useful during the initial stages of target costing, where it investigates the prices of competing products and conducts polls to determine the value of specific product features.

The Role of the Accountant in Target Costing

The accountant's role on a design team is to continually compile the projected cost of the product as it moves forward through the design process. He compares this cost to the total target cost, and communicates the variance between the two figures to management, along with qualitative information about where projected costs are expected to decline further, what design changes are most likely to achieve further cost declines, and how these design changes will affect the value proposition of the final product. Management uses this information to periodically monitor the progress of the design project, and to cancel the project if it appears likely that the product cannot be designed within the cost and value parameters of the project.

A key part of the accountant's role is to obtain cost information from suppliers, which in turn is predicated on the assumption of a certain amount of purchasing volume, which may not ultimately prove to be correct. If there are significant cost differences at varying purchase volume levels, it may be necessary for the accountant to present several possible product costs, one for each volume level.

EXAMPLE

Active Exercise Machines is designing a new treadmill for the home exercise market, and is having trouble pricing the laminated rubber conveyor belt. Since Active is creating a treadmill in a non-standard length, the conveyor belt supplier will incur a setup cost, and must spread this cost over the projected number of treadmills to be produced. Since the setup cost is significant, the cost per unit will decline dramatically if Active orders more conveyor belts. The cost is $95 per unit if Active only orders 5,000 belts, and drops to $50 if Active orders 10,000 belts. Since the total cost of the treadmill is projected to be $500, this difference represents 9% of the total cost, which is significant enough to bring to the attention of management. Consequently, the accountant presents management with two projected costs for the treadmill – one at a unit volume of 5,000, and another at a unit volume of 10,000.

The accountant's cost information is likely to be vague when the project is initiated, since he is working with general design concepts and rough estimates of production volumes. Consequently, initial cost reports are likely to be within a range of possible costs, which gradually tighten up as the team generates more precise designs and better sales estimates.

A final task is for the accountant to continue monitoring the cost of the product after its release and throughout its product life. This is a key role, because management needs to know immediately if the initial cost structure that the design team worked so hard to create is no longer valid, and why the cost has increased.

The tasks ascribed to an accountant in his role as a member of a design team are not minor. For a larger design project, it is entirely possible that he will be released for special duty to the project, so that no other routine tasks will interfere with his work on the team. In a larger company where product design is the lifeblood of the entity, the accountant may find himself permanently assigned to a series of project teams.

Data Sources for Target Costing

It may be difficult to obtain data from which to develop the cost of a new product design. Here are some of the data sources needed for a target costing project:

- *New components*. The design team may be creating entirely new components from scratch, so there is no cost information available. In this case, locate roughly comparable components and extrapolate from them what the new components might cost, including tooling costs.
- *Materials sourcing*. Some materials that the design team wants to include in a product may be difficult to obtain, or be subject to significant price swings. These issues should be highlighted, particularly by using outside sources of historical commodity prices to note the range of price swings that have occurred in the recent past. It is dangerous to only report to management the current market price of these materials, since management may decide to continue product development when it might otherwise drop the project in the face of large potential cost increases.
- *Competitor costs*. It is extremely useful to disassemble competing products to determine what they cost to produce. This information can be assembled into a database, which is useful for not only calculating the likely gross margins that competing products are earning, but also for comparing the design team's choice of components to those used by competitors. In many instances, the design team can copy some aspects of a competing design in order to quickly achieve a lower cost.
- *Production costs*. If a company has engaged in product design for a number of years, it may have developed a table that contains the cost to produce specific components or the cost of the production functions used to create those components. This type of information is difficult to obtain, and requires a great deal of analysis to compile, so having the information available from previous design projects is a significant advantage in the design of new products.

- *Downstream costs.* When the design team modifies a product design, there is a good chance that it will cause modifications in other parts of the design, in a ripple effect. The only source of information for what these changes may be is the design team itself.
- *Supplier performance data.* Suppliers are likely going to provide a significant proportion of the components of a new product, so obtain access to the company's database of supplier performance to see if key suppliers are capable of supplying goods within the performance constraints required by the new design. This is less of a cost issue than a qualitative review of the ability of a supplier to perform within the company's specifications.

These data sources may not contain a high degree of data accuracy, so the result is likely to be significant uncertainty in costing information, especially during the initial stages of product design.

The Product Life Cycle and Target Costing

Target costing generates a significant and immediate cost reduction at the beginning of a product's life cycle. Kaizen costing then generates an ongoing series of smaller cost reductions that gradually decline as several cost reduction opportunities are eliminated. A company that wants to stay competitive with its product offerings should carefully track the gradual decline in product costs, and replace the original product with a new one when there are minimal cost reductions still to be garnered from the old product. The new product is subjected to the same target costing approach in order to create a new value proposition for the consumer, to be followed by another round of kaizen costing.

In order to remain competitive over the long term, it is clear that a company must be aware of where its products stand within their product cycles, and be willing to replace them when there are minimal costs to be eliminated from the old designs.

Summary

Target costing is most applicable to companies that compete by continually issuing a stream of new or upgraded products into the marketplace (such as consumer goods). For them, target costing is a key survival tool. Conversely, target costing is less necessary for those companies that have a small number of legacy products that require minimal updates, and for which long-term profitability is more closely associated with market penetration and geographical coverage (such as soft drinks).

Target costing is an excellent tool for planning a suite of products that have high levels of profitability. This is opposed to the much more common approach of creating a product that is based on the engineering department's view of what the product should be like, and then struggling with costs that are too high in comparison to the market price. Given the extremely cooperative nature of target costing across multiple departments, it can be a difficult change for the engineering manager to accept.

Chapter 6
Cost Object Analysis

Introduction

A cost object is any item for which costs are separately measured. It may be necessary to track a cost object in order to derive pricing from a baseline cost, or to see if costs are reasonable, or to derive the full cost of a relationship with another entity. Here are several types of cost objects:

- *Output.* The most common cost objects are a company's products and services, since it wants to know the cost of its output for profitability analysis and price setting.
- *Operational.* A cost object can be within a company, such as a department, machining operation, or process. Examples are the design of a new product, a customer service call, or the reworking of a returned product.
- *Business relationship.* A cost object could be a business partner, such as a supplier or customer.

In this chapter, we address which costs to assign to a cost object that are relevant to decisions concerning that cost object. Several of the more common cost objects are described.

Factors in Cost Object Analysis

From a cost management perspective, why review cost objects? The main point is that there are vast differences in the amount of cost accumulated by each cost object, and the intent is to spotlight those cost objects that are soaking up more costs than their counterparts. The intent is not to spotlight slight differences in the costs of cost objects, since these could just as easily be caused by measurement problems as by actual differences in costs. Instead, the focus is on major spikes in cost that are causing significant profitability issues.

When reviewing cost objects, any of the following factors can be causing unusually high costs:

- *High complexity.* Any extremely complex cost object attracts more costs. This can include a higher initial investment, as well as more maintenance and training costs. For example, a large piece of automated equipment will attract more costs than a simpler device that can be manually operated.
- *High investment.* A high initial investment immediately applies a significant cost to a cost object, even if no additional costs accrue over time.
- *High support levels.* This concept applies specifically to customers, and refers to the greatly increased level of customer support that some

customers require. This concept can also involve the cost of bad debts, product returns, and warranties.

- *Low volume.* A cost object may attract a large amount of costs because there are so few units of it. Any costs incurred cannot be allocated across a large number of units, so the cost per cost object tends to be quite high.
- *Small lot size.* This concept mostly applies to production lines. When a significant amount of time is required to retool a production line, a small lot size will accumulate more setup costs on a per-unit basis than a larger lot size.

An unusually high cost in a cost object is not necessarily to be avoided, as long as a sufficient amount of profit can still be derived from the object. A business may intentionally invest in extremely expensive cost objects, with the intent of charging premium prices on products relating to these objects. For example:

- *Employees.* A company hires only the best programmers and rewards them with high-end compensation and a rich benefits package. The company then charges premium prices to customers for their services.
- *Machinery.* A company invests in a massively expensive automated factory that allows it to alter the production schedule on a moment's notice. The company then charges far more than the usual price for its products, based on its ability to customize orders and ship to customers on the same day.
- *Products.* A watchmaker manufactures very short production runs of premium watches and sells them to collectors at inordinately high prices.

However, all of these examples highlight the fact that only a premium pricing strategy can be used when cost objects collect unusually large costs. If a business pursues any other type of strategy, it must pay close attention to its cost objects.

The Assignability of Costs

The bulk of this chapter is concerned with the accumulation of costs for specific cost objects. When doing so, a key issue is which costs to include or exclude. The concept is not a minor one, for the resulting report may trigger a management decision to eliminate the cost object – which may be, for example, an employee, a store, a product, or a customer. Consequently, assigning the correct costs is crucial.

When assigning costs to cost objects, the rule is to do so if the elimination of the cost object in question would also eliminate the cost. Thus, the termination of employment for a single individual will certainly eliminate that person's compensation, but will not affect the additional costs of the payroll or human resources departments. However, the situation changes considerably when the scope of the cost object expands. Thus, if an entire production facility is considered a cost object, then it is entirely likely that the payroll and human resources departments of that facility should be included in the cost, since those departments would be terminated if the facility were to be eliminated.

Overhead costs should never be allocated to cost objects. The reason is that the most common management decision related to a cost object is whether to retain or eliminate it, so only costs that will verifiably be eliminated should be attached to a cost object. Since overhead is, by its nature, not associated with a cost object, it should not be assigned to a cost object.

EXAMPLE

The president of Grubstake Brothers is concerned that the cost reports for the company's new Trench Demon digger machine indicate that it is losing money. A close examination of the cost report reveals that one cost assigned to this cost object is not actually closely related to the product, and so should be stripped away. The revised report is noted in the following table.

	Assignable Cost or Revenue	Costs not Assignable	Notes
Revenue	$1,000,000		
Direct materials	350,000		
Direct labor	120,000		All direct labor staff work on this product, and so should be included
Corporate overhead		$150,000	No corporate costs would be terminated if the product were cancelled
Facility overhead	450,000		The facility would be shut down if the product were cancelled, and so should be included
Warranty costs	35,000		
Net profit/loss	$45,000	-$150,000	

Because the production facility would be shut down if the product were terminated, it is acceptable to assign all costs of the facility to the product. This is not the case for the corporate overhead costs, which should therefore not be allocated to the product. In short, once the corporate overhead cost has been excluded from the cost object, there is a discernible profit.

In summary, the assignability of cost will vary, depending on the nature of the cost object, and should always be restricted to the variable costs incurred by a cost object.

The Customer Cost Object

A major cost object is the customer, since the primary purpose of a business is to expend funds specifically to serve its customers. Unfortunately, the cost accounting system is not designed to track costs for individual customers, so new systems will be needed to track the customer service time devoted to each customer, salesperson time by customer, and the cost of returned goods. Consider the assignable costs in the following table.

Costs to Assign to a Customer

+/-	Assignable Cost	Commentary
+	Customer service	Only include the cost of customer service if there would be a reduction in this cost if a customer were to be terminated
+	Salesperson	Only include the cost of the sales staff if salespeople would be terminated along with a customer
+	Returned goods	Include the out-of-pocket cost to handle returned goods, which may include freight, repackaging, and the profit lost from reselling these goods at a reduced price
+	Credits	Include the cost of all credits claimed by a customer, which may include volume discounts, damaged goods claims, and so forth
+	Early payment discounts	All early payment discounts taken by a customer are a cost of doing business with that specific customer, and so should be included

When a customer demands a great deal of attention, management is most likely to hear complaints from all over the company regarding how much staff time this customer requires. However, the issue is irrelevant unless the termination of the customer would directly trigger a reduction in company support staff. If not, and despite all the complaining, there is no incremental staff cost associated with a demanding customer.

Thus far, we have only addressed the cost of *maintaining* a relationship with a customer. In addition, there is the cost of *acquiring* a customer, which can be extraordinarily high. There may be a marketing campaign that triggers a few expressions of interest from potential customers, followed by salesperson visits that further reduce the pool of prospects, followed by product demonstrations that finally yield a small number of actual customers. If the total cost of this acquisition process were to be spread across the few resulting customers, it would be apparent that an existing customer relationship is extremely valuable. Knowledge of this acquisition cost might trigger additional actions, such as:

- *More analysis of acquisition methods.* The profits garnered from newly-acquired customers may not justify the cost of their acquisition, resulting in the testing of alternative acquisition methods.

- *More initial analysis of customers*. Management is likely to spend more time reviewing the incremental cost of acquiring a new customer. It may pay to be picky about acquiring new customers in order to avoid those that will soak up an excessive amount of company resources.
- *More customer service*. Since it is less expensive to maintain an existing relationship than to acquire a new relationship, management could commit to spend more money on existing customers in order to improve the relationship, such as faster customer service response times or paying for faster shipping to customers.

The Employee Cost Object

One of the most commonly-reviewed cost objects is the employee, particularly in regard to those administrative positions that can be more easily culled in the event of a downturn in business. However, the typical analysis only includes base-level compensation and the related payroll taxes, which does not yield a complete picture of the situation. Instead, a more comprehensive view should be assembled. Consider the assignable costs in the following table.

Costs to Assign to an Employee

+/-	Assignable Cost	Commentary
+	Base compensation	Base compensation is always included in the cost of an employee
+	Historical overtime	If a person has a history of incurring overtime, then include the average amount of this overtime, plus applicable payroll taxes
+	Bonuses	Only include the amount of bonuses that are likely to be earned, plus applicable payroll taxes
-	Increased compensation elsewhere	If an employee is to be let go, consider the cost of increased overtime for those employees remaining, as well as the payroll taxes associated with that overtime
+	Payroll taxes	This includes the social security, Medicare, and federal unemployment taxes paid by the employer
+	Benefits	This is the net cost of benefits paid by the company, after employee payroll deductions are subtracted
+	Travel and entertainment	This includes the historical average cost of travel and entertainment incurred by the employee

Several costs should not be included in an employee cost analysis, since they would still remain if an employee were to be let go. Consider the following costs:

- *Cell phones*. If a cell phone is considered common property that is simply passed along to a different person when one individual leaves the company, then its cost should not be assigned to a specific individual.

- *Commissions.* In many cases, a customer will be assigned to a different salesperson if the original salesperson is let go, so the company continues to incur a commission. However, if each sale is unique and there is no transfer of customers to a replacement salesperson, then the cost of commissions could be assigned to an employee.
- *Depreciation.* The depreciation on computer equipment and furniture used by an employee will remain if the position is eliminated, so do not assign the cost to an employee.
- *Profit sharing.* If an employee were to be laid off, profits would simply be shared with someone else who remains on the staff.
- *Square footage allocation.* The department to which an employee is assigned may be charged for the square footage occupied by an employee. Since this cost would remain even if an employee were not on staff, it should not be considered an employee-specific cost.

A particularly large point that is frequently missed is to assign the *actual* net cost of benefits to employees, rather than the *average* net cost per employee. For example, it is entirely likely that an employee taking family medical insurance is much more expensive than one taking single coverage, since there is such a large disparity in the costs of these two variations on medical insurance.

The Product Cost Object

A common analysis is to accumulate costs for a product, and use this as the basis for a decision to cancel the product. In this case, the analysis should be entirely based on the variable cost of the product, and nothing else. Since most costs in the production area are fixed, this means that comparatively few costs should be assigned to a product. Consider the assignable costs in the following table:

Costs to Assign to a Product

+/-	Assignable Cost	Commentary
+	Direct materials	Always assigned as a product cost
+	Packaging costs	Always assigned as a product cost
+	Commissions	Only assigned to a product if the commission specifically relates to the sale of that product
+	Piece rate pay	Add the cost of labor and related payroll taxes when employees are being paid for the incremental production of each individual unit, as occurs under a piece rate pay plan
+	Outside processing charges	If a third party is being paid for some or all of the processing work on a product, include this cost
+	Licensing fees	When the company is paying a third party a licensing fee for each unit sold, include this cost

Several costs should not be included in a product cost analysis, since they would still remain if the product were to be eliminated. Consider the following costs:

- *Non-product commissions.* Do not assign to a product any commissions paid for other reasons than a product sale, such as a quarterly override or a bonus for managing a new sales region.
- *Direct labor.* Most direct labor is incurred to provide minimum staffing for a product line, rather than to produce an individual unit. Theoretically, direct labor costs could be incurred even if there is *no* production. Thus, this cost should be considered part of factory overhead.

The cost of many purchased components varies considerably, based on the quantities in which they are purchased. For example, when a widget is bought in a standard supplier's economy pack of 100 units, the supplier charges $5.00 per unit. However, if a smaller quantity is needed, this requires the supplier to break its normal packaging and ship the widget in a custom-sized shipping container; consequently, the price increases to $15.00. Further, if you need to buy in massive quantities, such as a truckload, the supplier can reduce the price further, to $3.50 per unit. Thus, the cost of a purchased component can vary substantially, depending upon the quantities in which it is purchased. It may be necessary to include this concept in the derivation of costs for a product.

EXAMPLE

Blitz Communications is considering developing a new desktop phone. The marketing department estimates that there is a 25% chance that the phone will sell 20,000 units or less, a 60% chance that it will sell between 20,000 and 50,000 units, and a 15% chance that it will sell more than 50,000 units. The phone is to be constructed almost entirely from purchased parts, with final assembly at the Blitz factory. The cost analysis is:

Component	(25% Probability) 20,000 Units or Less	(60% Probability) 20,001 – 50,000 Units	(15% Probability) 50,000+ Units
Price/Unit	$25.00	$25.00	$25.00
Base	3.00	2.50	2.00
Keypad	0.54	0.45	0.36
Microphone	0.78	0.65	0.52
Cord	0.96	0.80	0.64
Shell	4.50	3.75	3.00
Speaker	1.38	1.15	0.92
Direct labor	3.75	3.75	3.75
Overhead	8.00	4.20	2.00
Cost Total	$22.91	$17.25	$13.19
Profit	$2.09	$7.75	$11.81
Profit %	8%	31%	47%

The analysis uses the 20,001 to 50,000 unit range as the baseline. If product sales fall below the 20,001 unit level, the analysis shows that purchased component costs will increase by 20%, and that costs will decrease by 20% if the product sells more than 50,000 units. Further, the amount of fixed overhead costs must be spread over fewer units if the product sells 20,000 units or less, with the reverse effect if it sells more than 50,000 units.

The preceding example reveals the problem that management faces when evaluating product costs that could change with purchasing volumes; there is a possibility that profits could severely underperform. When this situation arises, management needs to decide if it should take the risk of releasing a product into the market, or of setting a lower price to attract more sales, or of reengineering the product to reduce its cost.

The Product Line Cost Object

It may be necessary to reach a decision regarding the termination of an entire product line. If so, the number of costs to include in the decision skyrockets, as compared to the meager cost listing for a single product. There may also be issues in the reverse direction, when costs must be added in order to expand a product line.

An entire facility may be used to create all of the products in a product family. If so, all of the costs of that facility are now considered variable when deciding whether to retain the product line. Consider the assignable costs in the following table, which are in addition to those listed in the last section for a product.

Additional Costs to Assign to a Product Line

+/-	Assignable Cost	Commentary
+	Direct labor	Direct labor is a fixed cost of the production line, and would be eliminated if the product line is terminated
+	Factory overhead	If the entire factory only manufactured that product line, then all factory overhead is associated with the product line
+	Marketing costs	There is usually a separate budget for marketing the product line, which therefore varies with the product line
+	Sales costs	If the sales staff only sells the product line, they are a variable cost of the line. If they sell other items as well, then do not include their cost.
+	Factory admin-istration costs	All of the administrative costs associated with running the factory are associated with the product line, if the factory only produces the product line

It is quite likely that the only cost *not* assigned to a product line will be the allocation of corporate overhead to the facility that produces these goods, since that would not necessarily be impacted by the termination of the product line.

Costs related to a product line can vary whenever they reach a step cost boundary. For example, a production manager finds that his facility can produce a maximum of 3,000 widgets per week if he uses one shift, but that he needs to start a second shift in order to meet any additional demand. When he adds the shift, the company will have to incur certain additional fixed costs, such as the salary of a supervisor for that shift.

When a company exceeds a step cost boundary and incurs a new step cost, how does this impact the cost of an individual unit of production? For incremental costing decisions, it does nothing at all, since the variable cost of producing a single unit has not changed. It has, however, increased the total overhead cost of the production system, as well as (presumably) the ability of the system to produce more units. The only way to see if a step cost has improved or reduced the ability of a production system to produce a profit is to subject it to constraint analysis, which we deal with in the Constraint Analysis chapter.

For the purposes of analyzing the impact of a step cost on a product line, the main consideration for the analyst is to point out to management the existence of any impending step costs, their amount, and how they impact the production system. Management then needs to decide if it has a long-term need for the additional production capacity that the step cost represents, or whether it makes more sense to avoid the step cost by either turning away additional business or outsourcing the work.

The Sales Channel Cost Object

Management may need to consider the cost of its various sales channels, to see if they are being operated in a cost-effective manner that produces profits. If so, the analysis should certainly include the costs of all goods and services generated by that sales channel, as well as the support costs required to maintain the channel, which could involve any separate distribution infrastructure. Consider the assignable costs in the following table.

Additional Costs to Assign to a Product Line

+/-	Assignable Cost	Commentary
+	Product cost objects	This is the cost of any products sold through the sales channel
+	Marketing costs	If there is a separate budget for marketing through the sales channel, consider it a variable cost of the sales channel
+	Sales costs	If the sales staff is assigned solely to a sales channel, then they are a variable cost of that channel. If they sell through multiple sales channels, then do not assign their cost to this cost object.
+	Logistics costs	If the storage and distribution of goods is separate for the sales channel, consider logistics a variable cost of the sales channel

This is not a minor topic, for a chain of retail stores can be considered a sales channel cost object. It is not uncommon for management to evaluate an entire cluster of retail stores and their supporting regional warehouse and marketing budget to see if the cluster should be retained or shut down. The same analysis can be applied to Internet stores, distributors, and other sales channels. Thus, the proper analysis of sales channels can result in some of the largest decisions that a business can make – and those decisions must be supported by the correct information.

Cost Object Termination Issues

Much of the discussion surrounding cost objects tends to involve their termination. If it is considered necessary to actually terminate a cost object, there are several additional issues to be considered regarding how that termination is conducted. Consider the following issues:

- *Inventory reduction.* When a product or an entire product line is being terminated, the remaining inventory of raw materials and work-in-process should be converted into finished goods, and the finished goods completely sold off. Otherwise, the company will end up holding inventory that it will only be able to liquidate with difficulty. Thus, planning regarding residual inventory levels must take place, which can impact the timing of a product or product line termination.

- *Inventory for warranties.* If a product is to be terminated and there is a warranty period associated with it, estimate the number of units to be held in reserve for warranty replacement purposes, and set them aside. Otherwise, production may have to be restarted at a later date to fulfill the company's warranty obligations.
- *Fixed asset maintenance.* If an entire production line is to be terminated, be sure to include fixed asset acquisition proposals in this decision. Ideally, maintenance of existing equipment should be enhanced during the final months of scheduled production, rather than spending funds on equipment that replaces worn-out machinery. This may mean that some production must be outsourced in order to sidestep production equipment that is no longer functional.
- *Severance costs.* If a product line or sales channel is being terminated, there will be associated severance costs for those employees impacted by the decision. Also, various laws may require that employees be given a certain amount of advance warning, which can delay the effective date of the shutdown.

These issues do no impact the decision to eliminate a cost object, but they can have an impact on the timing of the cancellation. Consequently, review these points on a regular basis as the termination date for a cost object approaches.

Which Cost Objects to Track

It is not necessary to track the cost of every conceivable cost object in a business. Some attract such a small amount of cost that there is no point in doing so, while there are no decisions that can be made in regard to other cost objects. The following table illustrates how to sort through the various cost objects in a business.

Tracking Concepts for Cost Objects

Cost Object	When to Track	When not to Track
Customers	When significant sales volume is concentrated with a small number of customers	When sales volume is widely dispersed among a large number of accounts
Employees	When specific sales can be traced back to an individual, or where pay levels are unusually high (examples: salespeople and engineers)	When there are a large number of employees whose pay is relatively low (example: retail clerks)
Products	When there is heavy pricing pressure that may drive product margins to zero	When product profitability is uniformly high
Product lines	When a product line is the sole focus of an entire production facility	When the product line has dispersed production and minimal targeted marketing or sales
Sales channels	When there is a large amount of supporting infrastructure, such as warehouses and a dedicated sales force	When the channel is incidental, with minimal ongoing costs

Summary

In essence, the study of cost objects is designed to focus attention on those aspects of a business that accumulate costs, and which therefore can interfere with profitability. This does not mean that the cost of all cost objects will be continually ground down over time to the bare minimum. On the contrary, management may conclude that *increased* spending on a cost object is needed in order to fulfill the corporate mission. However, these cases should be in the minority. In most situations, management should be made aware on a regular basis of how costs are concentrated throughout the business, and of any material changes in these costs over time.

Chapter 7
Constraint Analysis

Introduction

In cost management, the mindset is usually that a decision is to be based on a specific cost object. The decision does not take into account the greater corporate structure within which it takes place. For example, you may be called upon to judge whether a product should be cancelled because of an excessively low margin, or to choose between two possible capital investments based on their cash flows. However, the impacts of these decisions are rarely considered in relation to a company's *entire* capability, as an integrated unit, to earn a profit.

Constraint analysis does the reverse – its starting point is determining which company operation is constraining the entire company from earning a greater profit, and then focuses all decision-making upon how they impact this constraint (or "bottleneck"). To use the previous two examples, it may not be judicious to cancel a product that generates *any* amount of profit, since that profit helps to pay for the overhead cost of the entire system. Further, it may not be necessary to invest in any fixed assets unless it improves the capacity of the bottleneck operation.

This chapter gives an overview of constraint analysis, and then delves into a number of management decisions where using it can alter one's perception of how to manage the costs of a company.

Constraint Analysis Operational Terminology

Constraint analysis makes use of several unique terms, so we will begin with a set of definitions before proceeding to an overview of constraint analysis. The key operational terms are:

- *Drum.* This is a third variation of the *constraint* term, along with *bottleneck*. It is the operation, person, or (occasionally) the materials within a company that prevent it from generating additional sales. Since the ultimate profitability of the company depends on this one item, it sets the pace for how the company operates. Picture the drum beating on a rowed galley, and you can see why it is called a *drum*.
- *Buffer.* The drum operation should operate at as close to 100% of capacity as possible, but this is impossible when the flow of materials from upstream operations is unreliable. The buffer is inventory that is positioned in front of the drum operation, and which protects the drum from any stoppage in materials coming from upstream operations. The buffer may need to be quite large if there is considerable variability in the inflow of materials, or it may be of more modest proportions if the inflow is more stable.

- *Rope.* The rope represents the date and time when jobs must be released into the production process in order to have inventory arrive at the buffer just when it is needed by the drum; thus, it is really the total time duration needed to bring work-in-process to the drum.

These three terms are sometimes strung together in a single phrase, and are called the *drum-buffer-rope* system. As a group, they describe the essential operational components of constraint analysis.

Overview of Constraint Analysis

The key points in understanding constraint analysis are the following two concepts:

1. A company is an integrated set of processes that function together to generate a profit; and
2. There is a chokepoint somewhere in a company that absolutely controls its ability to earn a profit.

The chokepoint is also known as the drum operation (as defined above, or the bottleneck, or the constrained resource). We will refer to it as a bottleneck, since the word most clearly describes its impact on an organization.

The first concept, that of a company being an integrated set of processes, applies very strongly at the product line level, but less so at the corporate parent level. At the product line level, there is almost certainly a bottleneck that restricts the ability to generate more profit. At the corporate parent level, there may be multiple subsidiaries, each with a multitude of product lines. Thus, from the perspective of the corporate parent, there are still bottlenecks, but there may be a number of them scattered throughout the operations of the subsidiaries.

The second concept, that of the bottleneck, is most typically characterized by a machine that can only process a certain number of units per day. To improve profits, a company must focus all of its attention on that machine by taking such steps as:

- Adding supplemental staff to cover any employee breaks or downtime during shift changes
- Reviewing the quality of work-in-process going into the operation, so that it does not waste any time processing items that are already defective
- Positioning extra maintenance personnel near it to ensure that service intervals are short
- Reducing the amount of processing time per unit, so that more units can be run through the machine
- Adding more capacity to the machine
- Outsourcing work to suppliers

It is also possible that the bottleneck is not in the production area at all. It may be caused by a materials shortage, or by a lack of sales staff. In those rare cases where there is simply no bottleneck to be found, then the company has excess capacity, and can choose to either reduce its capacity (and the related cost) or try to sell more volume, possibly at a lower price.

EXAMPLE

Hammer Industries produces construction equipment. Its products are large, complex, and mostly sold through a request for proposals process. Its financial analyst has reviewed all production operations in detail and concluded that there is no bottleneck operation to be found. Instead, the real chokepoint appears to be in the sales department.

Hammer has a multi-tiered sales process, where one group makes initial contacts with prospective customers, another group of technical writers responds to requests for proposal (RFP), yet another group conducts sales presentations, and a final group conducts final contract negotiations. A brief analysis shows that the technical writers are completely overwhelmed with writing RFP responses, and have missed several RFP filing deadlines. The sales staff positioned ahead of them in the process flow, those making contacts with prospective customers, are aware of the problem and have scaled back their activities to meet with new customers, since they know the company is not capable of making timely RFP responses. Thus, it is evident that the sales department is the true company bottleneck.

The analyst reports this issue to management, and recommends a combination of additional technical writer hiring and the purchase of RFP response software to simplify the writing task.

It is usually easy to tell where the bottleneck is located, because it has a large amount of work piled up in front of it, while the work operation immediately downstream from it is starved for work.

A major part of the management of the bottleneck operation is the inventory buffer located immediately in front of it. Constraint analysis holds that there will always be flaws in the production process that result in variability in the flow of materials to the bottleneck, so a buffer must be built up to insulate the bottleneck from these issues. The buffer should be quite large if there are lots of upstream production problems, or much smaller if the production flow is relatively placid.

If production problems start to eat into the size of the inventory buffer, then the bottleneck is in danger of having a stock-out condition, which may cause it to run out of work. To avoid this, there should be a large *sprint capacity* in selected upstream production operations. Sprint capacity is essentially excess production capacity. There should be a sufficient amount of this capacity available to rapidly rebuild the inventory buffer. If the firm has invested in significant sprint capacity, then there is also less need for a large inventory buffer.

Finally, there is the concept of the *rope* that was mentioned earlier as a key definition. It is very important to only release new jobs into the production queue so that they arrive at the inventory buffer just in time to be used. The natural inclination of a production scheduler would be to release jobs too soon, to ensure that there is always a healthy flow of jobs arriving at the inventory buffer. However, doing so represents an excessive inventory investment, and also confuses the production staff, which does not know which of the plethora of jobs to process next. Thus, the rope concept represents a fine balance between overloading the system and starving it of work.

In summary, the bottleneck operation is the most important operation in a company. The management team needs to know where it is located, and spend a great deal of time figuring out how to maximize its operation so that it hardly ever stops.

The Cost of the Bottleneck

How expensive is it when a bottleneck operation is not running? The traditional cost accounting approach would be to calculate the foregone gross margin on any products that would otherwise have been produced if it had been operational. Under constraint analysis, the calculation is the entire operating cost of the facility, divided by the bottleneck's operating hours. We use the entire cost of the facility, because the bottleneck drives the profitability of the entire facility.

For example, a bottleneck operation is running 160 hours a week, which is three shifts, less eight hours for maintenance downtime. The facility has operating expenses of $1,600,000 per week. Therefore, the cost of *not* running the bottleneck operation is $10,000 per hour. When viewed from this perspective, it is very expensive indeed to stop a bottleneck operation.

EXAMPLE

Mole Industries incurs $250,000 of operational expenses per week for its Digger equipment line. The bottleneck work center is operational 150 hours per week, with the remaining 18 hours of the week being used for necessary maintenance. Thus, the cost of not running the bottleneck is $1,667 per hour ($250,000 operational expenses ÷ 150 hours per week).

The shift supervisor has received a demand from the union to give a one-hour lunch break to the three people working in the bottleneck operation, in each of the three shifts. The shift supervisor has the choice of shutting down the operation for 21 hours per week to accede to this request (7 days × 3 shifts × 1 hour per shift), or of bringing in additional staff at an astronomical $100 per hour per person to run the operation in their absence. Which is the better alternative?

Option 1, Stop the Bottleneck: The cost of not running the bottleneck is $1,667 per hour, so the total cost over 21 hours would be $35,000 per week.

Option 2, Use Supplemental Staff: The cost of using supplemental staff is $6,300 (21 hours × 3 staff × $100 per person).

Though the use of supplemental staff initially appears excessive, the cost is still far lower than shutting down the bottleneck operation.

The example makes it quite clear that a bottleneck operation should never be shut down. It is always less expensive to add staff to it, or do whatever else is necessary, to ensure that it keeps running.

An ancillary question is, what is the cost of running an operation that is not the bottleneck operation? It is zero. Since company operations do not hinge on any other operation, it is usually acceptable to shut them down for short periods. The only exception is when doing so may impact the bottleneck operation.

Local Optimization

The concept of the constraint is very much at odds with the traditional concept of local optimization, where management tries to improve the efficiency of every operation throughout a company. In many cases, these improvements do nothing to increase overall company profits, because the primary driver of profits is still the bottleneck operation. Consequently, if there is an investment in local optimization projects, profits do not improve, but the investment in the company increases, so the only logical outcome is that the return on investment declines. The following exhibit contains several examples of how constraint analysis alters the view of local optimization.

Examples of Local Optimization vs. Constraint-Based Solutions

Situation	Local Optimization Solution	Constraint Analysis Solution
Overtime is 10% of payroll	Restrict all overtime	Do not restrict overtime if it is being spent on the bottleneck operation, or on any operations feeding the bottleneck
A machine is not being utilized	Sell the machine	Keep the machine if it provides sprint capacity for the bottleneck operation
A product can be redesigned	Only do so if the product is at the end of its normal life cycle	Do so if the redesign reduces the product processing time at the bottleneck operation
The production staff is not fully utilized	Cut back on operations and lay off staff	If there is no bottleneck operation, then lower prices to attract more sales
A machine is reaching its maximum utilization	Buy an additional machine	Only buy an additional unit if it will provide more sprint capacity. Do not buy if it is located downstream from the bottleneck operation
A supplier is asking us to outsource production	Do so if it passes a cost-benefit analysis	Do so if it reduces the load on the bottleneck operation

In all of the cases noted in the table, it helps to step back from the individual decision and see what the impact will be on the entire company before the correct course of action can be determined.

In particular, be aware of two problems that are caused by local optimization:

1. *Excess inventory*. If a production operation is optimized that is not the bottleneck operation, then all you have done is give it the ability to churn out even more inventory than was previously the case, and which the bottleneck will be unable to process. Thus, you have not only needlessly invested in the operation, but also needlessly invested in additional inventory that must now wait to be processed.

2. *Overly efficient labor*. When a good manufacturing process was considered to be one with very long production runs, there was an emphasis on highly efficient labor. If you are instead focusing on maximizing the amount of production passing through the bottleneck – and nowhere else – then grossly overstaff the bottleneck operation to make sure that it is always operating, and pay much less attention to labor efficiency elsewhere. Employees should only work if inventory is actually needed. In short, it is better to have employees be underutilized and produce less inventory than to be more efficient and produce inventory that is not needed.

In summary, a company does not even have to be especially efficient in production areas located away from the bottleneck operation. Instead, the one and only focus is on maximizing the efficiency of the bottleneck. This change in focus alters most of the decisions that would be reached if you only focused on local optimization.

Constraint Analysis Financial Terminology

By now it should be apparent that constraint analysis is quite a valuable tool from an operational perspective. But what about from a financial perspective? How is the concept used to make decisions? There is a model for using constraint analysis in this role, but first we need to define the terms in the model. They are:

- *Throughput*. This is the margin left after totally variable costs are subtracted from revenue. This tends to be a large proportion of revenues, since all overhead costs are excluded from the calculation.
- *Totally variable costs*. This is usually just the cost of materials, since it is only those costs that vary when one incremental unit of a product is manufactured. This does not normally include the cost of labor, since employees are not usually paid based on one incremental unit of output. There are a few other possible costs that may be totally variable, such as commissions, subcontractor fees, customs duties, and freight costs.
- *Operating expenses*. This is all company expenses other than totally variable costs. There is no differentiation between overhead costs,

administrative costs or financing costs – quite simply, *all* other company expenses are lumped into this category.

- *Investment*. This is the amount invested in assets. "Investment" includes changes in the level of working capital resulting from a management decision.
- *Net profit*. This is throughput, less operating expenses.

Constraint Analysis from a Financial Perspective

When a company is examined from the perspective of constraints, it no longer makes sense to evaluate individual products, because overhead costs do not vary at the individual product level. In reality, most companies spend a great deal of money to maintain a production infrastructure, and that infrastructure is what really generates a profit – the trick is making that infrastructure produce the maximum profit with the best mix of products having the highest possible throughput. Under the constraint analysis model, there are three ways to improve the financial position of the entire production infrastructure. They are:

- *Increase throughput*. This is by either increasing revenues or reducing the amount of totally variable costs.
- *Reduce operating expenses*. This is by reducing some element of overhead expenses.
- *Improve the return on investment*. This is by either improving profits in conjunction with the lowest possible investment, or by reducing profits slightly along with a correspondingly larger decline in investment.

Note that only the increase in throughput is related in any way to decisions made at the product level. The other two improvement methods may be concerned with changes anywhere in the production system.

The Constraint Analysis Model

An excellent constraint analysis model was developed by Thomas Corbett, which is outlined here. The basic thrust of the model is to give priority in the bottleneck operation to those products that generate the highest throughput per minute of bottleneck time. After these products are manufactured, then give priority to the product having the next highest throughput per minute, and so on. Eventually, the production queue is filled, and the operation can accept no additional work.

The key element in the model is the use of throughput per minute, because the key limiting factor in a bottleneck operation is time – hence, maximizing throughput within the shortest possible time frame is paramount. Note that throughput *per minute* is much more important than total throughput *per unit*. The following example illustrates the point.

EXAMPLE

Mole Industries manufacturers trench digging equipment. It has two products with different amounts of throughput and processing times at the bottleneck operation. The key information about these products is:

Product	Total Throughput	Bottleneck Processing Time	Throughput per Minute
Mole Hole Digger	$400	2 minutes	$200
Mole Driver Deluxe	800	8 minutes	100

Of the two products, the Mole Driver Deluxe creates the most overall throughput, but the Mole Hole Digger creates more throughput per minute of bottleneck processing time. To determine which one is more valuable to Mole Industries, consider what would happen if the company had an unlimited order quantity of each product, and could run the bottleneck operation nonstop, all day (which equates to 1,440 minutes). The operating results would be:

Product	Throughput per Minute		Total Processing Time Available		Total Throughput
Mole Hole Digger	$200	×	1,440 minutes	=	$288,000
Mole Driver Deluxe	100	×	1,440 minutes	=	144,000

Clearly, the Mole Hole Digger, with its higher throughput per minute, is much more valuable to Mole Industries than its Mole Driver Deluxe product. Consequently, the company should push sales of the Mole Hole Digger product whenever possible.

The constraint analysis model is essentially a production plan that itemizes the amount of throughput that can be generated, as well as the total amount of operating expenses and investment. In the model, we use four different products, each requiring some processing time in the bottleneck operation. The columns in the model are as follows:

- *Throughput per minute.* This is the total amount of throughput that a product generates, divided by the amount of processing time at the bottleneck operation.
- *Bottleneck usage.* This is the number of minutes of processing time required by a product at the bottleneck operation.
- *Units scheduled.* This is the number of units scheduled to be processed at the bottleneck operation.

- *Total bottleneck time.* This is the total number of minutes of processing time required by a product, multiplied by the number of units to be processed.
- *Total throughput.* This is the throughput per minute multiplied by the number of units processed at the bottleneck operation.

This grid produces a total amount of throughput to be generated if production proceeds according to plan. Below the grid of planned production, there is a subtotal of the total amount of throughput, from which the total amount of operating expenses are subtracted to arrive at the amount of profit. Finally, the total amount of investment in assets is divided into the profit to calculate the return on investment. Thus, the model provides a complete analysis of all three ways to improve the results of a company – increase throughput, decrease operating expenses, or increase the return on investment. An example of the model follows:

Sample Constraint Analysis Model

Product	Throughput per Minute	Bottleneck Usage (minutes)	Units Scheduled	Total Bottleneck Time	Total Throughput
1. Hedgehog Deluxe	$80	14	1,000	14,000	$1,120,000
2. Hedgehog Mini	70	20	500	10,000	700,000
3. Hedgehog Classic	65	40	200	8,000	520,000
4. Hedgehog Digger	42	10	688	6,880	288,960
Total bottleneck scheduled time				38,880	
Total bottleneck time available*				38,880	
Total throughput					$2,628,960
Total operating expenses					2,400,000
Profit					$228,960
Profit percentage					8.7%
Investment					$23,000,000
Annualized return on investment					11.9%

* Minutes per month (30 days × 24 hours × 60 minutes × (1 − 0.10 maintenance time)

In the example, the Hedgehog Deluxe product has the largest throughput per minute, and so is scheduled to be first priority for production. The Hedgehog Digger has the lowest throughput per minute, so it is given last priority in the production schedule. If there is less time available on the bottleneck operation, the company should reduce the number of the Hedgehog Digger product manufactured in order to maximize overall profits.

In the middle of the model, the "Total bottleneck scheduled time" row contains the total number of minutes of scheduled production. The row below it, labeled "Total bottleneck time available," represents the total estimate of time that the bottleneck should have available for production purposes during the scheduling period. Since the time scheduled and available are identical, this means that the production schedule has completely maximized the availability of the bottleneck operation.

One calculation anomaly in the model is that the profit percentage is normally calculated as profit divided by revenues. However, since revenues are not included in the model, we instead use profits divided by throughput. Since throughput is less than revenue, we are overstating the profit percentage as compared to the traditional profit percentage calculation.

The constraint analysis model can be used in a before-and-after mode, to see what effect a proposed change will have on profitability or the return on investment. If the model improves as a result of a change, then implement the change. In the next few sections, we will examine how the constraint analysis model is used to arrive at several management decisions.

The Decision to Sell at a Lower Price

A common scenario is for a customer to promise a large order, but only if the company agrees to a substantial price drop. The sales department may favor such deals, because they bolster the company backlog, earn commissions, and increase market share. The trouble is that these deals also elbow out other jobs that may have higher throughput per minute. If so, the special deal drops overall throughput and may lead to a loss. The following example, which uses the basic constraint model as a baseline, illustrates the problem.

EXAMPLE

Mole Industries has received an offer from a customer to buy 2,000 units of its highly profitable Hedgehog Deluxe, but only if the company reduces the price. The new price will shrink the Deluxe's throughput per minute to $60. The analysis is:

Product	Throughput per Minute	Bottleneck Usage (minutes)	Units Scheduled	Total Bottleneck Time	Total Throughput
1. Hedgehog Deluxe	$60	14	2,000	28,000	$1,680,000
2. Hedgehog Mini	70	20	500	10,000	700,000
3. Hedgehog Classic	65	40	22	880	57,200
4. Hedgehog Digger	42	10	0	0	0
		Total bottleneck scheduled time		38,880	
		Total bottleneck time available*		38,880	
			Total throughput		$2,437,200
			Total operating expenses		2,400,000
			Profit		$37,200
			Profit percentage		1.5%
			Investment		$23,000,000
			Annualized return on investment		1.9%

* Minutes per month (30 days × 24 hours × 60 minutes × (1 − 0.10 maintenance time)

The baseline production configuration generated a profit of $228,960, while this new situation creates a profit of only $37,200. The profit decline was caused by a combination of lower throughput per minute for the Hedgehog Deluxe and the increased production capacity assigned to this lower-throughput product, which displaced other, more profitable products. Note that there was no production capacity available at all for the Hedgehog Digger product. Clearly, the company should reject the customer's offer.

The Decision to Outsource Production

One way to manage the bottleneck operation is to outsource work to keep some of the production burden away from the bottleneck. This option is always acceptable if the throughput generated by the outsourced products exceed the price charged to the company by the supplier, *and* the company can replace the throughput per minute that was taken away from the bottleneck operation. The following example, which uses the basic constraint model as a baseline, illustrates the concept.

EXAMPLE

Mole Industries receives an offer from a supplier to outsource the Hedgehog Classic to it. The supplier will even drop ship the product to customers, so the product would no longer impact Mole's production process in any way. The downside of the offer is that the supplier's price is higher than the cost at which Mole can produce the Classic internally, so the total monthly throughput attributable to the Classic would decline by $300,000, from $520,000 to $220,000. However, there is a large customer order backlog for the Hedgehog Digger, so Mole could give increased production priority to the Digger instead. The analysis is:

Product	Throughput per Minute	Bottleneck Usage (minutes)	Units Scheduled	Total Bottleneck Time	Total Throughput
1. Hedgehog Deluxe	$80	14	1,000	14,000	$1,120,000
2. Hedgehog Mini	70	20	500	10,000	700,000
3. Hedgehog Classic	65	40	200	N/A	220,000
4. Hedgehog Digger	42	10	1,488	14,880	624,960
		Total bottleneck scheduled time		38,880	
		Total bottleneck time available*		38,880	
			Total throughput		$2,664,960
			Total operating expenses		2,400,000
			Profit		$264,960
			Profit percentage		9.9%
			Investment		$23,000,000
			Annualized return on investment		13.8%

* Minutes per month (30 days × 24 hours × 60 minutes × (1 – 0.10 maintenance time)

Despite a large decline in throughput caused by the outsourcing deal, the company actually earns $36,000 more profit overall, because the Hedgehog Classic uses more of the bottleneck time per unit (40 minutes) than any other product; this allows the company to fill the available bottleneck time with 800 more Hedgehog Digger products, which require the smallest amount of bottleneck time per unit (10 minutes), and which generate sufficient additional throughput to easily offset the throughput decline caused by outsourcing. Mole Industries should accept the supplier's offer to outsource.

The Capital Investment Decision

In a large production environment, there are constant requests to invest more funds in various areas in order to increase efficiencies. However, it rarely makes sense to invest in areas that do not favorably impact the bottleneck operation in some way. In particular, investments in the capacity of operations located downstream from the bottleneck operation rarely yield a return, since improving them does nothing for the overall profitability of the entire system. The issue is addressed in the following example, which uses the basic constraint model as a baseline.

EXAMPLE

The industrial engineering manager of Mole Industries examines the entire production line, and concludes that he can double the speed of the paint shop for an investment of $250,000. This operation is located at the very end of the production line, and so is located downstream from the bottleneck operation. The analysis is:

Product	Throughput per Minute	Bottleneck Usage (minutes)	Units Scheduled	Total Bottleneck Time	Total Throughput
1. Hedgehog Deluxe	$80	14	1,000	14,000	$1,120,000
2. Hedgehog Mini	70	20	500	10,000	700,000
3. Hedgehog Classic	65	40	200	8,000	520,000
4. Hedgehog Digger	42	10	688	6,880	288,960
		Total bottleneck scheduled time		38,880	
		Total bottleneck time available*		38,880	
			Total throughput		$2,628,960
			Total operating expenses		2,400,000
			Profit		$228,960
			Profit percentage		8.7%
			Investment		$23,250,000
			Annualized return on investment		11.8%

* Minutes per month (30 days × 24 hours × 60 minutes × (1 – 0.10 maintenance time)

The only item that changes in the analysis is the amount of the investment, which increases by $250,000 and results in a reduced return on investment. Improving the capacity of the paint shop has no effect on throughput, since the entire production line can still only run at the maximum pace of the bottleneck operation.

There are some types of investment that can make sense, even if they are not associated with the bottleneck operation. In particular, if an investment can reduce the cost of an operation, then the investment is acceptable, as long as the return on investment percentage increases as a result of the change. The concept is illustrated in the following example.

EXAMPLE

Rather than proposing a capacity increase in the paint shop (as was the case in the last example), the industrial engineering manager of Mole Industries proposes to invest $250,000 in the paint shop, but only to add sufficient automation to reduce operating expenses by $5,000 per month. The analysis is:

Product	Throughput per Minute	Bottleneck Usage (minutes)	Units Scheduled	Total Bottleneck Time	Total Throughput
1. Hedgehog Deluxe	$80	14	1,000	14,000	$1,120,000
2. Hedgehog Mini	70	20	500	10,000	700,000
3. Hedgehog Classic	65	40	200	8,000	520,000
4. Hedgehog Digger	42	10	688	6,880	288,960
		Total bottleneck scheduled time		38,880	
		Total bottleneck time available*		38,880	
			Total throughput		$2,628,960
			Total operating expenses		2,395,000
			Profit		$233,960
			Profit percentage		8.7%
			Investment		$23,250,000
			Annualized return on investment		12.1%

* Minutes per month (30 days × 24 hours × 60 minutes × (1 – 0.10 maintenance time)

The investment creates a sufficient decline in total operating expenses to yield an increase in the annualized rate of return, to 12.1%. Consequently, this is a worthwhile investment opportunity.

The Decision to Cancel a Product

A common practice is to review all products issued by a company, carefully allocating costs to each one, to see if any are losing money. If so, management may agree to cancel them. However, when products are reviewed from the perspective of constraint analysis, they are almost never cancelled. The reason is that the basis of measurement should be throughput, which is revenues minus totally variable expenses, and since the cost of materials is really the only variable expense, there is *always* throughput. A company rarely prices its products at or below the cost of its materials, since that would result in catastrophic losses.

Since all products are likely to have throughput, the real question is not which products have the lowest throughput, but rather which ones have the highest throughput. By focusing on these high-throughput products, management can readily see which items to bring most forcibly to the attention of customers. If the result is an increased volume of production of products having high throughput, then the low

78

throughput products may be forced out of the production mix, simply because there is no production capacity left to manufacture them.

If you were to follow the more traditional approach of assigning overhead to products and then deciding if they are unprofitable, the result would be the ongoing elimination of products, as overhead costs are gradually shifted to fewer and fewer remaining products, driving up the cost of each one in turn and forcing management to conclude that each one should be cancelled. The following example illustrates the concept.

EXAMPLE

Mole Industries has three versions of a trench digging tool. The company has $4,000,000 of overhead that it allocates to the three products. The company allocates the overhead based on revenue. The cost characteristics of the products are:

Product	Revenue	Variable Costs	Overhead Costs	Margin
Hedgehog Classic	$2,000,000	$1,300,000	$800,000	-$100,000
Hedgehog Mini	3,000,000	1,600,000	1,200,000	200,000
Hedgehog Deluxe	5,000,000	2,400,000	2,000,000	600,000
Totals	$10,000,000	$5,300,000	$4,000,000	$700,000

Hedgehog's president decides that, since the full cost of the Hedgehog Classic results in a loss, he should cancel that product. This results in the next table, where the same overhead is now being allocated (based on revenue) between the two remaining products.

Product	Revenue	Variable Costs	Overhead Costs	Margin
Hedgehog Mini	$3,000,000	$1,600,000	$1,500,000	-$100,000
Hedgehog Deluxe	5,000,000	2,400,000	2,500,000	100,000
Totals	$8,000,000	$4,000,000	$4,000,000	$0

Hedgehog's president now sees that the Hedgehog Mini is losing money! Not knowing what else to do, he cancels that product, too. The result is shown in the next table:

Product	Revenue	Variable Costs	Overhead Costs	Margin
Hedgehog Deluxe	5,000,000	2,400,000	4,000,000	-$1,400,000
Totals	$5,000,000	$2,400,000	$4,000,000	-$1,400,000

Hedgehog's president gives up, closes down the company, and takes a cost accounting class to figure out what happened. He later learns that all three products were contributing toward the pool of overhead that needed to be paid for. As he successively stripped away each product, that left the remaining products to shoulder more of the overhead load.

Eventually, the Hedgehog Deluxe was left, and it did not generate enough of a margin to pay for all of the overhead.

Summary

Constraint analysis is one of the primary tools available for cost management. It makes quite clear where the bottleneck operation is located, the extreme expense associated with not maximizing it, and how to manage operations to maximize profits.

However, it can be a foreign concept to many managers, who have spent their careers working on local optimization issues, allocating overhead, and improving the efficiency of labor – all of which are concepts that constraint analysis teaches do not improve overall profitability. Accordingly, we suggest having a financial analyst trained in constraint analysis, and have this person use constraint concepts to render opinions on whether certain cost management decisions should be made.

Chapter 8
Process Analysis

Introduction

Even a smaller organization has several dozen key processes, while a major corporation may use several thousand processes. Each process evolved over time to meet the changing needs of the business, usually with little analysis to streamline the process. Consequently, processes tend to require too much time and too many resources, and so represent an enormous streamlining opportunity that can not only cut costs, but also reduce the time required to complete transactions.

There are a number of tools available for reviewing processes, which can be used to transform a business into one that operates in a lean manner while still retaining the capability to meet goals on a consistent basis. In this chapter, we make note of several tools that can be used to spot areas of potential process improvement.

> **Related Podcast Episodes:** Episodes 32, 67, and 72 of the Accounting Best Practices Podcast discuss accounting run charts, value stream mapping, and office work flow, respectively. They are available at: **accountingtools.com/podcasts** or **iTunes**

Process Analysis Tools

A process is a set of activities that transform an input into a useful output. Examples of key processes are the purchasing of goods, the shipping of goods to a customer, and issuing an invoice to a customer. Each process likely includes a variety of inefficiencies that can be detected with process analysis tools. Common types of inefficiencies are:

- An excessively long travel time to move a document to another person
- A long wait time before a document is reviewed
- A redundant supervisory approval
- A document copy that is filed and never used
- A type of information that is collected and never used
- Too many people are involved in the process

Through the remainder of this section, we make note of a number of process analysis tools that can be used to highlight process inefficiencies. Value stream mapping is used to document a variety of information in each step of a process. Flowcharts are used to provide an at-a-glance visual representation of a process. Run charts are useful for spotting changes in long-term trends that can indicate an out-of-control process. Check sheets are a simple technique for collecting information, usually about error rates. Root cause analysis is a tool for investigating why a problem occurs. Traffic analysis is used to reduce travel time by reconfiguring a work area. These tools can be used individually or as a group to accumulate the information needed to create tighter process flows.

Value Stream Mapping

A value stream map (VSM) reveals a considerable amount of information about the activities that we engage in to create value. Depending upon the format used, it can point out such information as:

- The work time and wait time required for each step in a process
- The amount of labor needed for a work step, including the identification of overtime
- The error rate by work step
- Downtime by work step

The resulting charts can be used to pinpoint areas needing improvement, such as reductions in errors, automation to eliminate staff time, and altered controls to shorten process flows.

The VSM concept is best explained with an example. In the following sample of the timekeeping process, we see that the accounting staff requires only a small amount of staffing and time to process two steps, which are issuing reminders to employees and verifying supervisory approval of time cards. However, the VSM indicates that the controller must allocate more staff to the tasks of reviewing received time cards and summarizing hours worked. These latter two tasks are so time-sensitive that they routinely require the use of overtime to be completed on time. The map also shows a high error rate. Further, the VSM reveals that a total of 25.5 hours are needed to complete this step, which is the lengthiest part of the payroll process.

Sample Value Stream Map – Timekeeping

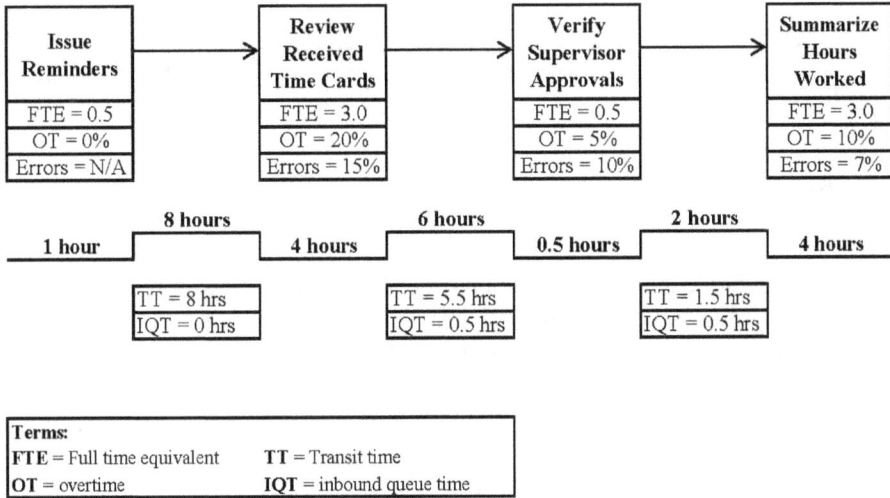

Issue Reminders	Review Received Time Cards	Verify Supervisor Approvals	Summarize Hours Worked
FTE = 0.5	FTE = 3.0	FTE = 0.5	FTE = 3.0
OT = 0%	OT = 20%	OT = 5%	OT = 10%
Errors = N/A	Errors = 15%	Errors = 10%	Errors = 7%

1 hour	8 hours / 4 hours	6 hours / 0.5 hours	2 hours / 4 hours
	TT = 8 hrs	TT = 5.5 hrs	TT = 1.5 hrs
	IQT = 0 hrs	IQT = 0.5 hrs	IQT = 0.5 hrs

Terms:	
FTE = Full time equivalent	TT = Transit time
OT = overtime	IQT = inbound queue time

Given the issues shown in the map, it would be reasonable to implement a more automated method of time tracking, such as a computerized time clock. By doing so, the two bottlenecks in the process can be eliminated, along with overtime and the high error rate. Automation will also likely reduce the total processing time by a substantial amount. The controller might not have realized the severity of the problems with timekeeping without a VSM to clarify the issues.

Consider focusing particular attention on the time periods in a VSM that are between processing steps. The amount of transit and inbound queue time listed in these areas likely exceeds the processing time by an enormous amount, and represents an excellent opportunity for time reduction. In the preceding example, the transit and inbound queue times represent 63% of the total process time. If this slack time can be reduced, the overall capacity of a process increases, which means that fewer resources can be allocated to a process.

Tip: The information in a value stream map is an aggregation of many transactions. If you drill down to individual transactions in a process, you will likely find that about 20% of the transactions cause 80% of the problems, usually because they represent unexpected or unusually complex transactions.

Value stream mapping is an especially effective tool when used to break down the elements of high-volume processes; these processes are completed many times in a typical year, so even small changes can yield large cumulative benefits. Conversely, there is little point in using VSM to analyze tasks that require little time and are only rarely completed, since there is only a modest opportunity for improvement.

> **Tip:** Errors are more likely when there are long inbound queue times, because the size of the work backlog forces employees to cut corners to complete work in a timely manner.

Flowcharts

A flowchart is extremely useful for creating a visual representation of how a process operates. It usually incorporates references to any forms and reports used, which is useful for seeing the complete scope of a process at a glance. Flowcharts are particularly useful for before-and-after views of a process, to see what will happen once a proposed improvement has been installed. For example, the following flowchart reveals what happens to the payroll timekeeping process flow that we just analyzed with a value stream map, after several improvements (noted in bold) are made to the process.

Sample Timekeeping Flowchart

```
              ┌─────────────────────┐
              │  Issue automated    │
              │  reminder to enter  │
              │     hours in        │
              │ timekeeping system  │
              └─────────────────────┘
```

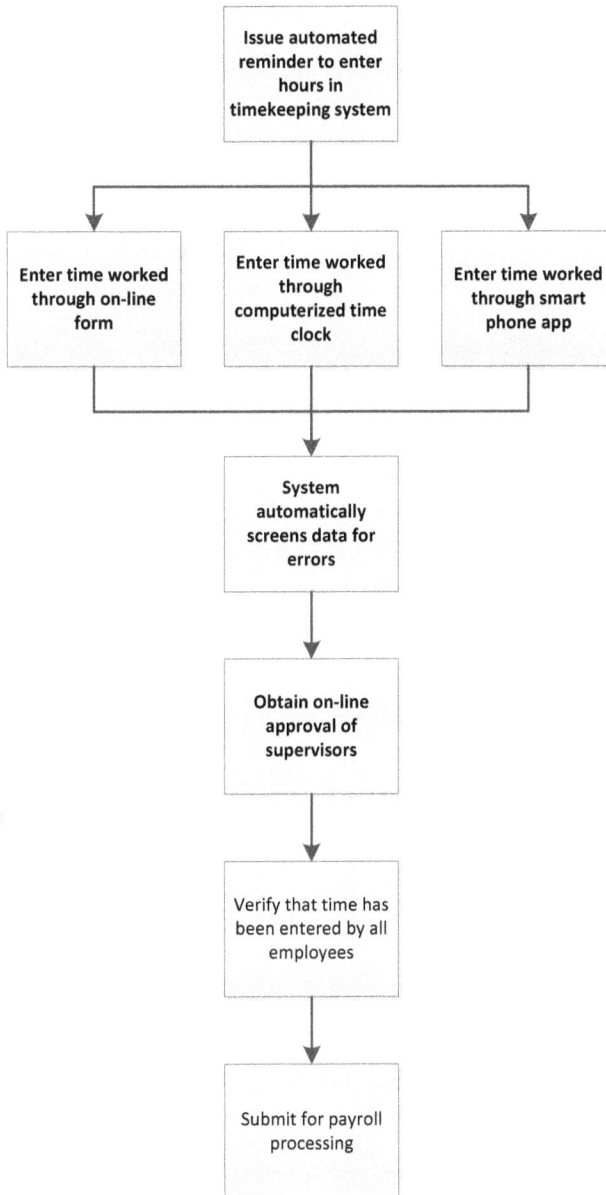

Flowcharting is useful for revealing the complexity of a process. Any process that requires many processing steps is a prime source of costly errors, which can be reduced by simplifying or eliminating the process steps.

Run Charts

A run chart shows the performance of a process on a trend line. It is used to high-light spikes or dips in process results that could indicate the presence of problems in the underlying system. This information would then serve as the trigger for a more in-depth investigation. The chart usually incorporates two trend lines, which are:

- *Average*. This is the short-term average results of the process, and should be a straight line across the chart.
- *Actual results*. This is the actual results of the most immediate set of time periods.

Examples of applications for run charts are:

- *Accounts payable*. The number of days to obtain approval of supplier invoices, or the number of supplier invoices paid late, or the number of early payment discounts not taken.
- *Customer billings*. The number of hours to issue a customer invoice, or the number of invoicing errors found by customers.
- *Payroll*. The number of payment errors found per payroll.

> **Tip:** There is always some natural variability around the average results of a process. Consider establishing the normal amount of variability, and then focus on results that fall outside of that range, especially if they remain outside the normal range for a series of consecutive measurements.

Run charts are most useful in applications where there are a large number of trans-actions, so they are most applicable to such areas as customer shipments, customer billings, and payroll.

Check Sheets

When tallying the number of errors or other events in a process, it is useful to use a structured format, known as a check sheet, to collect the information. This is a simple grid on which is listed down the left side the errors or events that are to be tracked, with columns for each day of the measurement period, and a totals column on the far right side. The intent of a check sheet is to allow someone to easily mark down the number of observed instances of an event within a certain period of time, so that the relative frequency of each item can be determined. Management will likely authorize further action to reduce the instances of whichever items have proven to be the most common.

In the following exhibit, we show a check sheet that has been constructed to compile different types of errors that employees are finding while observing a series of cycle counts in the warehouse.

Sample Check Sheet for Cycle Counting Issues Found

	Day					
	Mon.	Tue.	Wed.	Thu.	Fri.	Total
Incorrect unit of measure	II	IIII		I	IIIII	12
Incorrect quantity		II	IIII	I	III	10
Incorrect part number	III	I		IIIII		9
Incorrect bin location	I	I	III		II	7
Total	6	8	7	7	10	38

The sample check sheet reveals that incorrect units of measure have the largest number of observed errors, and so might be worth the most immediate corrective action.

Root Cause Analysis

Root cause analysis is the task of looking underneath the symptoms of a problem, to find the reasons why the problem is occurring. By correcting the underlying root causes of problems, the incidence of the problems can be greatly reduced or eliminated. Root cause analysis tends to uncover issues related to the failure of materials, an error by a person, or an organizational issue (such as an incorrect work instruction).

It is quite possible that finding and correcting a single root cause will not completely eliminate a particular problem. If so, root cause analysis can be conducted on a recurring basis, to gradually locate and eliminate a series of issues. Eventually, the number of times the triggering problem arises may decline to the point where additional effort is considered unnecessary, though there may be additional root causes still causing problems; the remaining issues are simply considered too immaterial to pursue, or their correction is not cost-effective.

EXAMPLE

Walker Inc. finds that there is a high return rate by customers for its baby stroller product, because there are repeated instances where the wheels fall off. After conducting a root cause analysis, the company finds that the nut used to tighten the wheels onto the axles has the wrong specifications, which it corrects in the bill of materials for the product. As a result, the company finds that product returns are reduced, but do not go away, due to the same complaint. Additional analysis finds that the axle onto which the nut is tightened can break off, due to metal fatigue. As a result, the company buys the axle component with more stringent specifications, after which the returns issue is eliminated.

Root cause analysis can be used in a variety of areas. For example, it can uncover the reasons for incorrect shipments, product failures, and inventory record accuracy issues. It is most heavily applied to the resolution of product failure issues, but can be readily adapted to the analysis of failures in company processes.

Root cause analysis may require a large amount of detailed investigation, not only to find a root cause, but also to generate several possible solutions that will correct the underlying issue. The solution selected will usually be the simplest or least expensive alternative available, and one that does not trigger a new root cause that leads to a new problem or reinforces an old problem.

Once a sufficient history of root cause analysis projects have built up within a firm, it is possible to apply this history to projected new processes to predict failures that may occur. Doing so allows a business to make corrections before an implementation begins.

Traffic Analysis

Traffic analysis involves observing the movements of employees through an area. Write down the tasks which are required within or outside of the target area, and the distances traveled while engaged in each one. These observations will likely highlight the need for several changes in the layout of a department, because of the following issues:

- Filing cabinets are clustered at one end of the department, requiring a long walk by those clerks located at the other end of the department.
- Office equipment is clustered at one end of the department, or is located outside of the department, which calls for more travel time by everyone.
- Employees are not clustered together by job junction, so they must travel within the department to confer on certain issues.
- Those employees that regularly interact with other departments are not located as close to those departments as possible.

A likely outcome of traffic analysis is the reconfiguration of the department into production cells. A production cell is a work area that is specifically configured to achieve a certain task with a high level of efficiency. The concept has been used for many years in the manufacturing area, where a set of machines may be clustered together to most easily create a particular component. The same concept can be used in other areas, which can be configured to most efficiently complete specific tasks. For example:

- *Billing.* A work area can include a computer terminal, all files relating to sales orders and bills of lading, ready access to customer folders, and a printer that is pre-loaded with a supply of the company's invoice form.
- *Cash receipts.* A work area can include a computer terminal, check scanning equipment, a small photocopier, and a safe in which checks may be stored.
- *Payroll.* A work area can include a locked cabinet containing payroll reports and confidential employee information, a computer terminal giving access to computerized time clocks, a printer that is pre-configured for

paycheck printing, a safe for the storage of paychecks, and a supply of overnight delivery packages for the issuance of payments to outlying company locations.

The production cell concept may still work even when there are only a few people in a department. A small number of cubicles can be set up in this manner, and employees simply move to a different location when they need to complete a different task.

Summary

We must introduce a note of caution in this discussion of process analysis. Do not attempt to arrive at an improved set of processes by enforcing a tsunami of change. Instead, we strongly recommend an experiment-and-test model. This approach involves the following steps:

1. Measure an unaltered process, so there is quantitative information about its performance.
2. Alter the process on a pilot basis with a new concept, and run the pilot for a sufficiently long time to be reasonably sure that the revised process has settled down and is producing consistent results.
3. Measure the altered process.
4. If the altered process yields improved results, expand or fully roll out the concept. However, if the alteration does not yield a verifiable improvement, either continue altering the process within the existing pilot project or cancel the change.

This type of carefully delineated testing makes it much more likely that you will indeed be able to eventually arrive at a more efficient and effective operating environment, though the necessary amount of testing will probably delay the end result.

Another consideration when evaluating a process is to only introduce those changes that make sense from a cost-effectiveness perspective. All too frequently, managers embrace advanced technological solutions when their operations are simply too small to make the investments worthwhile. For example, it is absolutely unnecessary to invest in a document imaging system when accounting records are already stored adjacent to the accounting staff, and the incidence of record searches is relatively low. Similarly, a small company that operates from a single location probably does not need to invest several million dollars in an advanced enterprise resources planning system that ties together the operations of every department. Instead, there are simple and inexpensive alternatives to many of these technology solutions that may not be quite as efficient, but which are vastly more cost-effective.

Chapter 9
Zero-Base Budgeting

Introduction

Zero-base budgeting is the process of conducting a thorough, top-to-bottom analysis of the need for expenditures in a budget period. The underlying concept is that a business must meet certain objectives in order to remain viable over time, so different packages of expenditures can be associated with each of these objectives. Managers can then decide upon which packages of costs to incur, delay, or avoid. This chapter addresses the basics of zero-base budgeting, how such a budget is assembled, the ancillary concept of conditional budgeting, and several other related topics.

Related Podcast Episodes: Episodes 71, 130, and 131 of the Accounting Best Practices Podcast discuss budget model improvements, the problems with budgeting, and operating without a budget, respectively. They are available at: **accountingtools.com/podcasts** or **iTunes**

Overview of Zero-Base Budgeting

A zero-base budget requires managers to justify *all* of their budgeted expenditures, rather than the more common approach of only requiring justification for incremental changes to the budget or the actual results from the preceding year. Thus, a manager is theoretically assumed to have an expenditure base line of zero (hence the name of the budgeting method). In reality, a manager is assumed to have a minimum amount of funding for basic departmental operations, above which additional funding must be justified. The intent of the process is to continually refocus cost management on key business objectives, and terminate or scale back any activities no longer related to those objectives.

The basic process flow under zero-base budgeting is:

1. Identify business objectives
2. Create and evaluate alternative methods for accomplishing each objective
3. Evaluate alternative funding levels, depending on planned performance levels
4. Set priorities

The concept of paring back expenses in layers can also be used in reverse, to delineate the specific costs and capital investment that will be incurred if you add an additional service or function. Thus, management can make discrete determinations of the exact combination of incremental cost and service for a business. This process will typically result in at least a minimum service level, which establishes a cost baseline below which it is impossible for a business to go, along with various gradations of service above the minimum.

One cost area that falls outside of the rigorous examination imposed by zero-base budgeting is the direct costs associated with providing a product or service. The zero-base concept addresses levels of service provided, whereas direct costs (such as the direct materials used in a product) *must* be incurred in order to generate a sale – there is no management decision involved.

Conversely, zero-base budgeting can be applied everywhere else in a business; such as corporate functions, research and development, engineering, maintenance, sales and marketing, procurement, and so forth. The concept is particularly applicable where costs must be expended in order to achieve a goal. For example, if a manager is assigned a budget of $1 million in the marketing area and only spends $980,000, was this good or bad? There was a cost savings, but did the manager achieve whatever goal was intended when the budget was assigned? Since zero-base budgeting establishes a link between a goal and an expenditure, you can tell if the amount spent was worthwhile.

Examples of the actions that can be taken under a zero-base budget appear in the following exhibit.

Zero-Based Budgeting Actions

Activity Area	Reduced Funding	Increased Funding
Accounting	Reduce collections and increase bad debt write-offs	Add collections staff to reduce bad debts
Information Systems	Eliminate desktop computer support	Roll out a work-from-home solution
Maintenance	Reduce to minimum maintenance level	Install preventive maintenance program
Marketing	Drop general awareness campaign	Add product survey program
Procurement	Eliminate competitive bidding	Implement supplier certification
Warehouse	Eliminate cycle counting program	Install wireless bar code scanners

The Zero-Base Budgeting Process

The key steps in zero-base budgeting are to develop *decision packages* and then rank the decision packages. The first step involves examining each discrete activity that a company engages in and associating funding with them in a document called a decision package, while the second step uses either cost/benefit or subjective analysis to rank the decision packages in order of importance. The decision packages that have been approved for funding are then assembled, assigned to a section of the budget (usually the responsibility area of a manager), and related costs are assigned to those budget sections. This results in the final budget. We will now expand upon the steps in this process.

Step 1 - Develop Decision Packages

A decision package is a document that provides management with sufficient information about a business activity to decide how to rank it against other activities, ultimately resulting in a decision to approve or reject it. The package should include the following information:

- Purpose of the activity
- Consequences to the business of not performing it
- Alternatives to performing it
- Costs and benefits associated with it
- Performance metrics related to it

A business may create a different decision package for a great many business activities. The following exhibit contains a sample list of business activities that may have decision packages built around them.

Decision Packages Associated with Business Activities

Functional Area	Business Activities
Accounting	Accounts payable, budgeting, collections, credit granting, financial analysis, fixed asset tracking, internal auditing, management reporting, payroll, record keeping, tax reporting, tax planning
Administration	Board of directors, building maintenance, grounds maintenance, janitorial, mail delivery, reception, safety, security, travel management
Engineering	Equipment procurement, operations analysis, plant design, process development, safety analysis, tool design, work measurement
Human resources	Benefits analysis, compensation analysis, job evaluations, labor relations, recruiting, training
Information technology	Backup management, equipment maintenance, program maintenance, system design and development
Legal	Contract reviews, contract negotiations, litigation, patent analysis, patent licensing, trademark analysis
Logistics	Inventory counting, materials transportation, putaways, picking, receiving, shipping
Procurement	Bid management, contract negotiation, purchase order processing
Production	Equipment planning, parts control, preventive maintenance, production planning, routine maintenance
Quality assurance	Finished goods testing, inbound testing, in-process testing, supplier certification
Research and development	Administrative support, equipment maintenance, research by project
Risk management	Claims management, loss prevention, insurance management, warranty claims analysis
Sales and marketing	Advertising, brochure management, catalog management, order processing, promotions, sales force management, sales forecasting, test marketing

Senior management should issue to the department managers an overview of the general level of activity that it expects the business to handle during the upcoming budget period. The department managers use this information as a guideline in the development of their decision packages. These guidelines could include such factors as:

- The estimated number of units of each product to be sold
- The identity of any new geographical regions to be served
- The number of new stores to be opened
- Changes in the size or location of company facilities
- Expected company headcount
- Planned changes to centralize or decentralize operations

When managers develop decision packages, the key item in the decision package is the discussion of activity alternatives. This can involve alternative ways to perform an activity, or different levels of effort to perform the activity. In the first case, describe the best way to perform the activity in detail, and then state other alternatives and why they were discarded. In the second case, state the minimum level of effort, and then address the result of different levels of effort in one or more additional decision packages. The minimum level of effort is considered to be at roughly 50% - 75% of the current level of operation. The alternatives presented under the level of effort classification should address the following levels of expenditure:

- Eliminate the activity entirely.
- Minimum level. This is the cost required to operate the activity at the minimum level; the company's objectives may not be achieved. This is the level below which any activity is no longer effective, and would likely be terminated.
- Current level. This is the cost required in the budget period to maintain the current level of activity. This may not be the historical cost level, since planned efficiency improvements may reduce costs, or inflation may increase costs.
- Increased level. This is the amount required to operate the activity at a higher level of performance.

When constructing a zero-base budget, it may be difficult to allocate overhead expenses to the various funding packages, because it is not possible to predict with certainty which cost packages management will select, and the levels of overhead arbitrarily allocated to the various packages may not reflect the amount of overhead that the business will actually incur. The best solution is to sidestep the problem by including all overhead expenditures in a baseline cost package that represents the minimum cost structure of the company. Any other overhead that would be incurred above this level should be associated with a higher-level cost package.

EXAMPLE

The controller of Quest Adventure Gear is developing a decision package for the accounts receivable collections activity. He describes the best way to perform the activity as follows:

Recommended decision package. Maintain the current method of using four dedicated collection personnel, at a cost of $40,000 each. This level of effort is needed to minimize bad debts and avoid shipping holds for orders currently in process.

Alternatives not recommended.

- *Shift collections to sales staff*. The sales staff has the best hands-on knowledge of customers, but engaging in collections research and contacts would reduce the time they could otherwise spend on sales activities.
- *Outsource collections*. An outside collections firm would apply aggressive pressure on customers and may therefore obtain payment sooner than usual, but might also exacerbate relations with customers, and would also be very expensive.

Level of effort.

1. **Minimum expenditure level**. Reduce the collections staff to two full-time employees. This ensures at least one contact with all customers having receivable balances over $25,000 in each month. There would be no contact with customers under this receivable balance level until receivables are at least 60 days old. **Cost = $80,000**.
2. **Current staffing level**. Retain four full-time collection employees. This ensures contact with all customers having receivable balances over $10,000, once receivables are at least 40 days old. **Cost = $160,000**.
3. **Expanded staffing**. Add an in-house attorney to the collections staff. Doing so allows us to file claims in small claims court as well as larger cases, and collect on judgments. This approach eliminates the need to outsource collections. The elimination of outsourcing fees will offset half of the incremental cost of this option. **Cost = $240,000**.

In the example, the controller could provide additional explanatory information associated with each option. For example, if he were explaining the third option under the level of effort, he might itemize the additional incremental cost associated with the third option for the next few quarters or years. By doing so, senior management would be apprised of any sudden changes in costs in later periods. The example shows that the cost of hiring the attorney in the third option was $80,000. But what if the controller expected to increase the attorney's pay by $20,000 in the following year in order to provide a competitive wage? That knowledge might lead senior management to not select the third option. In the following sample format, note that we do not present this information as a single line item, but rather at its gross cost, followed by any offsetting cost savings; we then provide the net cost to the company after both issues have been combined. This gives senior management more complete information about the decision package. Also, the gross cost is certain, while the projected cost savings are an estimate, and so may be worth discussing. Thus, it makes sense to separate the two items for examination.

Sample Cost Estimate Format for Decision Package

Level of Effort Option 3 – Add Attorney

	Quarter 1	Quarter 2	Quarter 3	Quarter 4	Quarter 5	Quarter 6
Gross cost	$20,000	$20,000	$20,000	$20,000	$25,000	$25,000
Related cost savings	-5,000	-9,000	-17,000	-22,000	-24,000	-25,000
Net cost	$15,000	$11,000	$3,000	-$2,000	$1,000	$0

The sample cost estimate format shows that the attorney will gradually ramp up his or her productivity to the point where there is no net cost by the fourth quarter, but that a projected annualized pay boost of $20,000 in the fifth quarter will make this an essentially breakeven proposition.

It may also be useful to include in the decision package an itemization of the metrics that will change as the result of making a decision. Only include this information if it may have an impact on the decision of the reviewer. Also, if it is included, be sure to include historical comparisons, so that a trend line of changes is shown. The following sample shows the impact on days sales outstanding (DSO) if senior management were to select the minimum expenditure level for the collections function. Note that two-year historical comparative information is included.

Sample Metrics Format for Decision Package

	Historical 2 Years Ago	Historical 1 Year Ago	Budget Period Year 1	Budget Period Year 2
Days sales outstanding	50	49	55	62

It is also possible that, depending on the circumstances, there is only one option available. If so, state the reason(s) for the lack of alternatives. It is more likely that there are a variety of sub-optimal solutions; if so, state those solutions and the reasons why they yield inadequate results, so that senior management gains a better picture of the situation.

Tip: When the manager of a functional area prepares a variety of cost packages for consideration by senior management and suspects that they may select the minimum service level, watch for cases where the manager *increases* the amount of expense at the minimum service level. Doing so allows him to actually provide the higher service level that he wants, rather than the true minimum service level that senior management wants.

The preceding example should make it clear that a vastly greater amount of work is required to prepare decision packages than would normally be the case under a traditional budgeting environment. A truly comprehensive and well thought-out set of decision packages will likely require the input of multiple people, so this approach tends to involve the opinions of more employees than just the department managers.

A manager who is directly responsible for an activity should prepare all decision packages associated with it. Senior management should evaluate all decision packages submitted and select which packages to use. That evaluation occurs in the next step.

Step 2 - Rank Decision Packages

Once the senior management team has received all decision packages from around the company, it must rank them in order of decreasing benefit or importance. This includes an analysis of the consequences associated with reducing funding from the current level for each decision package. The managers forwarding the decision packages should provide a preliminary ranking of the packages, based on their knowledge of the company's objectives. These opinions are quite valuable, since lower-level managers have the best operational knowledge of the company, and therefore of where changes in funding will have the greatest impact. In most cases, the senior management team will likely accept the recommendations of their subordinates. Only in cases where a clear change of direction or resource allocation is indicated will senior managers find it necessary to alter these recommendations.

In a large company, it may be necessary to consolidate sets of decision packages together, each describing a different scenario, and then make a decision for the entire set of decision packages. For example, the lowest level of a business may be its retail stores, for which there are separate distribution and sales systems by geographic region. Mid-level managers could select the best options for decision packages at the level of the geographic region in order to meet a company-wide goal of reducing costs. This may involve shuttering some stores and centralizing warehouses. At the executive level of the company, managers could decide among these consolidated decision packages, perhaps to pursue cost reduction in one region in order to fund more extensive growth through store expansions in a different region. This means that senior-level managers may not find it necessary to wade through each individual decision package; instead, they can select from a small number of pre-selected groupings, based on general company objectives.

Tip: Be sure to include expenditures for fixed assets in the decision packages, so that managers can see the complete set of cash flows associated with a decision. This may also involve the disposition of existing fixed assets if management decides to scale back on or eliminate existing activities. You can also include in the decision packages different ways to acquire fixed assets, such as through outright purchases, leases, or short-term rentals.

In most cases, a company is constrained in its selection of decision packages by the amount of available funding. In this environment, senior management will likely only have a modest amount of discretionary funds available, and so will need to rank the decision packages to determine where to allocate funds. This is not necessarily a case of assigning funds to the decision package that has the largest monetary payback. Instead, the ranking system should highlight those areas in which additional or reduced expenditures have the greatest and least impact on company objectives, respectively. Based on both a quantitative and subjective analysis of the rankings, senior management then decides where to allocate funds.

The following table illustrates the incremental cost levels associated with a variety of decision packages. It does not include a discussion of which objectives will be met (or not) at each funding level, but does show the aggregate levels of funding included in the decision packages. This information is useful for determining the range of potential funding requirements, as well as the minimum level of funding at which a company can operate.

Summary of Decision Package Funding Levels

Decision Unit	Last Year Actual Cost	Minimum Package	Current Level	Increased Level
Accounts payable	$230,000	$170,000	$55,000	$25,000
Budgeting	60,000	0	62,000	78,000
Collections	120,000	60,000	65,000	25,000
Credit granting	50,000	0	52,000	23,000
Financial analysis	38,000	15,000	25,000	30,000
Fixed asset tracking	25,000	5,000	20,000	0
Internal auditing	48,000	24,000	25,000	15,000
Management reporting	35,000	10,000	27,000	20,000
Payroll	92,000	80,000	14,000	11,000
Record keeping	39,000	20,000	19,000	3,000
Tax reporting	65,000	50,000	15,000	7,000
Tax planning	35,000	0	40,000	30,000
Totals	$837,000	$434,000	$419,000	$267,000
Cumulative total		$434,000	$853,000	$1,120,000
Cumulative % of last year actual		52%	102%	134%

Once the management team selects the various funding levels it wants in all functional areas, it assembles its selections into a budgeted income statement. This income statement includes the usual revenue and direct costs normally found in any income statement, but then the remainder of the document is comprised of the various decision packages. The following sample is an extremely simplified version of what this income statement might look like, using just a few decision packages.

Sample Budgeted Income Statement

	Package Type	Amount	Totals
Revenue		$8,000,000	$8,000,000
Direct materials		2,500,000	
Direct labor		1,000,000	
Fixed overhead		2,200,000	
Cost of goods sold			5,700,000
Accounting:			
Accounts payable	Current	60,000	
Collections	Minimum	40,000	
Payroll	Increased	93,000	
			193,000
Logistics:			
Putaways	Current	80,000	
Picking	Increased	45,000	
Receiving	Minimum	64,000	189,000
Production:			
Production planning	Current	155,000	
Routine maintenance	Current	109,000	
			264,000
Sales and marketing:			
Advertising	Increased	300,000	
Order processing	Minimum	100,000	
Sales force management	Current	550,000	
			950,000
Total expenses			7,296,000
Net income before taxes			$704,000

Advantages of Zero-Base Budgeting

There are a number of advantages to zero-base budgeting, which include:

- *Alternatives analysis.* Zero-base budgeting requires that managers identify alternative ways to perform each activity (such as keeping it in-house or outsourcing it), as well as the effects of different levels of spending. By forcing the development of these alternatives, the process makes managers consider other ways to run the business.

- *Budget inflation.* Since managers must tie expenditures to activities, it becomes less likely that they can artificially inflate their budgets – the change is too easy to spot.
- *Communication.* The zero-base budget should spark a significant debate among the management team about the corporate mission and how it is to be achieved.
- *Eliminate non-key activities.* A zero-base budget review forces managers to decide which activities are most critical to the company. By doing so, they can target non-key activities for elimination or outsourcing.
- *Mission focus.* Since the zero-base budgeting concept requires managers to link expenditures to activities, they are forced to define the various missions of their departments – which might otherwise be poorly defined.
- *Redundancy identification.* The review may reveal that the same activities are being conducted by multiple departments, leading to the elimination of the activity outside of the area where management wants it to be centered.
- *Required review.* Using zero-base budgeting on a regular basis makes it more likely that all aspects of a company will be examined periodically.
- *Resource allocation.* If the process is conducted with the overall corporate mission and objectives in mind, an organization should end up with strong targeting of funds in those areas where they are most needed.

In short, many of the advantages of zero-base budgeting focus on a strong, introspective look at the mission of a business and exactly how the business is managing its costs in order to achieve that mission.

Problems with Zero-Base Budgeting

The main downside of zero-base budgeting is the exceptionally high level of effort required to investigate and document department activities; this is a difficult task even once a year, which causes some entities to only use the procedure once every few years, or when there are significant changes within the organization. Another alternative is to require the use of zero-base budgeting on a rolling basis through different parts of a company over several years, so that management can deal with fewer such reviews per year. Other drawbacks are:

- *Bureaucracy.* Creating a zero-base budget from the ground up on a continuing basis calls for an enormous amount of analysis, meetings, and reports, all of which requires additional staff to manage the process.
- *Gamesmanship.* Some managers may attempt to skew their budget reports to concentrate expenditures under the most vital activities, thereby ensuring that their budgets will not be reduced.
- *Intangible justifications.* It can be difficult to determine or justify expenditure levels for areas of a business that do not produce "concrete," tangible

results. For example, what is the correct amount of marketing expense, and how much should be invested in research and development activities?

- *Managerial time.* The operational review mandated by zero-base budgeting requires a significant amount of management time.
- *Training.* Managers require significant training in the zero-base budgeting process, which further increases the time required each year.
- *Update speed.* The extra effort required to create a zero-base budget makes it even less likely that the management team will revise the budget on a continuous basis to make it more relevant to the competitive situation.

In short, the key downside of zero-base budgeting is the increased level of bureaucracy associated with it.

Conditional Budgeting

A variation on zero-base budgeting is the concept of *conditional budgeting*. Under conditional budgeting, management does not authorize spending the full amount of a budget for a budget period. Instead, associate a certain amount of specific expenditures with a certain level of revenue, gross profit, or net income. Because of the structure of this type of budgeting, it is very important to segregate the various types of revenue by probability of occurrence. These levels can include:

- *Secure revenue.* This revenue is very likely, even under the most pessimistic projections. The sources of this information are likely to be the current order backlog and an analysis of historical sales that are very likely to occur again.
- *Event-driven sales.* This revenue is based on very specific events, such as a promotional campaign, opening a new store, or creating a new sales region.
- *Incremental revenue.* This category is where the less-likely items are placed that arise from such factors as an estimate of increased same-store sales, increased market share, or sales to new customers who are currently serviced by competitors.

When creating the various levels of expenditure that are associated with revenue levels, there will be a minimum revenue level below which it is difficult to go, because the company's fixed costs must be incurred at the baseline cost level, and there will be substantial losses if revenues cannot offset the fixed costs.

Different types of costs are more likely to appear in the various expense tranches. The following cost layers might be used:

- *Minimum cost layer*. Contains all fixed costs, plus the bare minimum expenditures required to keep the company operational over the short-term. This level pares equipment maintenance, does not advocate new fixed asset acquisitions, and may reduce pay levels.
- *Long-term existence cost layer*. Contains those costs required to keep the company in operation over the long term. This includes adequate levels of equipment maintenance, moderate capital expenditures, and market rates of compensation.
- *Robust growth*. Contains those costs required to attain a leading position in the industry. This level includes enhanced training, funds for acquisitions, and a strong research and development department.
- *Incidental items*. Contains those items useful for "rounding out" a company's expenditures, but which are not needed to be a long-term competitive business. This level includes significant donations, improved corporate facilities, enhanced employee benefits above the level needed to normally retain employees, and so forth.

If you were to use the conditional budgeting approach to release a large amount of expenditures as soon as a specific revenue target was reached, the result would appear to be a massive step cost that may cause a major profit decline. Instead, it is more prudent to set up a ranking system within each cost tranche, and then gradually authorize expenses based on this ranking as revenues increase through a predetermined range.

In summary, conditional budgeting reacts to the revenue levels being experienced by a business, releasing funds as revenues reach certain predetermined target levels. Zero-base budgeting, on the other hand, involves the specific targeting of certain expenditure levels in advance of the beginning of the budget period, so that expenditure levels are locked in during the budget period.

Summary

Zero-base budgeting is more of a management technique than strictly a budgeting system, since it calls for a periodic re-examination of the way in which a company does business. As such, it is extremely time-consuming, and may be considered a threat by those managers whose areas of responsibility could be reduced by it. Even if you do not choose to use it for these reasons, or are trying to avoid budgeting in general, it may be worthwhile to use the concept occasionally, for these reasons:

- To review the priorities of the business and how expenditures address those priorities
- To delve into the cost structure of the company's service and support activities

- To avoid across-the-board cost cutting, in favor of highly targeted and well thought-out reductions in less-critical areas
- To have plans in place for differing expenditure levels, which can be quite useful in the event of a sudden change in revenues

In short, the work required for zero-base budgeting is significant, but it may still make sense to engage in this process from time to time, just to ensure that the business is appropriately spending funds in support of its objectives.

Chapter 10
Cost Reduction Strategy

Introduction

A company may find itself in a position where the business is clearly failing, and it appears that costs must be reduced in order to ensure survival. There are a number of reasons why a business may be failing, and each one calls for a different cost reduction strategy. In this chapter, we delve into the various types of cost reduction strategies, as well as the general types of cost reductions that *do not* work.

> **Related Podcast Episodes:** Episodes 150, 151, 152, and 153 of the Accounting Best Practices Podcast discuss managing in financial adversity. They are available at: **accountingtools.com/podcasts** or **iTunes**

Failing Business Scenarios

There are situations where a business may be experiencing financial adversity. The amount of cost reduction that results from these situations depends upon the nature of the crisis. Usually, financial adversity arises from one of the following three causes:

- *Unrelated business segments.* Company management wanted to keep growing the company, but found that the original market niche was not large enough. Consequently, they added a number of side businesses. The result was a divergence away from a single core business that was reliably profitable to a cluster of somewhat related businesses. The organization in its present form is so muddled that management does not know which segments are profitable and which lose money.
- *Failing business model.* The original business model no longer works, so the company is in the midst of shifting its resources to a new business model, where it hopes to achieve profits again. This is a calculated move into a new competitive space. Alternatively, management may choose to remain with the same business model, but to alter how the company is structured in order to be more competitive.
- *Expense drift.* Management has consistently stayed with the original business model, but does not pay attention to expenses. Perhaps too much corporate infrastructure has been added, or money is being spent sponsoring the owner's favorite racing team. Whatever the case may be, expenses have been added that are not central to the mission of the business.

In the following sections, we will explore how to reduce costs (or not) to match each of these failing business scenarios.

Dealing with Unrelated Business Segments

A company may have built up a number of lines of business, resulting in an environment where the results are so tangled that management cannot discern where the business is making or losing money. In this case, the goal is to sort through the information and determine which costs can be pared back immediately in order to avoid shutting down the business.

This is a case where cost accounting can literally save a company, because the main point of this exercise is to use direct costing to determine the incremental cost of essentially every activity in a business. Direct costing refers to assigning only variable costs to cost objects, and is discussed in the Direct Costing as an Analysis Tool chapter. A cost object is anything for which you want to separately measure the cost. The concept is best illustrated with several examples:

- *Cut products scenario.* A business has fallen on hard times, and it produces an enormous number of products. Management asks if it might be possible to save money by cutting back on some of these products. Each product is a cost object. The accounting staff reviews the situation to see which costs will be eliminated if certain products are cancelled. Using direct costing reveals that only direct material costs will be eliminated if the products are cancelled. So, unless the products are selling at below the cost of their direct materials, it may not make sense to cancel the products. This concept is addressed in more detail in the Cost Management at the Product Level chapter.
- *Cut product line scenario.* An entire line of products is manufactured from a single production facility, where the same set of production equipment is used to make a dozen different models. In this case, the logical cost object is the entire facility and everything produced in it. So, the accounting staff could use direct costing to determine the incremental cost of this entire bundle, which includes the product costs, the facility, everyone working in the facility, and the related selling, marketing, and distribution costs. If the entire cluster of costs more than offsets the revenues being generated, it may make sense to terminate the entire product line.
- *Cut a retail chain scenario.* A company operates a chain of retail stores. Initially, management only wants to conduct a direct costing analysis at the individual store level. However, it then becomes apparent that a large part of the expense incurred by the retail chain is the distribution system that supports the stores. Accordingly, the analysis is expanded to cover the entire retail chain, which includes the cost of the regional store manager and his staff, the chain's accounting and finance staff, warehouses, and distribution trucks. At this level, what had previously been considered overhead costs are now direct costs of the entire chain; that is, if the chain is eliminated, so too are all of the related "overhead" costs.

- *Cut a sales channel.* A business sells through a variety of sales channels, including distributors, retail stores, and a web site. Each of these channels can be considered a cost object. The company finds that it is spending an inordinate amount of programming labor to support the web site and run fulfillment for it, as well as pay for Internet advertising. When netted together, it is apparent that this sales channel is losing money, so the company shuts down the entire channel.
- *Cut a customer.* A customer can be considered a cost object, since a business expends money to service the needs of its customers. This is one of the more difficult analyses, since a large amount of customer service overhead may apply to a customer, but little of it is actually a direct cost; that is, if the company stops doing business with a specific customer, not that many expenses will be eliminated. The amount of direct costs associated with a customer, other than the cost of products shipped, tends to be quite low.

When making decisions about cutting costs related to business segments, the decisions should be binary. That is, either a segment is entirely retained, or it is terminated or sold off. If management wants to hedge its bets by retaining a business segment, it must also retain much of the associated overhead, so the effect on costs is minimal. If management is truly committed to reducing costs, it should get out of certain businesses entirely and commit to the remaining business segments. This calls for decisive decision making.

This discussion requires the management team to pare down the business with vigor, rather than making a timid attempt to shave a few expenses here and there while retaining the bloated overall structure of the business. Aggressive action to eliminate business segments should allow management to focus its time and any remaining funds on the segments that it has elected to retain, which can result in a surge in profits.

Unfortunately, a company that finds itself with a muddled mix of products and businesses reached this position through unfocused management that did not attend to the strategic direction of the core business. Consequently, it is unlikely that the senior management team that got the company into this mess has the ability to pull it back out. This is a particular concern when managers are personally attached to the business segments that must be dropped. Thus, the board of directors may find that the best approach to resolving the situation is to replace the senior management team, and then pursue the cost accounting analysis advocated in this section.

Failing Business Model: Remain in the Same Business

A business may find itself in a difficult situation where competitive pressures, reduced customer demand, or increased costs are making it more difficult to generate a profit. Management may decide to remain in the same general business area, which means that it must recast its cost structure in order to generate profits.

There may currently be a relatively high proportion of fixed costs, which means that the company must attain a certain amount of sales each month in order to pay for the fixed costs. If management wants the business to operate profitably at a lower sales level, a possible option is to convert the fixed costs to variable costs, so the costs are only incurred as activity levels increase. Here are several ways to convert from fixed costs to variable costs:

- *Outsource production.* Have a third party manufacture goods for the company. Ideally, this means the third party ships goods directly to the company's customers (known as *drop shipping*), so the company has no warehousing obligations. Outsourcing production can result in a cost of goods sold that varies in lockstep with sales, which is an ideal way to eliminate fixed costs.
- *Outsource administration.* It may be possible to outsource a variety of administrative activities, such as payroll processing, information technology, and marketing. The resulting expenses will vary with activity levels, rather than sales, so there is not a perfect correlation between changes in these costs and sales. For example, payroll processing will vary by number of employees on the payroll, as will an off-site sales management software package for which the company pays by the number of users.

Outsourcing is a classic method for switching from fixed to variable costs. However, it also requires a completely different mindset for how a business is run. Consequently, it is useful to question whether the management team can stomach this ultra-lean approach, and whether it wants to operate a business in this manner. Also, outsourcing can be more expensive on a per-unit basis than employing in-house resources. However, because the billing structure is a variable one, it allows a company to operate at a profit at a lower sales level than would be the case if it were to keep all functions in-house and have higher fixed costs. This concept is developed further in the Cost-Volume-Profit Analysis chapter.

After considering every possible cost reduction alternative, load them into a pro forma income statement and see if the resulting business configuration will allow the company to turn a profit. If not, it may be necessary to shut down the business entirely.

However, before doing so, consider that the competition is still in business, so they have obviously figured out cost structures, products, and price points that allow *them* to turn a profit. Consequently, investigate how they achieve profits and see if any aspects of their business models can be copied by the company.

Tip: When it appears necessary to lay off employees as part of a strategic shift, consider discussing the matter with employees. Their suggestions for how and when a layoff should be conducted may lead to a different competitive structure than management had initially contemplated.

Failing Business Model: Shift to New Model

There are many situations where a company's original business model no longer works, so management is in the midst of shifting its resources to a new business model, where it hopes to achieve profits again. This means that profits are falling or gone, and management is trying to keep the business operating until profits from a new revenue source begin to appear. Management already knows the company is in serious trouble, and is doing everything it can to cut expenses and keep the company running long enough for the new model to prove itself.

From a cost management perspective, the question is whether profits from the new model will appear in time, and can the company afford to wait that long? If not, the owners should shut down the business right now, before it burns through any more cash. Otherwise, the company is losing money that should go to creditors or investors. The latter advice may not appear overly optimistic, but it is realistic; if a new business model gives little indication of working, management can either prolong the pain and suffer a disorderly company collapse at some point in the future, or close it down early and in a more orderly manner.

Clearly, the key issue is how to make the decision to keep a business running or to shut it down. Making the right decision is based on collecting the right information, which falls into the following two categories:

- *Cash burn*. Management must know at all times the exact amount of cash outflow that is occurring on a daily basis, and exactly when it can expect to run completely out of cash. This information establishes the time period over which management can make decisions.
- *New business measurements*. Collect information about any initial evidence of success for the new business model, such as initial customer orders, size of customer orders, initial sales per store, and customer retention rates.

The cash burn figure is a "hard number," and so can reliably reveal the time period over which the existing operations will last. The new business measurements are much less reliable, since they pertain to new operations that may barely be functional. There are several ways to make decisions based on this high level of uncertainty for the new business. Consider the following options:

- *Information table*. Construct a table that itemizes all of the information needed to properly make decisions, along with the source of the information. Also note on the table any substitute information that can be used to make decisions.
- *Competitors*. If the new business model is not yet functional, use the metrics reported by competitors. When doing so, keep in mind that a number of factors, such as product quality, marketing, and price points could be giving the competitor different results than might be expected from your own business model.

- *Extrapolation.* When the actual results for any key metric begin to arrive, extrapolate that number for the initial results throughout the business model. Since the initial results will be based on a minimal number of data points, the extrapolation may not be valid, so continue to revise the extrapolations as actual results begin to accumulate.

If the new business can survive long enough, all of the extrapolations, guesses, and competitor information can be swapped out of the business model and replaced by actual metrics generated by the new business, which yields the best information. However, it may take months or even a year to obtain this level of high-grade information, so management will likely have to make decisions about whether to continue operating the new business based on relatively weak information.

EXAMPLE

Sharper Designs wants to shift from its existing industrial saw blade business to a new retail-focused operation that sells cutlery through a web store. Management constructs an information table that contains the key information required to decide if the new venture will work. Key items in the table are:

- *Page views.* Sales will only occur if the website attracts a sufficient number of page views. This information is directly accessible from Google. As a substitute, the company can estimate the possible range of page views from those being generated from the websites of competitors.
- *Conversion rate.* The number of page views on the site must convert to actual sales at a certain minimum rate, or else sales will not be sufficient to turn a profit. This minimum amount can be plugged into the model and then matched against initial results.
- *Sales per customer.* The number of sales per customer must be at a certain minimum level in order to generate a profit. This amount can initially be estimated from the results of competitors.
- *Average gross margin per sale.* As was the case with the conversion rate and sales per customer, the gross margin resulting from each sale must be sufficient to generate a profit. The gross margin can initially be estimated from the results of competitors.
- *Advertising.* The company must engage in a certain amount of advertising in order to generate page views. This is a fixed cost, so any significant change in this amount will alter the breakeven point for the web store.

The initial model for the new business requires that the following metrics be achieved in order to break even:

- Page views of 50,000 per month are required in order to achieve a conversion rate of 5% that generates 2,500 sale transactions.
- Sales per customer transaction are expected to be $35, with an average gross margin of 55%, to achieve gross profits of $48,125 per month.

Of these metrics, the one most in question is the 5% conversion rate. As the first results come in, the actual conversion rate turns out to be 3%. When entered into the business model, this results in gross margins of only $28,875, which is well below the breakeven level. Management continues to operate the website for an additional two months to verify that the same conversion rate is occurring, and then elects to shut down the business, since it cannot generate a sufficient gross profit.

If management decides to include in its business model the metrics being generated by competitors, be aware of the differences between the business models of competitors and the one being contemplated by the company. It is entirely possible that the differences can create large variations in the results achieved by the different models. For example, a company may not be able to mimic the sales per square foot being achieved by a competitor's retail stores, because the competitor has already garnered leases on all of the prime retail locations in the target market.

These concepts mean that the key issue driving the switch to a new business model is the reliability of the information on which the decision is based. The model may initially be based on complete guesses, for which management needs to understand which guesses are most critical to the financial outcome of the new business. As time passes and results begin to arrive from the new business, the guesses can be replaced by extrapolations of initial results, which may or may not validate the business model. If not, management has a choice of either:

- Tweaking the model for a short time to see if the initial results can be altered; or
- Waiting for an extended period to see if the initial results continue to be achieved; or
- Shutting down the new business.

In summary, the cost reduction strategy for a change to a new business model does not necessarily focus on reducing any costs. Instead, the focus is primarily on identifying the key information that will indicate the most likely success or failure of the new model. This means operating with sometimes paltry amounts of information, or using substitute information derived from other entities.

Dealing with Expense Drift

One of the areas that can require an expense reduction strategy is expense drift, where too many expenses have been added to a business. One option is to call a meeting and attempt a general cutback in spending by soliciting suggestions from employees. This approach may yield minimal results, since it can be extremely difficult for employees to part with their favorite expenditures.

A better alternative is to conduct historical research by reviewing the company's earlier financial statements. Assemble the income statements into at least a decade-long comparison, where expenses are shown as a percentage of sales. Then use a ruler to focus on each individual row of expenses, and look across each row to see when each percentage increased. When there is an upward spike in expenses, investigate the cause of the expense increase, and log the reason for the change.

Each of these expense increases represents decisions that the company made over the years that have cumulatively brought the company to its present financial problems. A case can probably be made that a number of these expense increases represent good decisions. However, the company had less money in its early days, and yet managed to generate a profit with lower expenditures. Consequently, it is entirely reasonable to assume that the business can return to its roots by stripping away the specific expenses it has since incurred.

The result of this analysis should be a list of specific expense increases that have occurred over the years, and the reasons for the increases. The management team can review the list and decide which expenses to eliminate. Some of the expenses may represent critical aspects of the company's infrastructure and so should be maintained.

It is useful during this exercise to create a pro forma income statement that incorporates an expense rollback for *all* of the indicated items. If the result is a company that has returned to profitability, this is an indicator that following through on the expense reductions may actually work. However, if the pro forma results still reveal poor results, then the company is suffering from other issues, such as declining gross margins, that may not allow it to survive at all.

Once the expense reductions have been made, are there ways to ensure that the expenses do not return? Here are several alternatives:

- *Proportional limitation.* Routinely review expenses as a percentage of sales, and do not allow the larger expenses to exceed a certain proportion of sales. For example, do not allow compensation expense to exceed a fixed percentage that has historically proven to be sufficient to run the business. However, this approach assumes that the business can be run in the same manner, year after year.

- *Mandatory wait.* If someone wants the company to incur a significant new expense, impose a mandatory waiting period, such as for 90 days, before the expenditure is made. For example, waiting to hire a new position may reveal that the company has been able to function adequately without that new hire during the waiting period, and so perhaps does not need to hire anyone.

- *Approval for long-term commitments.* Some expenses are particularly difficult to pare back once they have been made, and so should require a higher level of approval. Any expense that requires a multi-year commitment certainly falls into this category, such as a facilities lease. If these commitments involve a noticeable increase in expense, have a company policy that specifically requires a comparison of the old and new expense levels, and a justification for the increase.

EXAMPLE

The profit margins of Hassle Corporation have been slowly falling for years, so the controller is tasked with investigating the reasons for the decline. She assembles the following five-year historical income statements of the business, where expenses are expressed as a percentage of sales:

	20X1	20X2	20X3	20X4	20X5
Sales	$5,000,000	$5,250,000	$5,500,000	$5,900,000	$6,300,000
Cost of goods sold	40%	**43%**	43%	43%	43%
Gross margin	60%	57%	57%	57%	57%
Compensation	22%	**26%**	26%	26%	26%
Marketing & advertising	2%	2%	**5%**	5%	5%
Rent	8%	8%	8%	**11%**	11%
Travel & Entertainment	6%	6%	6%	6%	**9%**
Other	4%	4%	4%	4%	4%
Net profit	18%	11%	8%	5%	2%

Highlighted in the table are those points at which there was a sustained increase in an expense type. The explanations for these increases are:

- Cost of goods sold permanently increased 3% in 20X2. Caused by an increase in the cost of raw materials.
- Compensation permanently increased 4% in 20X2. Caused by hiring a marketing department.
- Marketing and advertising permanently increased 3% in 20X3. Caused by sponsorship of a professional sports team.
- Rent increased 2% in 20X4. Caused by a move to a newer company facility that has a higher cost per square foot.
- Travel and entertainment increased 3% in 20X5. Caused by the rental of a company plane.

Of the causes noted here, only the increase in the cost of raw materials is one that probably cannot be reversed. In all other cases, an argument can be made that an expense can be rolled back. The result may be somewhat lower sales, especially if the marketing expenses are cut, but this may be acceptable if the result is a large increase in profits.

In short, it can be very useful to review the decisions that were made in the past to incur expenses, and to see if these decisions can be reversed, thereby reverting the cost structure of the company back to where it was during earlier and more profitable times.

Incorrect Cost Reduction Strategies

The analyses advocated in the preceding sections represent an intelligent approach when circumstances mandate that cost reductions take place. Unfortunately, many businesses take more broad-based approaches to cost reductions that can have serious negative consequences.

One way not to deal with a financial crisis is the concept of doing more with less. This concept usually means that a number of employees are laid off, and the remaining employees are expected to take on the work load of the departed staff. While this approach may initially reduce expenses, it can lead to the following problems:

- *Culture degradation*. Because the work day is longer and the work load is larger, there is no time for employees to mingle. Also, there is no time for company-sponsored events, such as after-work parties. The result is that all of the subtle reasons for making a workplace enjoyable fade away, which impacts the level of employee turnover.

- *Employee burnout*. Work days are extended, and weekends become work days. After a few of these massive work weeks and the accompanying pressure, employees start making mistakes. Efficiency improvements disappear, because no one has the time to think about installing best practices. For these reasons, productivity declines.

- *Work knowledge*. The remaining employees are being asked to perform work for which they are not trained, since the people specializing in these areas have been let go. There is no time to conduct the necessary amount of training, since there are no trainers remaining on the payroll. The result is that productivity declines and error rates increase. Further, employees know that their performance in these new areas is marginal, so their morale goes down.

- *Employee exits*. The best employees know that they have better alternatives with other companies, so they are likely to be the first ones to depart the company. This leaves less experienced or lower-performing employees, which negatively impacts productivity.

For all of these reasons, the impact of laying off employees without a fundamental restructuring of the business is the inevitable appearance of massive work hours, plummeting morale, employee departures, and lost productivity.

Another way not to deal with a financial crisis is when management decides to be "fair" to all parts of an organization, and requires the same percentage of expense cutbacks all over the company. Doing so results in the following issues:

- *Good management penalized*. Some department managers are better than others at controlling their expenses, so a tightly-run department could be devastated by a mandatory expense reduction. Meanwhile, someone who has been very loose in managing another department may find that it is quite simple to accommodate an expense reduction request, since there is so much excess spending already going on in the department.

- *Budgetary slack.* A side effect of a series of mandatory expense reductions is that managers begin to introduce budgetary slack into their annual budgets. Budgetary slack occurs when expenses are deliberately set at a level higher than is actually needed. By doing so, managers will be able to more easily accommodate requests for expense cuts, but at the cost of maintaining a higher expense level than necessary.
- *Key areas penalized.* Every business has a few areas that are central to its success. For example, a well-funded research and development lab may be the core generator of profits. Imposing an across-the-board cut on these areas can have a long-term negative effect on revenues and profits.

Yet another less-useful reaction to financial trouble is when management imposes a wage reduction on everyone in the company. This may initially appear to be a prudent and humanitarian decision, since it avoids a layoff. The concept may work if there is a reasonable expectation that the situation will improve in the near future, after which compensation will be restored to its normal level. If so, paring back wages allows the business to retain talent, and it can build trust with employees. The problem is that it does not work well if management is simply *hoping* that sales will improve. There may be no basis for such a belief. If so, several negative effects can be expected:

- *No planning.* Management may not be taking any other steps to deal with the crisis, which is hardly proactive behavior. If a competitor is undergoing the same issues but reacts to the situation by fundamentally restructuring its business, the first company may find itself at a serious competitive disadvantage.
- *Duration.* No one knows how long the pay cut will be in effect, which will cause an increasing amount of employee discontent as time passes. Eventually, expect to see the best employees leaving for more promising positions elsewhere.

Consequently, if management is contemplating a universal wage cut, at least set up a mandatory review date to examine the situation. When that date arrives, make a realistic assessment of the situation, and decide whether to prolong the pay cuts to another review date, or take more decisive action.

Summary

The key point when dealing with situations that call for large-scale cost reductions is to take an intelligent approach to selectively paring away expenses, rather than attacking the entire business with a meat cleaver (figuratively speaking). The end result should not be a devastated work force that spends the bulk of its time trying to find employment elsewhere. Instead, the result should be a core group of business segments on which management wants to place its financial bets for long-term success. All other business segments should have been shut down or sold, with any proceeds used to nurture the surviving segments.

Chapter 11
Compensation Cost Reduction

Introduction

Depending on the type of business, the cost of compensation may be the largest cost incurred. This is particularly the case in service industries, and where highly-skilled employees are required to design products, such as in the software and airliner construction businesses. Compensation can be a particularly pernicious cost, because it tends to increase every year through inflationary increases, even in the absence of improvements in employee productivity to offset the costs. In this chapter, we look at more than 40 techniques for mitigating the cost of compensation. These techniques are divided into the areas of employee hiring, temporary cost reductions designed for financial downturns, and more permanent solutions. There are also discussions of changes specifically designed to improve employee productivity, and to improve the conduct of an employee downsizing.

Proactive Hiring Solutions

Some compensation costs can be avoided by being extremely prudent about hiring decisions. The initial compensation level at which someone is hired is extremely important, for it sets the base case upon which future pay raises will be founded. There are also options available for completely avoiding or delaying the hiring of employees. Consider the following techniques:

- *Temporary workers for overflow work.* When activity levels are increasing within a business, do not automatically hire new full-time employees to assist with the work load. If you do, a result may be that the current activity level is not sufficient to keep the new staff busy. Instead, bring in temporary staff to handle the incremental work load. If the activity level drops, remove the temporary workers with a call to the temp agency that supplied them. If activity levels prove to be more permanent, then it is time to replace the temporary workers with permanent positions.
- *Temporary workers for evaluation.* New hires are typically based on several interviews, a background check, and phone calls to a few references. While useful, these activities do not give a sufficiently clear impression of the work habits and knowledge base of a prospective employee. An alternative that will provide this information is hiring people on a temporary basis, and then hiring them into a full-time position after a probationary period. This approach gives the existing staff a much more detailed view of an applicant, and so tends to result in hires that are less likely to result in an early termination. The trouble with this approach is that people applying for the more senior positions are not likely to agree to a temporary

work arrangement; consequently, it is more commonly used for hiring into lower-level positions.

- *Interns for evaluation.* It is a time-honored tradition in some businesses to hire summer interns. This is a useful approach that allows both the company and the intern to examine each other and see if a longer-term arrangement might work. The intern concept is an accepted part of the college experience, and so has a less dim reputation than the temporary-to-hire path.
- *Subcontract work.* If there are tasks to be done that are not central to the mission of the business, is it possible to subcontract the work to another company? Doing so means that the business is only paying for work that needs to be done, and that the contract work can be shifted elsewhere to a different provider if the work product does not meet the company's standards. This approach is particularly effective when an entire department of non-core activities is subcontracted, since the larger amount of work gives the company enough leverage to impose higher levels of performance and reasonable contract prices.
- *Delay start dates.* If new recruits have been offered positions with the company, consider asking them to start several months later. This approach can be made less unpalatable by issuing signing bonuses that the recruits can use to cover some portion of their expenses until the delayed start date arrives. A delayed start date is a better long-term solution than terminating offers that have already been extended, since the latter alternative creates a bad reputation for a company on college campuses.
- *Require lengthy hiring review.* When a new hire does not work out, it can take months or even years for management to overcome the usual reluctance to fire someone, resulting in a long-term waste of cash while the person is still being employed. One way to avoid this is to require multiple interviews by a number of the staff, psychological testing, and an extensive background check before anyone is hired. The intent is to spend a moderate amount of time and money up front in order to detect flaws in recruits, thereby saving much more cash later on related to lost productivity and termination costs.

The main thrust of these points is to only hire on a full-time basis when absolutely necessary, and to be extremely careful when hiring into those positions that absolutely must be filled.

Temporary Cost Reductions

When a company has encountered financial problems, the most common solution is for the president to enact some form of temporary compensation cost reduction, which is only intended to be in effect for the duration of the crisis. The intent of these measures is to retain as many employees as possible, on the theory that the knowledge base of the pool of employees is too valuable to lose. If this approach is taken, consider using a mix of the following tactics:

- *Stop hiring.* For the duration of the crisis, simply stop all hiring. Instead, as some employees leave the company, allocate their work among the remaining staff. This is not the best solution, for a significant imbalance may develop between the amount of work to be done and the number of available employees, resulting in large amounts of overtime and employee stress.
- *Cut bonuses.* If there is no obligation to pay bonuses, issue a notice that bonuses will not be paid. This should not be a problem for those employees whose base pay is adequate, but could be an issue if bonuses comprise a large part of their annual compensation. An alternative is to defer bonuses, so that they are paid on a later date. In the latter case, do not announce a specific date by which bonuses will be paid, so the company has the leeway to continue to defer the payments.
- *Cut management compensation.* When there is financial hardship, the management team should always set an example by taking the largest compensation cuts in the company. Doing so focuses the attention of managers on correcting the business, and also makes it easier for other employees to accept any pay cuts that may be assigned to them. Reductions in management compensation should certainly involve large portions (or all) of their bonuses, as well as notable reductions in their base pay. The level of pain inflicted should progressively increase for the higher levels of management.
- *Cut pay in general.* It may be necessary to institute a pay cut throughout the company. If so, avoid promising to pay back employees for lost wages when the good times return, since doing so merely imposes a large burden on the company at a later date. Instead, make it clear that the pay cut will continue in effect, and will be reviewed at regular intervals to see if an improvement in the company's fortunes will allow it to reinstitute the original pay levels at some later date.
- *Freeze pay.* It may be possible to simply freeze the pay of employees for the duration of the crisis. Doing so does not severely impact employees, since their current compensation is untouched. However, it is rarely sufficient from a cost management perspective, since a financial crisis implies that costs must be reduced, not just held steady. Consequently, a pay freeze is usually accompanied by other methods that more directly impact costs, such as a layoff. The key element in this approach is to not back-date any pay increases that are instituted after the financial crisis has been weathered. By simply stopping all increases for a period of time, the business has avoided the impact of inflationary increases until such time as pay raises are started again.
- *Reduce the amount of planned pay increases.* If the financial decline is a modest one, it may be sufficient to merely reduce the rate of planned pay

increases. The resulting cost savings will initially appear to be relatively minor, but also have a beneficial long-term effect, since future pay increases will be based on the somewhat lower compensation of employees.

- *Shift to part time*. The work situation of some employees may allow them to accept part-time status for a certain period of time, perhaps due to a family situation, such as supporting elderly parents. The amount of benefits paid to them can be negotiated. This approach should be treated as a call for volunteers, rather than a mandatory cut-back to part-time status. In the latter case, many employees simply cannot survive on part-time pay, and so would have to look for work elsewhere.

- *Shift between departments*. It is possible that one department is experiencing a decline in its activity level at the same time that another department is experiencing an increase. For example, the shipping department for a snow blower company may be swamped until the end of the calendar year, after which the customer service department experiences an increase in call volume. In these situations, it may be possible to shift personnel between departments to handle shifts in demand. However, this is only likely to be possible when the training needed within a department is relatively low, so that people contributed to a department can become productive in short order.

- *Cut working hours*. If the overall amount of work to be completed declines, consider reducing the work hours for the entire company, such as switching from an eight-hour day to a seven-hour day. This approach means that management wants to retain all employees for a certain period of time, after which it expects to be able to ramp up activity to the normal work period again. This approach may not work well when the work force is mostly comprised of low-wage employees who cannot afford even a small reduction in their pay. Cutting work hours can be a smart long-term solution for a retail establishment, if it appears that few customers are in stores near the beginning and end of normal store hours.

- *Use vacation time*. The company can strongly recommend to employees that this would be a good time to use their accrued vacation time. Doing so does not reduce the amount of cash being paid as compensation to employees, but it does reduce the company's obligation to pay employees for unused vacation time if they were to be laid off at a later date. Thus, this is good advance preparation for reduced cash payouts if a downsizing is considered possible.

- *Institute unpaid vacations*. Give employees the opportunity to take an unpaid vacation. This approach is particularly palatable when the financial crisis is likely to be a short one. The main issue with it is that some key employees whose services are needed may take advantage of the offer, which could lead to a scramble to cover their work loads during their absences.

- *Offer voluntary unpaid days off*. If there is clearly too much work capacity available within a business, it may be possible to simply offer unpaid days off to all employees, and see who takes the offer. There may be employees who want to take occasional days off to supplement their vacations, and whose financial circumstances make an unpaid absence an agreeable alternative. However, be aware that this may result in a dearth of employees in the workplace in the periods adjacent to major holidays and weekends.

- *Require furloughs*. If employees do not volunteer to take time off, then require them to do so with scheduled furloughs. A furlough is a mandatory period of unpaid leave. There is a risk that someone on furlough will spend the time looking for a new job. However, if furloughs are limited to a short period of time (such as one or a few weeks), employees will be more likely to return. Also, by shifting furloughs among the staff over a period of time, it is easier to schedule enough staff to keep the organization manned in most areas on a continual basis. When furloughs are used instead of layoffs, this allows a business to retain its core staff and be better prepared for an upturn in business. However, furloughs are not allowed or are restricted in some government jurisdictions.

- *Lay off employees*. If no other alternatives appear to yield sufficient cost savings, it may be necessary to lay off employees. Before doing so, consider the full cost of a termination, which includes residual benefit payments, termination pay, increased unemployment insurance, and so forth. If this step is taken, review the Cost Reduction Strategy chapter for tips on how to select employees for a layoff.

- *Offer a hire-back bonus*. If there is an expectation that business will eventually pick back up, and if the people to be laid off have significant skills, it may make sense to offer them a bonus if they are hired back. This means that the company incurs no immediate cost, but will pay a bonus if it hires back an employee. The advantage of doing so is that employees may be more willing to subsist on temporary work until they are hired back. Of course, convincing employees to wait around in this manner requires a sufficiently large hire-back bonus to grab their attention.

While these methods are useful for retaining staff during difficult economic times, employees cannot subsist on reduced compensation forever. Consequently, expect the effectiveness of these measures to gradually decline over time, as increasing numbers of employees abandon the company to find work elsewhere.

Permanent Cost Reductions

The most valuable compensation cost reductions are those that represent permanent cuts that will not be given back to employees. Here are several alternatives:

- *Pay more commissions*. Moving a larger proportion of employee pay to a commission basis means that the company is only obligated to pay if a sale is made. Though useful, there are still several problems to consider. First, not many employees generate revenue, so a commission plan will not apply to most of the staff. Second, commission payments must be made as stated in the commission agreement, which may call for cash payments when the company has no cash. And finally, an excessive focus on commissions can lead to incorrect behavior that drives away customers.

- *Pay more bonuses.* If employees are accustomed to a large proportion of their pay being in wages and salaries, then there is an assumption that this form of pay will at least receive a boost to compensate for inflation, so there is an ongoing spiral of increasing compensation costs. To avoid some of the inflationary impact, shift a large part of compensation into bonuses, which are only paid when the company's results are sufficiently good to generate the cash for the bonuses. Also, bonuses are not necessarily subject to inflationary increases.
- *Restrict bonus eligibility.* An alternative to the last point is to restrict the number of people who are eligible to receive bonuses. Ideally, only those people who have a direct impact on the performance of the company should be eligible for a bonus. If other positions have gradually crept into the bonus pool, even though these employees are essentially being paid extra in exchange for no performance, then weed them out of the bonus pool.
- *Pay more small bonuses.* The reverse of the last point may also work, from the perspective of improving employee morale and reinforcing good behavior. The typical bonus plan is that a few senior managers earn large bonuses, which does nothing to incentivize the rest of the staff. Instead, consider paying a large number of small bonuses to many employees, very frequently. For example, gift certificates could be used to reward excellent customer service. The net total paid out may actually decline, while the largesse is spread more broadly through the organization.
- *Pay more stock options.* When a company is publicly held, a viable alternative to the basic compensation package is to pay lower wages in exchange for stock options. This approach works best in a startup company, where there is a reasonable prospect that the options will gain appreciably in value, resulting in major gains for the recipients. An added benefit is that the company not only has no cash payout obligation, but is *paid* cash when employees convert their shares to options. They pay the company the exercise price at which a stock option allows them to buy shares from the company, and then sell the shares to investors on the open market. The main downside of this approach is that it reduces the ownership percentage of existing shareholders.
- *Stop paying overtime.* Any overtime payment requires a substantial boost over the normal pay rate, so it is tempting for employees to delay their work somewhat in order to stay later and qualify for overtime pay. To prevent this behavior, mandate senior management approval for any overtime hours worked. Doing so eliminates the temptation to delay work, and can reduce the total cost of labor. However, a negative result may be that crucial work is not completed in a timely manner.

- *Eliminate overtime drivers*. Some organizations use an excessive amount of overtime within certain departments, sometimes for years. Consider delving into the reasons for overtime within these parts of the business and working on resolving the underlying issues. For example, there may be poor work scheduling, rework due to nonconforming materials, late deliveries by suppliers, or inefficient processes – all of which can be corrected.

- *Tighten merit pay criteria*. The top-performing employees should certainly be paid in accordance with their abilities. However, outsized pay increases should be confined to the most deserving group. All too frequently, merit pay criteria are reduced to the point where far too many employees are receiving merit pay increases. This is an especially pernicious problem, since the merit increases enhance their base pay, so that their compensation over time becomes much too high. In short, be very critical in reviewing merit pay criteria and employee evaluations, to ensure that only the deserving few receive outsized compensation.

- *Revise job classifications*. The human resources department may have developed a set of job descriptions for employees, with pay rates tied to those job descriptions. It may be possible to revise the job descriptions to more precisely define the types of work performed, so that some employees are shifted into a lower job classification that pays less. Since this approach involves an outright pay reduction, it can meet with employee disapproval, so consider offering counseling on the training that would be required for employees to move up into their former job classifications. Also, expect increased employee turnover if pay levels are reduced.

- *Put hard cap on pay ranges*. If employees are classified as having certain types of jobs, put a hard cap on the maximum wage or salary that can be paid. Thus, an engineer grade three might be allowed a maximum salary of $90,000. Any pay above the hard cap is prohibited, though bonuses may be allowed. The concept is intended to avoid stratospherically high compensation levels for those employees who have been in the same job classification for a long time, and who have been receiving routine pay increases that no longer equate to their underlying skill sets.

- *Swap titles for pay*. It may be possible to award a larger number of higher-ranking titles in exchange for keeping pay levels relatively low (witness the number of vice presidents in the banking industry). This cannot be done to too great an extent, since doing so would water down the effect of using the titles. Still, it may allow for a limited reduction in compensation.

- *Install a two-tier wage structure*. If some of the work force is protected from a wage reduction, it may still be possible to set up a two-tiered structure where new hires are paid substantially less than the workers who were hired at an earlier date. This approach is most common where employees are unionized. Though effective, it can engender difficult relations between the two groups of employees.

- *Designate employees as core or administrative*. In a business where most of the business is generated by a small group of core employees who have specific skill sets, it may make sense to direct most of the compensation at them. All other employees are designated as administrative support staff, and are paid substantially less. In essence, the wage structure is designed to drive down employee turnover among a small group of employees, while accepting much higher turnover among the administrative staff. In aggregate, total compensation may be somewhat lower under this approach.

- *Only pay for hot skills.* There are imbalances in the labor market between supply and demand that result in a certain number of positions having what are considered "hot" skills, and for which employers are willing to pay substantial amounts. In these cases, pay whatever amount is required to acquire and retain the needed skill sets. However, this does not apply to the vast majority of positions, where pay rates are much more competitive, and there are a large number of possible recruits available. Thus, management should make a conscious decision to identify hot skill positions and only pay high rates for these positions.

- *Support hot skill positions.* When there are employees who are classified as having hot skills, examine their jobs to see if any portions can be stripped away and given to administrative staff. Doing so means that these highly-paid employees can focus solely on their primary skill sets, which allows the company to employ fewer of them. The increased cost of administrative staff should be much less expensive than the cost savings from employing fewer hot skill positions. An additional step is to continue monitoring the work of people in hot skill positions to see if they are still engaging in low value-added tasks. If so, continue to restructure their jobs and hand off any low-value work to other employees.

- *Match pay to target turnover levels.* If turnover levels are inordinately low, it may mean that the company's compensation levels are so high that employees would be foolish to leave the company. This is not necessarily a cost-effective solution to employee turnover. Instead, derive an acceptable target turnover level, and gradually allow compensation levels to drift down to the point where that employee turnover level is achieved. This analysis may also find that excessively high turnover in some key areas may warrant an increase in compensation levels.

- *Outsource work.* It may be substantially less expensive to shift some work to a low-wage location, where an outsourcing firm handles local hiring and management on behalf of the company. An alternative is for the company to open its own facility in a low-wage location, so that it can impose its own human resources practices on the local staff. While this approach may initially appear like a major cost reduction, there are several issues to consider. First, off-site management time may be required, as well as a substantial increase in travel costs and training time. Also, low-wage locations tend to have much higher employee turnover, so the quality of the replacement staff becomes an issue. Further, competition by other companies for these low-cost workers tends to drive up the cost of labor over time, so outsourcing may not seem so cost-effective in a few years.

- *Pay hiring bonuses.* If a quality candidate for a position is pushing for an initial pay level that is too high, the result will be a base rate of pay on which merit and inflationary increases will subsequently be based, so that the company bears the burden of the increased cost for years to come. To avoid this issue, offer a standard rate of pay, plus a hiring bonus. Doing so drives down the recruit's initial base pay, which reduces compensation levels in future years.
- *Encourage early retirement.* It may be cost-effective to increase the company's pension payout to a sufficient extent that older employees can be encouraged to retire from the company early. Doing so eliminates the most expensive pay bracket in the company, and allows for the hiring of less expensive newer employees in their place. Also, there is no unemployment cost associated with a retired employee. However, there are a number of issues with this concept. First, the pension payout may have to be substantial in order to be sufficiently tempting to older employees. Second, the company may find that some quite valuable employees accept the offer. And third, the net change in experience from the departing to the incoming employees could be so large that the company's operations suffer to a noticeable extent.

There is no single tactic that is likely to trigger a decline in compensation costs. Instead, a broad range of concepts may have to be followed, and even then the impact may be only a reduced rate of increase in compensation costs. To achieve any favorable results, the management team must consistently follow selected compensation control tactics for a long time, with few exceptions.

Productivity-Based Solutions

An essential problem with compensation expense is that it tends to increase in step with the general rate of inflation, year after year, and so represents an inexorable increase in cost over time. Here are several alternatives to break this conundrum:

- *Profit sharing.* Swap scheduled pay increases for direct sharing in company profits. By doing so, compensation costs do not take up an increasing proportion of company expenses over time, but instead are incurred only if the company earns a profit. This concept should allow all employees to share in a single profit sharing pool, so that everyone is incentivized by the same goal. Only allowing profit sharing for a subset of employees reduces the overall level of motivation to increase company profitability. However, an extended period of profit stagnation may drive employee compensation down so low that employee turnover will increase.
- *Allow turnover.* There are job positions where only a certain level of expertise and/or experience is required, and yet employees will continually

expect pay raises over time. In these situations, it may make sense to restrict the pay level, and accept a larger amount of employee turnover. This is a common concept in the tax, auditing, and consulting professions, where only a small proportion of employees are promoted into more senior positions, and the remaining staff is counseled out in order to make room for new hires.

- *Forced rankings.* If productivity levels must increase in order to pay for wage increases, then one option is to rank the entire workforce every year and terminate the employment of those ranked at the bottom of the standings. Doing so constantly eliminates the least productive staff, allowing the business to extend pay raises to the more productive employees. This concept may appear brutal, especially to a long-term, entrenched work force, but is a valid method for increasing productivity. A good accompanying measure is to issue outsized pay raises to the best employees, thereby sending the message that the organization places a strong premium on productivity, and will reward the best staff.

- *Publicly rank employees.* An amalgamation of the last two points is that the performance of employees can be publicly ranked. Doing so may encourage those near the bottom of the list to either improve their performance or find work elsewhere. This approach is only effective where performance can be specifically tied to an individual, as is the case with a salesperson.

- *Enforce time standards.* Employees may have been given no targets for how long to complete a task. If time standards are formulated and imposed on various activities, employees will be more likely to strive toward attaining the standards. This approach works best when a task is highly repetitive, and especially when an internal analysis team can examine the tasks periodically to see if the work can be reconfigured to enhance efficiency. Given these criteria, the use of time standards is more common in the production area. However, it can be used in administration to measure such activities as processing purchase orders and reviewing contracts.

Tip: Prioritize the development of time standards in areas where labor content is greatest, so that the firm generates the greatest return on the effort involved in creating time standards.

When there is a strong focus on productivity improvements, it is useful to track total compensation costs as a percentage of sales on a trend line, and implement whatever productivity enhancements are required to ensure that the compensation percentage does not increase past a target threshold.

Total Labor Cost Analysis

Most of the preceding recommendations are targeted at outright reductions in the amount of compensation paid to employees. However, an unrelenting focus on low pay does not always result in the best overall performance by a business. Low compensation levels can drive away top-notch employees and engender low morale among the remaining staff, to the point where the following conditions arise:

- Absenteeism is higher, since employees will tend to view sick time as a form of compensation that they should maximize.
- Overtime is higher, since productivity levels are so low that extra work is required to meet demand.
- Scrap rates are higher, since there is little incentive to drive down the scrap rate.
- Best practices are not installed, since doing so reduces the available work for employees.
- Innovation is extremely low, since the most productive employees have long since been driven away by the low pay rates.

Under these circumstances, a better solution may be a significant boost in pay, to upgrade the quality and morale of the workforce. Doing so may mitigate so many other issues that the total cost of labor actually declines.

An issue to consider is that a simple across-the-board pay boost may not be sufficient, since the company is still employing that residual group of employees who were *not* driven away by the prior low-pay practices. It may be necessary to replace the existing staff with an entirely new group of more motivated and higher-quality employees before the full effects of the higher pay rates become apparent.

Timing of Compensation Changes

Compensation may be considered the sacred cow of a business. Once a compensation level is initially set, employees will react poorly to any significant restructuring of the basic type of compensation, unless there is a clear indication that the outcome will result in *more* compensation.

Because of the strong attachment to the status quo for compensation, the best time to radically overhaul the system is in a time of crisis. In this case, employees understand that their jobs are at risk, and so will be much more amenable to major alterations. Consequently, treat a crisis as a major opportunity, and enact as thorough an overhaul of compensation as possible, all at once. If the election is instead made to roll out a series of changes over time, employee resistance to the changes will likely increase, especially if the financial situation of the company begins to improve.

Given the large cost savings that can be found in compensation, and the timing required to retrieve these savings, it may make sense to have the ideal compensation plan ready well in advance of an impending crisis, so that a polished solution can be released when the time is right. Conversely, altering the compensation system in an overnight scramble ensures that the outcome will not strike a proper balance between employee acceptance and maximized cost savings.

The Downsizing Process

Downsizing the workforce is not always a good idea, since it triggers severance, outplacement, and rehiring costs, as well as the potential for employee lawsuits and long-term distrust of management.

> **Tip:** If an employee is to be granted stock on specific future dates and is laid off, the terms of the stock grant may require the company to accelerate the grants and award them to the employee as of the termination date.

Also, the remaining employees are likely to be more paranoid about their jobs, and therefore more risk-averse. Nonetheless, if downsizing is necessary, consider the following issues when planning for it:

- *Selection process.* The single most important element in a corporate downsizing involves the selection process for who is to be downsized. As explained in the Cost Reduction Strategy chapter, the best approach is to pare away entire business units or other cost objects, rather than imposing a percentage cutback throughout the business. Nonetheless, there will be situations where management decides to impose cutbacks throughout the business. If so, there should be a well-defined process for determining who is to be let go, such as by the seniority of employees. By acting consistently, employees will know how at risk they may be in the event of future layoffs, and so can decide whether they should start looking for new work.
- *Impact on work environment.* A key consideration when downsizing is how it will impact the work environment. A deep across-the-board cutback is virtually guaranteed to crush any remaining corporate culture, since the remaining staff will be scrambling to preserve their jobs and working through the immense backlog of work that they must now handle with fewer resources. To mitigate these effects, communicate constantly with the staff and try to accommodate their needs whenever possible. If the downsizing was not too large, it may still be possible to preserve the work environment by working closely with the human resources staff.
- *Union rules.* If the workforce is unionized, consult with the local union representative at once, to ensure that any downsizing rules in the union agreement are followed. Otherwise, the union is more likely to challenge who was laid off, which can result in litigation, a more aggressive union in the future, or even a strike.
- *Decisiveness.* There is nothing more agonizing for the staff than to suffer through an ongoing series of downsizings, since a high level of uncertainty permeates the work environment. Instead, management should act decisively to complete the entire downsizing at one time, so that the remaining staff can put the upheaval behind itself as fast as possible.

When a downsizing is conducted, and a company's circumstances later improve, it may be necessary to conduct a large amount of rehiring. When rehiring occurs, the business will have to incur a number of additional expenses, such as:

- Recruitment costs
- Training costs
- Market premium for qualified new hires, if the prior downsizing reduced the company's reputation in the marketplace
- Additional supervisory costs while new hires are learning their jobs
- Lower productivity of new hires during the training period

These additional costs can be substantial, and are worth considering when contemplating a layoff. The added cost may be so large that management elects to pursue other alternatives before engaging in a downsizing.

Summary

When confronted by a downturn in profits, the knee-jerk reaction for many managers is to conduct a layoff. This is not always the best solution, since the business loses the investment already made in its employees, and must also deal with residual turnover from the remaining staff, who may feel betrayed by the company.

While there are times when a corporate restructuring and layoff are certainly necessary, there are many other alternatives available for reducing compensation expense that do not involve the departures of large numbers of employees. This chapter has laid out dozens of alternative paths that are worthy of consideration before taking the more drastic step of conducting a layoff.

Chapter 12
Benefits Cost Reduction

Introduction

The cost of employee benefits tends to be spread among a number of line items on the income statement, and paid to many suppliers, which means that management does not always understand the sheer size of this cost area. In some organizations, the cost of benefits may be second only to the cost of compensation. Even when management *does* understand the extent of its benefit costs, there may be a tendency to avoid any aggressive cost reductions, on the grounds that a comprehensive and competitive set of benefits is needed to attract and retain quality employees.

As we will note in several places in this chapter, the cost of benefits should not be considered an untouchable area. Instead, there are a variety of ways to shift and reduce costs to arrive at a benefits package that is the most effective at providing just those benefits most desired by employees.

Benefit Cost Sharing

Perhaps the most common form of benefits cost reduction is to shift some portion of their cost to employees. In this section, we describe several ways to do so, and also make note of some of the pitfalls that can arise from cost sharing. Possible options include:

- *Require co-pays.* Require employees to pay a high co-pay for a variety of benefits, such as for prescriptions, doctor visits, and hospitalizations. The theory is that higher co-pays will prevent employees from seeking treatment for minor ailments, thereby reducing the total amount of medical bills. However, high co-pays may also prevent employees from seeking treatment in the early stages of an illness, resulting in vastly higher expenses later, when they are in much worse condition. Consequently, co-pays should not be set at inordinately high levels.

- *Require cost sharing.* The company can require employees to take on a larger share of the cost of any type of benefit. For example, it may be possible to shift from requiring 10% employee payments for medical insurance to 30%. The same approach may be applied to dental insurance, disability insurance, and life insurance. By shifting an increased amount of costs to employees, it is also more likely that some coverage will eventually be moved to the benefits plan of a spouse. However, this approach can be taken too far. It may result in lower-wage employees having to back out of coverage entirely, if they cannot afford their share of the costs. It can also be a problem when a recruit is comparing the benefit plans of possible employers, since a lower cost-sharing percentage may lead to a decision to work for a competitor.

- *Charge higher premiums to smokers.* Employees who smoke are more likely to become sick and therefore cost the company more money in insurance costs. This cost can be shifted back to smokers by charging them a higher premium than the rate charged to non-smokers. This approach could also be coupled with a corporate wellness program, so that smokers are more likely to avoid the premium through a smoking cessation program.

- *Offer a consumer-directed plan.* There are health plans available that allow employees to elect either lower deductibles and higher premiums, or the reverse. A low-deductible situation is more likely to be attractive to an employee who has health issues, while a high-deductible plan may be more useful to a person who rarely has health issues. This approach does not necessarily save money for the employer, but can save money for employees.

- *Charge more fees to 401(k) plan.* A company must pay a number of service charges and audit fees related to any 401(k) plan that it has established for its employees. The company can choose to absorb these costs itself, or it can charge some or all of the fees to plan participants. The main downside of charging 401(k) fees to the plan is that the effective rate of return experienced by employees on their invested funds will be lowered, which makes this form of pension plan less attractive to them.

Benefit Reductions

In some cases, it may be possible to reduce the amount of benefit coverage, though consider the impact on employees of engaging in excessively severe cutbacks. The following are all variations on the concept of benefit reduction:

- *Pay no benefits.* At the far end of the spectrum of benefit solutions is to pay no benefits at all. This is not an acceptable alternative when competing firms offer rich benefit packages, since the company will have difficulty attracting or retaining employees. However, it can work in situations where the compensation level is so high that employees can readily divert some of their compensation to the purchase of benefit packages. It may also work when a high proportion of employees are obtaining benefits through their spouses, who work for other companies.

- *Reduce base-level benefits.* If the majority of employees are young, they may not have a great need for those benefits that may be considered more critical to older employees, such as disability insurance, life insurance, and a rich medical plan. In this case, an economical option is to reduce the base-level benefits to what is considered acceptable to the younger employees, and then offer an upgrade to the basic package for an additional charge. This concept will be less effective as the average employee age increases, when a better benefit plan is considered more important by a larger proportion of employees.

- *Expand plan after initial service period.* If the company experiences a large amount of employee turnover, it may make sense to offer only a basic level of benefits during the first year or two of employment, after which employees are eligible for a more comprehensive set of benefits. Dangling richer benefits in front of new employees may also create an incentive for them to stay with the company, thereby reducing turnover. The same approach can be used with accrued vacation, where there is a significant increase in the amount of vacation accrual after an employee has worked for the company for at least one or two years.

- *Reduce pension match.* Many businesses have set up 401(k) plans, to which employees contribute funds for their retirement. A company may choose to match some portion of the funds contributed by employees, and advertise it as a major benefit. While the existence of a pension match is a notable benefit, it probably will not make the difference between hiring a key recruit or not. Consequently, a more prudent course is to monitor the amount of pension matching offered by competing firms, and offer a roughly comparable figure. Pension matches can be rather expensive, so an inordinately high match is not recommended. Also, the match percentage must apply to all employees covered by the plan, so using a high match to target a specific employee is an extraordinary waste of cash; instead, offer more specific compensation to the targeted individual.

- *Move to a health maintenance organization (HMO).* There can be a notable cost reduction when a business shifts all of its employees to an HMO. Doing so concentrates the benefits purchasing power of a company with a single benefit provider. The provider may do quite a creditable job of servicing the needs of employees. However, we categorize this change as a benefit reduction, since it does not give employees the power to choose their own doctors.

- *Charge 401(k) loan fees to employees.* Employees may want to borrow funds from their 401(k) accounts. If so, the company can charge the employees a small fee for this service, which compensates it for the charges imposed by the plan administrator.

- *Do not pay for non-core benefits.* The key concept behind offering benefits to employees is to offer those benefits that are most crucial to employees; the company could pay a large proportion of the costs of these items, while simply offering all other benefits to employees without paying for any of them. By doing so, employees still have access to the other benefits, but must pay for their entire cost. For example, the company may pay for most of the cost of medical insurance, while only making dental insurance available for purchase.

Benefit Limitations

A variation on benefit reductions is to place a cap on the maximum amount of a benefit that is paid out, some of which can yield large cost savings. The following points illustrate the concept:

- *Cap the benefit offered.* Some benefits are guaranteed to increase as employees stay with the company for longer periods of time. For example, the costs of life insurance and disability insurance will increase as employees become older and their base compensation increases. For these types of benefits, the company could establish a maximum benefit amount that it is willing to pay, over which employees must pay the remaining benefit cost. The primary downside is that the cost differential paid by employees may eventually become so great that they drop certain benefits entirely.

- *Cap lifetime limits.* The cost of medical insurance declines if the company accepts lower lifetime limits for medical insurance. Doing so reduces the protection of the insurance coverage, so very low lifetime caps are not recommended. Still, some prudent reduction of lifetime limits might be possible, as long as the limits are set high enough to still provide coverage for major medical situations, such as for cancer treatment and organ replacement.

- *Pay cash for benefits.* The company could issue a fixed cash amount to its employees as part of their ongoing compensation, which is designated as payment for benefits. Employees are then responsible for obtaining any type of benefits they want with this cash. The company can direct employees to a list of benefit providers from which they can purchase benefit packages. This approach completely caps the amount of benefits expense that a business will pay, because all risk of benefit inflation, as well as administrative chores, are shifted to employees. This is not a very employee-friendly approach, but could work in situations where a very young work force is more interested in receiving extra cash than in receiving benefits.

- *Limit vacation carryovers.* When employees are allowed to carry over their vacation hours to later years, this means that the company will eventually have to pay them for the vacation hours at the (presumably) higher rate of pay in existence when the vacation hours are eventually used. It also calls for the recordation of a vacation liability on the company's balance sheet that will carry over for however long employees do not use their vacation hours. To mitigate this liability, require employees to use their accrued vacation time within a certain period of time, or only allow a small carryover into the next year. However, be aware that this restriction may cause employees to take vacation at the end of the year, when their services may be quite urgently needed. Also, it may be illegal to impose a "use it or lose it" rule where vacation time is cancelled if not used, since vacation time is considered an earned benefit that cannot be taken away. If there is some question of legality, an alternative is to stop accruing the benefit once a certain number of accrued hours is reached.

- *Terminate cash-out option.* If the company allows employees to demand a cash payment for any unused sick time, this policy merely encourages them to work through situations when they are sick and should be home, thereby infecting their co-workers and causing more sickness. Consequently, do not offer payment for unused sick time to employees.

Benefit Exclusions

There may be ways to limit the issuance of benefits to just employees, avoiding coverage for other dependents. Examples are:

- *Encourage use of spouse benefits.* In many families, both spouses work on a full-time basis, and both parties are eligible for the complete benefits packages offered by their employers. Logically, the spouses should purchase whichever benefits package is more cost-effective to them, and ignore the other benefits package. A company can encourage its employees to use the benefits provided by the other spouse's employer by offering an extra payment that rewards such behavior.
- *Terminate eligible spouse coverage.* As an extension of the last point, a company could even terminate the coverage of any spouse that is eligible for coverage through their own employer. This can be tricky to implement, since spouses may have already declined coverage by their employers.
- *Only provide coverage to employees.* A smaller business with limited funding might opt to just offer benefits to its employees. All dependents would be excluded from coverage. This approach is more common in businesses that are scaling up their operations, and intend to provide more comprehensive coverage once their cash flow improves.

In essence, benefit exclusions are designed to take advantage of the more generous benefits of other employers. This concept does not work well if large numbers of employers adopt it, since coverage may not be available for any dependents.

Benefit Swaps

Some employees do not need certain benefits, and so may be willing to cancel them in exchange for other benefits that are less costly for the company. Several examples are:

- *Swap time off for benefits.* If employees do not have a need for certain benefits, encourage them to take other benefits in exchange that are less costly to the company. For example, a younger person may feel that life insurance is not necessary, and so may be willing to swap it for an extra day off, perhaps even at a reduced rate of pay.

- *Swap lower drug co-pay for generic purchases.* Generic drugs are much less expensive than name-brand formulations, so offer employees a lower co-pay if they buy generic drugs.
- *Swap lower drug co-pay for mail order purchases.* When employees have long-term prescriptions, the most cost-effective way to fill these prescriptions is to assign them to a mail-order operation that mails the drugs at regular intervals, and at lower cost than the neighborhood pharmacy. To encourage the use of mail-order prescription fulfillment, offer a lower co-pay to employees if they use this service. In essence, the company is swapping a portion of the co-pay for a lower overall drug cost.

Benefit Aggregation Concepts

There are situations where a business may be able to concentrate its benefits purchasing power, thereby wringing price reductions from its benefit suppliers. Consider the following alternatives:

- *Purchasing coalition.* It may be possible for several organizations to create a coalition for the purchase of benefits. By creating a larger pool of employees, they can obtain better rates from benefit providers. However, doing so may require that some overhead costs be incurred to manage the coalition, as well as a commitment to remain in the coalition for a certain minimum period of time.
- *Benefits bundling.* Consider shifting a large bundle of benefits to a single service provider. By doing so, the increased volume of business should entitle the company to lower fees. For example, payroll service providers also offer 401(k) plan administration services, while some medical insurance providers also provide other types of insurance. The main downside of bundling is that some plans favored by employees may be dropped when benefits are shifted into a bundled arrangement.
- *Subsidiary aggregation.* A company may have a number of subsidiaries, each with its own benefits plan. If so, centralize benefits administration and require all subsidiaries to use the same benefit providers. By aggregating the number of employees using a smaller number of benefit plans, the company may obtain better benefit pricing. This concept may not work for outlying company locations where benefit coverage is not available from a selected provider, but could still be implemented for other company locations.

Benefit Terminations

The one type of benefit plan that is downright egregious from the perspective of the company is the defined benefit pension plan. This is a pension plan under which retired employees are guaranteed specific payment amounts. Because the exact amount of the benefit to be paid is defined in the plan, this puts the onus on the company of not only paying funds into the pension plan, but also of paying in more funds if subsequent investment returns are not sufficient. Also, the terms of these plans frequently provide a benefits boost to those employees who remain with the company for a long time, and base payments on an average of their compensation during the last few years of their employment prior to retirement, when their pay is presumably at its highest level. The result can be a massive pension burden for the company. A more fair arrangement is the defined contribution pension plan, where the company is only responsible for an initial payment into the pension plan, and not for the amount of cash that is eventually paid to the recipient. Thus, a defined contribution plan passes the risk of pension plan performance to retired employees.

Another benefit that can be terminated is free snacks and drinks for employees. Some employees graze on company-provided snacks to an inordinate extent, resulting in startlingly high food costs. Also, if the snacks and drinks are of the high-calorie, processed food variety, the company is essentially paying to reduce the health of its employees. Consequently, if this benefit is to be provided at all, it should only encompass healthy foods that can improve employee health.

Workers' Compensation Issues

The cost of workers' compensation can be considered an employee benefit, even though this insurance is mandatory. Within the requirements of state-level workers' compensation programs, there is still room to manage the cost. Consider the following options:

- *Job classification analysis.* The cost of workers' compensation is based on the job classification assigned to each employee. For example, the cost of workers' compensation insurance is much higher for a production employee than for an administrative person, because of differences in the inherent dangers of these positions. Consequently, it is useful to examine the job classifications of all employees just prior to the insurance renewal date, to ensure that the classifications fairly represent the actual work of each employee.
- *Screen new hires.* Conduct a complete review of each job candidate to see if there has been any history of workers' compensation fraud. Indicators could be a former felony conviction or a positive drug test. It is much less expensive to pay for these up-front reviews in order to avoid hiring someone, than to later be saddled with false injury claims.
- *Require drug testing.* The use of illegal drugs may have led to an employee injury that the company must then pay for under its workers' compensation insurance. To guard against this issue, institute a policy that requires a drug test following any employee injury. If the test result is positive, this gives the company grounds to terminate employment, thereby avoiding any additional claims in the future.
- *Alter jobs.* Employees may be experiencing a number of stress-related injuries that result in workers' compensation claims. If so, consider altering

their jobs to avoid those aspects of the work that are triggering the injuries. Alternatively, make these employees aware of less stressful jobs elsewhere in the company, and encourage them to apply for these positions.

- *Outsource work.* There are usually a small number of locations within a company from which most workers' compensation claims arise. Given the inordinate cost of some claims, it may make sense to selectively outsource the work conducted in these areas to a third party, thereby eliminating the insurance expense. This approach will only work if the locations involve non-core activities, and third parties are available to provide this type of work.

Corporate Wellness Programs

Consider instituting a corporate wellness program. This is a program that encourages employees to engage in activities that improve their level of fitness, dietary habits, and so forth. This can include free health screenings, on-site flu shots, smoking counseling, disease management, and access to a gym. Essentially, the company expects to offset the cost of the wellness program with reductions in employee medical claims. In addition, there may be a reduction in the number of sick days taken, and perhaps even in employee turnover. A wellness program requires a long-term commitment, since favorable results may require a number of months (or years) to materialize. The following additional pointers can assist in maximizing the benefits of a corporate wellness program:

- *Marketing.* Market the wellness program to employees to gain more comprehensive participation. This can include information about the benefits of weight loss and smoking cessation on life span, as well as the reduced likelihood of illnesses in the future.
- *Reward staff.* Offer bonus or base pay increases to employees if they participate in the corporate wellness program for a certain minimum period of time, or reach certain goals.
- *Offer monitoring.* Offer to pay for a series of private monitoring sessions, so that employees can track their progress toward reaching their wellness goals.

An expansion on the corporate wellness concept is to also offer it to the spouse and children of employees. The cost of doing so should be offset by the reduced medical costs of these dependents. The cost savings from a broader wellness program may be so extensive that it could pay to even offer a bonus to any families that elect to join the wellness program.

A variation on the corporate wellness concept is to include doctor's house calls in the standard package of medical benefits. Doing so has the advantage of keeping sick employees away from the office, where they might infect other employees and trigger a large number of sick days and lost productivity. House calls can also be used to treat ailments for which employees might otherwise be tempted to visit the local emergency room, which is much more expensive than a house call. A further benefit is that a house call tends to take longer than a standard office visit, so the doctor is more likely to derive the correct diagnosis of an employee's illness. This approach works best when there are a large number of employees located within a relatively small area, which allows the company to cost-effectively contract with a local medical firm to provide house call services.

Training Benefits

Training can be considered a benefit, since it increases the skill level of employees, which they can use to obtain higher levels of compensation. Training is an area rife with inefficiencies, and where careful alignment of employee needs and company resources can produce a substantial improvement in the cost-benefit of training expenditures. Consider the following possibilities:

- *Terminate mandatory training.* The company may require that employees submit to certain types of training when they are hired, and at regular intervals thereafter. If the training is enforced for legal or safety reasons, then mandatory training is probably necessary. However, there may be other instances where employees already have the appropriate training, so requiring the same training again only means that an extra training cost is being incurred while the time of these employees is being wasted.
- *Determine exact training requirements.* Evaluate each employee for their specific training needs, rather than assigning training based on job title, years in grade, or other more generic criteria. Doing so will highlight specific issues that can be addressed to improve the performance of employees, and avoids the cost of unnecessary training.
- *Provide one-on-one training.* If the skills to be gained from certain types of training are extremely valuable, it may make sense to provide one-on-one training of employees, to ensure that they comprehend the information being imparted. This is a particularly useful approach when the employees in question are billable, and their billable rates can be increased as a result of the training. The cost of training in this manner will be higher than for group training sessions, so it should only be used when there will be a clear improvement in the company's profitability.
- *Post video training sessions.* If the training to be provided can be broken down into relatively small snippets, it may be possible to create separate videos for each session, and make the videos available to the staff for viewing at their convenience. This approach has the advantage of allowing employees to access the training during any stray periods when they are not engaged in other activities. They can also avoid those training topics for which they already have sufficient knowledge.
- *Provide teleconference training.* When training is only available off-site, the associated travel cost can be substantial. A way to avoid this cost is to arrange for a teleconference, where employees access training sessions

from their computers, and can post on-line questions to trainers. This approach works well for short courses, but not for lengthy training sessions. Also, because employees have not left their desks, they may be distracted by daily work events, such as incoming e-mail.

- *Provide self-training modules.* If a company uses a comprehensive accounting or enterprise resource planning module, the software may include self-training modules that walk users through the process of operating the software. Consider setting up a training program for any employees using the software, and monitor their progress through the training modules.

- *Create internal trainers.* It may be possible to only pay for outside trainers until a group of employees have received sufficient training to take over the task of providing training to other employees. While this approach will reduce the cost of outside trainers, it may not be cost-effective, since the internal trainers may be significantly less effective than the outside trainers. Also, the internal trainers are no longer completing their original tasks while engaged in training other employees. Consequently, only use this cost management technique with caution.

- *Terminate general training reimbursement.* Do not offer training unless it directly benefits the company. Any policy to reimburse employees for their advancement through a degree program is unlikely to directly benefit the company, can be quite expensive, and may even trigger employee departures for higher-paying jobs once they have completed their degrees. The only exception is when an employee requests reimbursement for a class that can be of assistance in his or her specific work area.

Eligibility Audits

When a business extends benefits to the family of an employee, the benefits are only intended for those family members who qualify. Over time, children grow up and become too old to still be covered by the corporate benefit plan, and spouses may divorce. However, employees do not always notify the employer when these transition events take place, so the company continues to pay for benefits. Consequently, an obvious cost reduction technique is to conduct an eligibility audit from time to time, to see if any employee dependents can be removed from the corporate benefit plan. An eligibility audit can encompass the following areas:

- *Dependent eligibility tracking.* Review the process by which dependents are initially reviewed for acceptance into the corporate benefit plan, as well as the process by which the status of dependents is subsequently tracked. Ideally, the process should result in the prompt elimination of benefits as soon as a dependent is no longer eligible.

- *Eligibility documentation.* Review the documents that were originally provided as proof that someone is an eligible dependent, such as marriage certificates, birth certificates, adoption papers, and so forth. The review may reveal situations where someone is not eligible for benefits, such as a spouse who is now divorced, and children who are now too old to receive benefits.

- *Overpayment recovery.* Review the process for obtaining repayment from employees in those situations where benefits were extended to a dependent that is no longer eligible.

An element of eligibility auditing is the development and distribution of a policy that states the exact circumstances under which dependents are eligible to receive benefits, and the company's commitment to ensure that these standards are upheld. Doing so informs employees of the company's standards, and makes it less likely that they will attempt a circumvention.

The concept of an eligibility audit for benefits may not sit well with employees, since they may feel that it requires an excessive degree of company interference in their personal affairs. If so, it can help to point out that eligibility audits reduce the total cost of benefits, and so allow the company to continue offering benefits to employees at a reasonable cost.

A likely response to an eligibility audit is the occasional request for a waiver, so that an unqualified dependent can be provided with coverage. These requests should be rejected in all cases, since a waiver would violate the terms under which third parties provide benefits to the company, and because one waiver opens the door to additional requests for waivers from other employees.

Benefit Cost Administration

Benefit plans can require an inordinate amount of staff time to administer, especially when there are many types of benefits, and lots of options are offered to employees. Here are several ways to reduce the cost of benefits administration, while still retaining the essential benefits:

- *Reduce the number of options.* When a company offers its employees a virtual blizzard of benefit options from which to choose, there is a natural temptation to continually tweak the benefits being taken. When a large number of employees are constantly adjusting their benefits, the administrative staff must spend an inordinate amount of time recording these changes, modifying benefit deductions in the payroll system, and notifying benefit providers of the changes. A less expensive approach from an administrative perspective is to vastly reduce the number of options available to employees, which in turn reduces the number of staff needed to monitor the benefit plans. A variation on this concept is to only allow employees to change their benefits once a year.
- *Minimize deduction updates.* Employees are commonly asked to pay for a portion of each benefit offered to them, where their portion is deducted from each of their paychecks. Whenever there is a change in the cost to the company of a benefit, this means that the employee portion of the deduction must be updated in the payroll system, which can be a massive undertaking that is also subject to error. One way to mitigate this

administrative headache is to offer some of the lower-cost benefits to employees for free, while increasing the deduction for a few of the higher-cost benefits. Doing so reduces the total number of deductions that must be updated. Another alternative is to offer a single benefit deduction that applies to an entire package of deductions, so that only one deduction must be updated each year.

- *Provide on-line access.* Create a corporate intranet that is accessible to all employees, and which provides them with up-to-date information about their benefit plans, deductions, forms, the answers to frequently asked questions, and so forth. They should also be able to apply for benefit changes through an on-line form. In essence, this approach shifts some of the administrative burden to employees and away from the administrative staff. However, creating such a system may not be cost-effective for a smaller organization.

Other Cost Management Concepts

This section contains several additional cost management concepts applicable to employee benefits that did not slot into any of the earlier topic areas. These concepts are:

- *401(k) match vesting period.* When a business sets up a 401(k) pension plan for its employees, the company typically offers a matching program where it matches a certain proportion of the cash contributed to the plan by employees. The amount of this match is usually earned, or vested, over several years. If an employee leaves before vesting is complete, then some or all of the employer matching funds for that employee are now made available for matching the contributions of other employees. Thus, a longer vesting period results in lower matching costs for the company. Vesting may also play a role in convincing employees to stay with the company for longer periods of time, thereby reducing employee turnover.
- *401(k) match at year-end.* Only match the employee contributions to a 401(k) pension plan at the end of the year, rather than immediately after employees make their contributions. If employees leave the company prior to the end of the year, they do not receive their matching funds. This approach can be considered penurious, but only has a direct impact on those employees leaving the company.
- *Benefit reporting.* A business may pay for any number of additional benefits that may be incurred only for a few employees, or only at long intervals. Examples are health club memberships and tickets to sporting events. To bring more attention to these costs, record them in a separate general ledger account, and routinely report on their annualized cost to senior management. Also, whenever possible, charge these costs directly to those departments most directly benefiting from them, rather than charging them

to general corporate overhead. These actions will at least increase the awareness of these costs, and may lead to some cost reductions.

- *Self-funding.* Another option for controlling benefit costs is to self-fund a portion of medical insurance. The usual approach is to build up a cash reserve, from which employee claims are paid. If the total amount of claims exceeds a certain amount, a purchased stop-loss insurance package is triggered, which pays for all remaining claims above the threshold amount. A variation on the concept is to hire a third party to administer claims on behalf of the company, which leaves the business in the role of providing funding, rather than wasting time dealing with medical claims paperwork. Self-funding can reduce costs over the long term, since it eliminates the profit that an insurance company would add to its pricing structure. However, the amount of payouts will vary over time, depending on the presence of an occasional large claim, so do not expect to achieve lower costs in all periods.

- *Create a captive insurance company.* A variation on the self-funding concept is to create and fund a captive insurance company. This approach is less expensive than buying insurance from an independent insurance entity, which must include a provision in its pricing for an adequate profit. There are also tax advantages to using a captive insurance company. Given the costs to set up and manage a captive insurance company, as well as the cost to obtain an insurance license, this approach is usually only cost-effective for mid-sized or larger organizations.

- *Smoker avoidance.* Some businesses go to the extreme of not hiring smokers. This can even include periodic tests to ensure that employees have not taken up smoking. By doing so, a business can reduce its health care costs, as well as incur fewer employee sick days. Before implementing such an approach, be sure to consider how any smokers currently on the payroll are to be treated, as well as any legal considerations.

Summary

When reducing benefit costs, keep in mind that there is a limit to how far cost reductions can be taken. If the company is perceived by employees to be a parsimonious spender in this area, it could damage the ability of the business to hire new recruits, and gives existing employees less reason to continue working for the company.

Rather than cutting costs everywhere, a good approach is to canvas employees to determine which benefits are most critical to them, and to also review the offerings of competitors; based on this information, focus spending only on the most critical areas, and cut back much more on all other types of benefits. The result could be a signature set of benefits that the company can boast about, where nearly all benefits funding is concentrated. If this approach is followed, be sure to revisit the allocation of benefit expenditures at regular intervals, and adjust it to bring benefits into alignment with employee expectations.

Chapter 13
Sales and Marketing Effectiveness

Introduction

The title of this chapter focuses on effectiveness, rather than the outright reduction of costs that are advocated in other chapters. The reason is that much of the spend in the sales and marketing areas is poorly defined, so that the payoff in increased sales is not optimal. Consequently, the focus in this chapter is not necessarily on the reduction of costs, but rather on the more targeted use of these funds. In the following sections, we discuss ways to improve the management of costs in the areas of sales, marketing, and customer service. We also make note of the possibility of increasing prices.

Sales Effectiveness Improvements

There are a number of ways to improve the effectiveness of the sales function. In this section, we break down these improvements by classification. A behavior-related improvement is designed to incentivize the sales staff to alter their selling behavior, while activity-related changes focus on altering the types of activities that the sales staff should be engaged in. The process-related changes emphasize how sales resources are deployed to generate sales activity, while the analysis-related items focus on specific selling activities that can be targeted to increase profitability.

Behavior Related

- *Focus commission plan on profits.* The typical commission plan states that a salesperson will receive a certain percentage of the price of each product sold. However, this plan does not focus on the amount of profit associated with each sale, so a salesperson could be vigorously pursuing a sale that will result in little overall profit for the company. Instead of this approach, consider altering the terms of the commission plan to pay higher commissions on those products and services that generate the highest profits. Since the sales staff is not likely to have detailed information about product profitability, the simplest way to direct their attention to these items is to set up a small number of product classifications, each based on underlying product profitability, and assign a different commission rate to each one. The main problem with this approach is that the accounting for commission calculations will become more complicated, since a single customer order may include several different commission rates.
- *Avoid special commission deals.* There may be a temptation to adjust the commission plan to an excessive extent to incentivize certain types of

behavior. Always review the implications of these alterations to see if they may be damaging other parts of the company. For example, offering a higher commission on sales to new customers may have the unintended effect of reducing sales efforts directed at existing customers, for which sales are usually much easier to generate. Or, a bonus for last-minute sales to close out the quarter places undue pressure on the production department at the end of the quarter, results in more overtime costs, and also trains the sales staff to delay recording orders until the bonus is offered.

Activity Related

- *Focus on declining customers.* Most organizations do not focus on those customers whose orders have declined or vanished over time. Instead, they focus on obtaining the next big sale, no matter who the customer may be. However, the cost of re-selling to an existing customer is much less than the total cost of locating a new customer, so it makes sense to monitor declines in order volume to see what can be done for existing customers. Accordingly, the sales manager should review a report that states customer order volumes over time, and have the sales staff contact those customers whose orders have not kept pace with their historical averages. The result may be the discovery that these customers are dissatisfied with a particular aspect of the company's products, services, field support, or other issues that can be readily rectified. Not only can these corrections bring back long-term customers, but they can also improve the experience for other customers, who will then be less likely to abandon the company.

- *Avoid strategic sales.* A strategic sale is a transaction that is considered important to the market positioning of a business, but which has an unusually low profit or no profit at all. Classifying a prospective sale as a strategic sale is usually considered because the target customer is well-known, or the sale can build the production volume of the business. There are several problems with these types of sales. First, the customer's price point is now set so low that the company will never earn a profit on subsequent sales to that entity. Second, word of the price point allowed may spread to other customers, who will also demand the same price point. Third, the company's overall profits will decline, since some of its production capacity is being reserved for deliveries to a customer that generates no profits. Instead, allow competitors to "win" these strategic sales, so that their profits suffer.

- *Avoid collections by the sales staff.* The sales staff can be unusually effective at collecting overdue payments from customers, since they have the best contacts within the customer organizations. However, their time is usually more effectively spent on generating more sales. Consequently, reserve the use of sales personnel on collections work for only the largest and/or most intractable collection problems.

- *Evaluate trade shows*. Attending trade shows can be quite expensive, especially if a company is renting booth space. Evaluate the outcome of each trade show to see if it produces an incremental increase in the company's sales. An additional benefit of not attending a trade show is that the sales staff who would otherwise attend the show can now be re-targeted toward more productive activities.

Process Related

- *Emphasize more inside sales*. The nature of the sales call is always changing, so continually evaluate the need to place sales people in front of customers, versus doing so with contacts made by inside sales personnel. The net cost of an inside salesperson is massively lower than that of a travelling salesperson, since the cost of travel is eliminated, as well as the downtime while in transit to a customer. The inside sales concept is becoming much more acceptable to customers, as they become used to video communications in many of their other business and personal interactions. This concept can be extended to the sales support staff. For example, customers may find it quite acceptable for a salesperson to come to a product demonstration, while the sales engineer demonstrating the product is doing so online. At an extreme, it is possible that there may not be a need for an outside sales force at all. The concept can be extended even further, so that inside sales personnel work from their homes, thereby eliminating the need for office space. However, the shift to inside sales requires hiring for a different skill set that emphasizes more product knowledge and less emphasis on interpersonal skills, so it is not always possible to repurpose existing outside salespeople into this type of position.
- *Focus on sales bottlenecks*. The sales process flow for some organizations is complicated, involving such activities as initial customer contacts, sales visits, a product demonstration, and contract negotiations. Each step in this process may involve a different specialist, so that work is handed off from one employee to another. It is entirely likely that there will be bottlenecks somewhere in this process flow that restrict the amount of sales transactions that can be completed. For example, a common constriction point is the product demonstration, since it takes time to train sales engineers, resulting in there being too few sales engineers available. Consequently, the sales manager should continuously review the backlog of work at each stage in the sales process; any backlogged activity is a bottleneck, and must be resolved before sales can be increased. For example, it makes little sense to increase the number of junior sales staff conducting cold calls to prospective customers if there is a backlog in the proposals group that prevents the company from issuing proposals to any of the newly generated leads.
- *Eliminate order hitches*. Consider the company's sales process flow from the perspective of the customer. It should be incredibly easy for a customer

to place an order, perhaps to the extent that customers prefer to buy from the company just because it is so much easier to do so than to buy from a competitor. This can include the use of an automated credit application process, immediate feedback on product availability, and free overnight delivery. In particular, avoid any process steps that give customers an opportunity to back away from placing an order.

- *Focus on internal salesperson efforts.* It is entirely possible that some aspects of a company's operations may be so inefficient that the sales staff rightfully feels that it must shepherd each customer order through the maze of internal credit reviews, production schedules, and shipping procedures to ensure that customers are satisfied. While constant salesperson attention certainly can improve customer satisfaction, it is massively inefficient in terms of the time spent by the sales staff. If this scenario sounds familiar, institute a top-to-bottom review of the time required for a customer order to pass through the company, and take whatever actions are necessary to create an environment where orders are processed in a speedy and reliable manner. Only then will the sales staff return to their normal selling activities.

Analysis Related

- *Sell based on customer profitability.* The sales manager should closely monitor the amount of contribution margin generated by each customer. Contribution margin is sales minus all direct costs, such as direct materials, unreimbursed shipping charges, and commissions. This periodic review should result in decisions to refocus the efforts of the sales staff toward those customers generating the most profits. Perhaps even more important, it means the company should consider terminating its relationship with any customers that are unprofitable and for which there is no prospect of generating more profitable sales. A further subdivision of this analysis can be the amount of time that the administrative staff spends on low-profit customers, since their time could potentially be re-deployed toward more profitable customers if the low-profit customers were to be terminated.
- *Focus on incremental selling costs.* Some salespeople are more cost-effective than others in their travel arrangements, resulting in more sales for the amount of travel funds expended. Thus, a detailed review of the incremental selling costs required to close a sale should certainly be conducted. However, there are a multitude of additional factors to consider before judging a salesperson based on this analysis. For example, the build out of a new sales region requires more sales calls, since there will initially be no repeat customers. Also, a less-populated and geographically larger sales region requires more travel time and costs to reach customers. Further, it may take a number of months or even several years before a new salesperson reaches a high level of sales effectiveness. Consequently, full

consideration must be given to all mitigating circumstances when using this analysis.

Marketing Effectiveness Improvements

In this section we address ways to improve the effectiveness of the marketing function. Please note that we are not necessarily advocating the reduction of costs in the marketing area, but rather the repurposing of the expenditure to maximize market awareness of the product. All too frequently, the marketing budget is slashed in the midst of a financial downturn, leading to long-term damage to a brand. Instead of such behavior, our suggestions are:

- *Copy competitors*. If the company's marketing efforts do not appear to be paying off with increased sales, take a hard look at the characteristics of the marketing programs being used by the industry's market share leaders. They have likely worked through many variations on how to spend their marketing funds, and have hit upon a combination that is most effective for them. Copying some or all aspects of their general marketing concepts could be a reasonable way to improve the effectiveness of marketing expenditures. However, this approach is less useful if the company's product offerings or market image are substantially different from those of the market leaders.

- *Survey customers*. It is essential to understand how customers are hearing about the company, so conduct ongoing surveys to collect this information. It is entirely likely that the majority of expenditures are being made in areas such as television advertising that are immensely expensive, and which are not registering with customers. It may be worthwhile to spend what may appear to be an inordinate amount to understand how customers hear about the company, since the amount of funds that could be wasted on marketing through the wrong channels is even greater.

- *Explore new channels*. The channels through which a company can transmit its marketing message to customers is continually changing, with television advertising in decline, and a multitude of alternative channels springing up on the Internet. Consequently, continually allocate a small amount of funding to alternative marketing experiments, and survey customers to determine whether the alternative channels used are worthy of additional funding.

- *Avoid special promotions*. Customers love special promotions, because they can buy at reduced prices. These arrangements are not so attractive to companies, for several reasons. First, they train customers to expect lower prices, so the customers withhold their purchases until the next promotion comes along. Also, the production department is placed in the uncomfortable position of having to ramp up in anticipation of a promotion, followed by a production decline thereafter, resulting in uneven manufacturing flows that are difficult to manage. Also, production costs related to overtime and maintenance for overused machines may increase as part of these promotional periods. Thus, a marketing system that is built around an ongoing series of special promotions may not be optimizing company operations or profits. One of the few situations in which promotions may be justified is when old products must be cleared from stock in anticipation of the sale of a replacement set of products.

- *Reduce breadth of product offerings.* When there are a vast number of un-related products, it becomes difficult for the marketing staff to create a reasonable number of marketing campaigns that address all of the products. The result is likely to be a relatively small amount of marketing attention to each individual product, while spending an outsized amount for the marketing budget in total. Further, because of the reduced amount of spending on a per-product basis, it is less likely that any particular product will attain the top position in its market niche. A reasonable alternative is to cut back on the stray products that are soaking up an excessive amount of the marketing budget. A variation is to ignore these outlying products and concentrate all marketing expenditures on clusters of related products. The end result should be either reduced marketing expenses in total, or much more effective marketing that is targeted at particular segments of the company's lineup of products.

- *Make packaging cost-effective.* A product's packaging can have a major impact on how well it sells, so the marketing department may have a significant influence over the packaging design. The marketing staff may have to deal with many other factors besides how well packaging improves a sale, such as being tamperproof, stackable, and made of recycled materials. An additional concern is whether the design is cost-effective. This means that the design is sufficiently robust that it does not contribute to product damage, while not being so over-designed that it contributes no additional protection to the product. This approach may result in substantially less packaging material. When packaging designs reduce the overall volume or weight of a product, a secondary benefit is that shipping costs may also decline.

- *Quantify payback.* It may be useful to introduce a more quantitative analysis viewpoint to the allocation of marketing funds. This can involve budgeting the incremental increase in unit sales that are estimated from an investment in a certain marketing activity, followed by a feedback loop to see if the estimated unit quantity was attained. The concept can be expanded to estimate the maximum amount of marketing expenditure that should be made in a certain activity before the incremental contribution margin from doing so begins to decline. The following example illustrates the concept.

EXAMPLE

The owner of the Crumb Cake Café wants to start up an Internet advertising campaign for the mail order delivery of her crumb cakes, for which there is an incremental profit of $1 per cake sold. She constructs the following analysis of the projected return from search engine advertising, which is based on a trial run.

Incremental Block of Expenditures	Funding Increment	Incremental Unit Sales	Profit per Dollar Expended	Total Incremental Margin	Total Cumulative Margin
1	$5,000	15,000	$2.00	$10,000	$10,000
2	5,000	10,000	1.00	5,000	**15,000**
3	5,000	5,000	0	0	15,000
4	5,000	4,000	-0.20	-1,000	14,000
5	5,000	2,000	-0.60	-3,000	11,000

Based on this analysis, it is apparent that the most optimal use of Internet advertising would be to spend $10,000 per month on this activity, since any additional expenditures would have a net zero or negative payback.

A cost reduction issue worthy of investigation is the prices charged by a company's ad agency. Their pricing is usually based on a percentage of the total amount of company spend that they control, which means that there is no link between the cost of their efforts and the price charged. Instead of this arrangement, look for an ad agency that is willing to accept a billing arrangement that is based on hours worked. The result should be a notable decline in the cost of ad agencies. However, if an existing ad agency is unusually effective and refuses to accept such an arrangement, then it may be more effective in terms of overall impact to continue with the current billing situation.

Customer Service Issues

In this section, we address several general concepts that are useful for more closely aligning customer service with the overall strategic direction of a business, as well as how to drive decision-making down into the organization and use automation in the most effective manner possible. The suggested improvements are:

- *Match service to strategy*. Customer service is yet another aspect of sales and marketing where an unrelenting focus on cost reduction is not necessarily a good idea. If customers are paying high prices for premium products or services, then the customer service function of the company should also be premium. Conversely, a low-margin business with cut-rate prices may need to adopt every conceivable method to reduce the cost of its customer service function.

- *Automate customer service.* Within the boundaries of the last point regarding matching customer service to strategy, it can be extremely cost-effective to automate large amounts of the customer service function. Consider the following options:

  - *FAQs.* Prominently display on the company website a link to a lengthy list of frequently asked questions, along with detailed answers. Customers may very well find what they need on this page, and will not trouble the company further with additional questions.

  - *Automate service for low-profit customers.* When a customer calls the company's customer service system, have them enter their customer number, which will route the lowest-profit customers to an automated response system and the highest-profit customers to actual customer service representatives. This routing recognizes the realities of differences in customer profitability, and that a personal touch is needed to retain the most important customers.

  - *Shift workload to customers.* In general, shift as much of the work load to customers as possible, thereby reducing the time required by the customer service staff to deal with customers. This concept can include posting product manuals on-line that customers can peruse, setting up spare parts ordering forms on-line for customers to fill out, and on-line product return request forms that customers can complete.

- *Increase authorization levels.* Allow the customer service staff to settle as many customer problems as possible, rather than annoying customers by routing issues around the company for senior levels of management approval. For example, the customer service staff can approve credits to customers, the return of goods, and warranty claims. This approach also reduces the amount of unresolved issues that the customer service staff must deal with.

Product Return Issues

Product returns can result in the imposition of significant costs on a business. Returned items may have to be reworked or destroyed, or require new packaging. At a minimum, a business must incur labor costs to return those goods to the shelf that were returned in perfect condition. There are also cases of fraud, where someone shoplifts goods from a store and then returns it for cash, having claimed that the receipt was lost. These costs can be reduced by imposing restrictions on product returns, such as restocking fees, the requirement of an accompanying receipt, and/or allowing only a short time window within which returns are allowed. The imposition of a short return window is especially important for fashion or seasonal items that lose value within a short period of time.

The problem with these restrictions is that they can annoy a company's most loyal customers, who only rarely return goods. It may be possible to walk a fine line between these issues by only applying restrictive return policies to the likeliest offenders; the company can then impose few (if any) product return restrictions on its other customers. A firm can maintain a database of product returns and aggregate the data to determine who is clearly abusing its return policies. Abusers can be found by examining return frequency and the proportion of purchases that are returned. If the level of returns is destroying the profits otherwise earned from sales to a customer, then this customer is a clear candidate for a restrictive returns policy. By taking this more nuanced approach, a company can maximize its profits while also maintaining good relations with the vast majority of its customers.

Raise Prices

This entire book is concerned with techniques and tips for keeping costs as low as possible. However, it would be unwise not to make some mention of improving profits by raising prices. Managers have a tendency to assume that prices are fixed or trending downward, and so spend a massive amount of time focusing instead on cost reduction activities. In reality, there may be a large amount of room available in which to raise prices. This is particularly the case when a company has a strong brand image, and it does not sell commodity products. If so, it is certainly worthwhile to experiment with targeted price increases or reductions in the use of special discounts, with the goal of improving the net revenue per product sold.

When engaging in price increases, do so on an experimental basis. This means setting up a pricing experiment to measure how unit sales decrease in response to a price increase. If there is a net increase in overall profitability despite a decline in unit sales, then broadly roll out the price increase. Conversely, if there is a sharp decline in unit volume during an experimental price increase, then terminate the experiment and return the price to its original level.

A variation on the theme of raising prices is to add prices for services that are currently free. This can include the following:

- *Rush fee.* If a customer wants delivery sooner than the promised date, add a substantial additional charge, and increase the fee further for overnight delivery.
- *Fuel surcharges.* The cost of energy is always increasing, so why not pass it along to customers in the form of a fuel surcharge?
- *Credit card fee.* These fees usually start at 3% of a transaction's price and go up from there, and so can be a significant burden on the profits of a seller. However, adding a surcharge to a purchase transaction is commonly viewed in a negative manner by customers, since it is essentially a penalty for using a credit card. A reasonable way to deal with the situation is to raise list prices enough to cover the cost of credit card fees, and then offer a discount for cash payments.

- *Shipping and handling fees.* Unless there is competition in the industry based on free delivery, be sure to charge a reasonable amount for shipping and handling. Do not overcharge in this area – the prevalence of free shipping in some areas has made consumers more sensitive to this type of fee.

Summary

This chapter focused on the general principles for improving the effectiveness of expenditures for sales and marketing, rather than itemizing a massive list of ways to pare costs in these areas. Sales and marketing managers are likely already cognizant of what expenditures are being made and how to control them, so the real issue is how to allocate costs in the most effective manner in order to maximize profitable sales. The recommended items tend to require more detailed analysis and intensive implementation efforts to overcome what may be deep-seated opposition to changes in the way that these functions have "always" been handled.

Chapter 14
Production and Maintenance Cost Reduction

Introduction

The production function has traditionally been built around the concept of long production runs that are designed to drive down the cost of each unit produced by spreading overhead costs among the largest possible number of units. While this approach may appear correct from a cost accounting perspective, its real-world application is flawed. Lengthy production runs tend to result in large investments in inventory, high scrap rates, and any number of production inefficiencies that are masked by the high inventory levels.

The maintenance function was originally designed to be an emergency-oriented group of experts who swoop down upon malfunctioning equipment and fix it in record time. While exciting to watch, this approach is not cost-effective, since machinery downtime is still involved, parts may be needed on a rush basis, and the system is practically designed to incur overtime costs.

In this chapter, we describe a range of options that dismantle the long production run concept and instead focus on short production runs and lean production techniques. We also address a more practical methodology for scheduling maintenance operations, and include a number of recommendations for reducing the cost of parts and supplies.

Production Cost Reduction

In this section, we address a large number of cost reduction concepts related to production. We begin with a few general comments regarding the reduction of complexity in several areas that impact production, and then proceed to more specific areas of improvement, including manufacturing systems, production cells, production lines, quality concerns, bottleneck analysis, outsourcing, and similar topics.

Complexity Reduction

- *Reduce the number of products.* When a company manufactures a massive number of products, it is difficult to optimize the production process, and employees will have a difficult time learning about ways to improve the production process for each one. The result will likely be an ongoing low level of manufacturing efficiency. To improve the situation, consider dropping those outlier products that earn minimal profits, and yet tend to clutter up the production process. This concept will require the cooperation of the marketing manager, who is usually trying to expand sales by offering a broader range of products to customers.

- *Design for production*. Products can be designed to incorporate fewer components, which reduces the amount of assembly work. Another option is to outsource some of the manufacturing work, leaving less labor for the final assembly staff. Yet another option is to design a product to be shipped in the absolute smallest possible container size, which can reduce shipping costs.
- *Idiot proof the assembly process*. When the engineering staff designs a product, it should ensure that the parts can only be assembled one way; that is, the parts will not fit together properly if anyone attempts to assemble them in a different way. By paying attention to this issue, the risk of improper unit assembly is eliminated, which in turn reduces product defect rates and warranty costs.

These issues are not ones that can be resolved by the production manager. Instead, they involve fundamental marketing or product design issues that must be addressed well before products ever appear in the production area.

Manufacturing Systems

- *Adopt a pull system*. The traditional production system is a "push" system, in which a production scheduler guesstimates the amount of various products that will be needed, and then authorizes the production area to produce these units. The trouble with the push system is that this forecast may not bear much resemblance to the quantities that customers actually want, resulting in significant amounts of finished goods inventory that are not purchased, and therefore in obsolete inventory write-downs and/or the sale of these items at reduced prices. A better alternative is to wait for customer orders to arrive and *then* produce the goods, which is called a "pull" system. This approach essentially eliminates the investment in finished goods inventory. However, the pull system is not easy to install, since it requires that the production processes work together in a highly coordinated manner to ensure that just enough goods are produced to meet customer demand.
- *Implement a kanban system*. A kanban is essentially an authorization to produce more goods. A kanban can take many forms, such as a colored card, a bin, or some other visual signal. Kanbans are employed in conjunction with a pull system, so that each downstream workstation authorizes an upstream workstation to produce a certain additional amount of goods. In essence, the concept is used to ensure that only enough parts are manufactured to exactly fill a customer order. Once that order has been completed, no additional kanbans are issued, so no upstream work stations are allowed to produce any more goods. The result is an extremely low investment in inventory. A kanban system may be incorporated into a computer-controlled production system, or it can be an entirely manual notification system.

- *Use an MRP II system.* If it is not possible to implement a just-in-time pull system as just described, at least install a manufacturing resources planning (MRP II) system, which matches the production schedule to the capacities of the various production workstations, and also schedules the flow of inventory through the production system. Though these systems are expensive and require constant monitoring, the result is a well-run production process in which inventory levels are reduced.

- *Mistake management.* In a typically complex production environment, there are a vast number of opportunities to make a mistake. When a mistake occurs, there must be a system in place for dealing with it immediately. Otherwise, the issue will travel up and down the management chain, and may be resolved weeks later; meanwhile, the mistake still exists, and is likely causing product defects or production inefficiencies. In some production environments, employees are authorized to halt production if they see a serious issue, and a repair team swarms over the problem until it is resolved. Alternatively, it may be sufficient to note the problem on a nearby whiteboard, which is closely monitored by repair teams. The key element in whatever solution is adopted is the *immediate* recognition and correction of problems. An elaborate reporting system is not needed, and could even introduce so much bureaucracy that it slows down the correction of mistakes.

- *Employee training.* Each processing step in a production environment requires that a certain number of steps be taken in a particular order. These steps may be second nature to experienced employees, but could be unfathomable to new hires. Accordingly, trace back operator errors to specific work stations and individuals, and see if the use of detailed operator instructions or specific training might eliminate the issue.

- *Ban expediting.* A manufacturing "system" is the use of expediters. These employees are assigned customer orders that are considered high priority, and are authorized to override all current jobs while ramming their orders through the production process as fast as possible. The inevitable result is that allocated materials are swept up by each expedited order, work queues are bypassed, and machine setups are overridden. Thus, an expediter leaves a debris trail of interrupted work and missing parts throughout the production area that makes it more difficult for normally scheduled work to be completed. Though the customer benefiting from an expedited order may be happy, everyone else will find that their estimated order completion dates have now slipped. The only way to avoid this level of chaos is to completely ban the use of expediting. Instead, focus on reducing the amount of time required for a standard order to work its way through the production system, so customers will not feel the need to demand more rapid delivery.

The concepts noted in this sub-section are among the most critical cost management issues for the production department. If these concepts are not implemented, then the full range of cost reduction opportunities that are available will be reduced to a notable extent.

Production Cells

- *Create production cells.* A production cell is an arrangement of workstations that are laid out in a cluster and designed to allow a small number of employees to walk a part through a series of finishing steps. This approach eliminates the need for a production line, since it is possible for a single employee to handle many production activities. By doing so, any out-of-specification conditions can be immediately spotted and corrected, which massively reduces the amount of scrap cost incurred. Also, there is very little work-in-process in this arrangement, because there is no need for work to pile up in front of each workstation. The result is a notable reduction in the amount of working capital investment related to inventory.

- *Assign product families to cells.* As just noted, only a small number of employees are needed in a production cell, and each one may be trained to work on multiple machines. To improve employee familiarity with the parts being produced, assign groups of similar products to each production cell. Not only does this increased volume eventually lead to more cell efficiency, it also tends to create a reduced number of defective parts.

- *Install quick changeovers.* A production cell will not work unless the machines in it can be configured to change over to a new setting with only a few moments of effort. Otherwise, someone walking a part through a production cell will spend an inordinate amount of time changing over each machine in turn, which will result in significant effort to produce one part. If quick changeovers cannot be completed, then the production cell concept is not viable. Consequently, it is critical to implement quick changeovers for every machine in a production cell. The following steps are usually required to effect a quick changeover:

  1. If any changeover activities can be completed before the end of the last production run, be sure to do so.
  2. If any changeover activities cannot be completed until the last production run has been completed, see if they can be altered in order to complete them before the end of the last production run.
  3. Simplify all remaining steps that can only be completed after the end of the last production run.
  4. Document the changes and train the staff on how the new process operates.
  5. Continually review the process to see if additional improvements can be made. The ideal changeover is one in which operator movements are minimized and only a few seconds are required.

- *Move cells close together.* When there is some physical distance between production cells, parts completed in an upstream cell are typically allowed to pile up for a time, after which a materials handling person arrives with a forklift and shifts the parts to the next downstream production cell. There are several problems with this. First, the amount of inventory that is allowed to pile up represents an extra investment in inventory. Second, the materials handling person could damage the parts while transporting them. Third, a defective process in the upstream production cell might not be noticed until the entire batch is moved to the downstream process and used by the staff at that production cell, resulting in the entire batch being declared defective. The solution is to move the cells closer together and connect them with conveyors. By doing so, units can be shifted to the next production cell at once, there is no need for any materials handling staff, and the production area requires less floor space.

- *Favor small machine purchases*. An inherent requirement of a production cell is that it be comprised of a small number of machines that can be configured over time to match the changing needs of a business. Ease of configuration means that a machine be on the smaller and lighter side, so the cost management objective is to avoid acquisitions of the larger and more complex equipment that is typically positioned once and never moved again. This latter type of machine is called a *monument*, and leads to several types of suboptimal results. Consider the following:

  o *No backup*. When a large investment is made in a monument machine, this usually implies that there was only enough cash to buy one unit. Therefore, when this machine is down for maintenance, there is no backup unit available to continue production, resulting in a complete stoppage.

  o *Production runs*. Since a monument tends to take longer to set up, there is an inclination to have longer production runs, to justify the time required for the set up. The result is more inventory than the company actually needs.

  o *Breakdown rate*. A more complex machine is more likely to break down, so expect it to have more down time and more maintenance staff time applied to it than would be the case if a simpler machine had been acquired.

- *Stock inventory next to production cells*. A traditional production system involves the storage of raw materials in a warehouse, which are then transported to the production area as needed. Doing so requires that the company expend cash to maintain the warehouse space and pay the warehousing and materials handling employees. To avoid these costs, consider having suppliers deliver their goods directly to the production line, thereby avoiding the need for the receiving function, warehouse, and materials handling staff. While an attractive concept, this is not easy to implement. Suppliers must first be certified for having sufficiently high-quality goods, and they must have access to the company's production schedule, so that they can deliver the exact items as needed within a particular time slot. Consequently, this is considered an advanced production technique.

- *Cross-train employees*. The cost of labor can be excessively high when the production staff is governed by work rules that specify the precise tasks that each person is allowed to perform. The result is downtime for some employees and massive overtime for others. Where possible, eliminate these work rules and cross-train employees so that they can perform multiple functions. By doing so, pockets of labor inefficiency within a facility can be eliminated.

The use of production cells is a significant concept that requires a large amount of time to implement and fine tune. Given the level of knowledge required to establish a well-run system of production cells, this is a good area in which to bring in a consultant to provide advice.

Production Line Issues

- *Adopt a serpentine line*. In cases where goods are being produced in high volume, it may be most efficient to install a classic production line, where employees start with raw materials at one end and issue a completed product at the other end. While efficient, a straight production line has been proven to yield relatively high defect rates. The trouble is that the sheer distance covered by a production line makes it difficult for employees throughout the line to communicate with each other. As a result, someone finding a defect near one end of the line may have trouble communicating back up the line to determine the source of the problem. A good way to improve upon the situation is to install a serpentine production line configuration, so that the longest straight-line distance from one end of the line to the other is vastly shortened. The result is a much easier environment for communicating across the entire production line. However, this approach calls for a complete revision of the existing production line layout, which could be expensive to adjust.
- *Shorten the line*. When a company installs a long production line, more space is allowed for employees to move around. However, it also means that there is space *between* employees. If parts are traveling down the line at a steady pace, the extra space means that there are a large number of work-in-process parts on the line at any one time that are not being worked on by employees. These extra parts represent an increase in the company's investment in inventory. This investment can be reduced by shortening the production line. The ideal arrangement is when the number of parts traveling down the line equals the number of employees on the line, which means that every item in process is being worked on at any given moment. Shortening the line to this extent will require some work load balancing by the industrial engineering staff, and may not be achieved at once. However, continual attention to this issue can reap benefits, not only in

inventory reduction, but also by reducing the space taken up by the production line.

- *Parts assignment.* When a product or part is needed, the production planning staff will likely assign it to the next available machine. However, that machine may have slightly different tolerances or setup characteristics from the machine on which the item was usually produced. Consequently, the equipment changeover person assigned to the machine will likely have to engage in additional testing to ensure that the changeover is properly set up to produce the new item within allowable specifications. To avoid this extra work, the scheduling staff should try to run the same items on the same machines on a repetitive basis, so that a consistent set of changeover notes can be relied upon to produce an in-specification unit with minimal machine fine tuning.

The preceding comments are intended for those situations where the high volume of goods produced makes a production line the most cost-effective solution. In all other cases, the earlier comments regarding production cells would apply.

Shift Issues

It can be tempting to meet increased production demands by adding one or more shifts. However, if the first shift is inefficient and works at low capacity utilization levels, then adding shifts merely expands the problem into shifts that historically experience even lower levels of efficiency. Instead, it can make more sense to concentrate on squeezing the maximum output out of the first shift operations and *then* copying this enhanced production scheme over to additional shifts.

> **Tip:** Monitor the efficiency levels of each separate shift, to see if it makes sense to continue operating a second or third shift. If there is a substantial decline in efficiency in the later shifts, it may make sense to concentrate on just a single shift.

When calculating the costs associated with a second or third shift, there are several additional costs to consider, which (in aggregate) can make the operation of these shifts unprofitable. Consider the following costs:

- The shift is starting from scratch with new people, so it will take an unusually long period of time to bring these people up to a reasonable level of efficiency.
- Because of the large proportion of new employees, a late shift may require more supervision than the first shift.
- Equipment may have more downtime than on the first shift, since there may not be any repair people on staff during the late shifts.
- Employees are usually paid a premium to work on a late shift.
- Employees working on a late shift have more health problems and a higher rate of absenteeism.

157

- Utilities expenses may be higher, if additional lighting is needed to illuminate the workplace.

An additional concern is that the second and third shifts tend to live longer than they are actually needed. They may have been instituted in order to handle a short-term increase in demand, after which demand has gradually declined. Thus, it pays to monitor the need for additional shifts on a regular basis, and be willing to curtail them.

Quality Issues

- *Reduce defects at the source.* One of the largest sources of costs in the production area is scrapped inventory that is caused by defective processes. If these goods escape the attention of the in-house inspectors, they may then turn into warranty claims, which are even more expensive to handle, and which cause customer ill-will. Consequently, it is especially important to adopt production cells (as noted in a prior point) or other methods for triggering an immediate stoppage in production activities when a defective process is found. When production cells are used, the work station operator stationed at the beginning of each cell should conduct a manual inspection of incoming parts, and immediately warn the upstream workstation staff if a defective condition is detected.
- *Reduce quality inspections.* This point may seem counter-intuitive after the last item, but the way to reduce defects in a production process is *not* to install more quality inspection points. These inspections require additional staff, and the inspectors are not adding value to the product. Instead, spend more effort on eliminating defects at the source, so defect rates are reduced to such a low level that there is no need for formal quality inspections. The result can be reductions not only in the cost of quality assurance staff, but also of the overall amount of defective materials produced.

The preceding comments can be implemented to too great an extent, where *all* quality assurance workstations are eliminated. This may not be possible, especially when more detailed tests must be conducted than it is possible for the workstation employees to handle. Also, a company may have to establish a history of quality tests for legal or safety reasons, which mandates the continuing use of some quality assurance personnel.

Bottleneck Analysis

- *Rebalance the production line.* In any production process, there is likely to be at least one process where incoming work-in-process piles up, creating a bottleneck. These bottlenecks impede the ability of the company to produce a profit, since they place an upper limit on the amount of goods that can be produced. While it may be impossible to work around some bottlenecks (due to the capital cost associated with an upgrade), others can be eliminated by regularly reviewing the production area and adjusting the layout and materials flow. Bottlenecks can be caused not only by the inherent restrictions of a work station, but also by changes in the types of production required by customer orders, so rebalancing is an ongoing process.

- *Test quality before bottleneck.* Having just advocated a reduction in quality inspections, we must note one exception, which is to ensure that no defective parts reach the bottleneck operation. The bottleneck limits the amount of total production that can be achieved, so running a defective part through the bottleneck means that the time of the bottleneck operation has just been wasted, which will reduce overall company profitability. Consequently, a location just in front of the bottleneck is an excellent place to set up a quality review station.

- *Overstaff the bottleneck operation.* Since the bottleneck operation restricts the ability of a company to earn additional profits, it is fundamental that the run time of the bottleneck operation must be maximized. This means that there should always be a sufficient number of personnel operating the bottleneck at all times. Consequently, someone should fill in when there are scheduled operator breaks, and the maintenance staff should prioritize its work on the bottleneck, so that it is non-operational for the shortest possible amount of time.

- *Outsource bottleneck work.* The bottleneck operation in the production area is typically a large and expensive machine that management does not want to duplicate by making a large investment. To avoid any additional expenditures in this area to expand capacity, consider shifting excess work to a third party. Even if the unit cost of the outsourced work is high, doing so still allows the company to effectively increase the capacity of the bottleneck operation, which typically equates to greater overall profits.

In essence, the goal of bottleneck analysis is to devote a large amount of management attention to the bottleneck operation to ensure that it is operating constantly.

Outsourcing Issues

- *Outsource work requiring large investments.* When a business must make a substantial investment in equipment in order to conduct a particular manufacturing process, it may be more cost-effective to outsource the work in order to avoid investing in the underlying fixed asset. The situation may change over time, if the amount of work being outsourced is so consistently large that it is obvious that the company can fully support such equipment, and the cost of doing this work in-house is substantially less. Thus, outsourcing should be used to initially avoid large investments until rising demand makes it more cost-effective to bring the work in-house.

- *Outsource to avoid step costs.* As an extension to the last point, only invest in large fixed-cost production equipment to the extent that current demand warrants the investment. If demand increases to a level only slightly higher than the in-house capacity level, it may be better to outsource this additional work until such time as demand has been proven to be consistently higher. Otherwise, the company may incur a substantial step cost and then find that the new equipment is rarely used.

In essence, outsourcing can be a useful tool not only for the long-term shifting of production costs outside of the company, but also for short-term overflow demand situations that cannot be handled internally.

Inventory Reduction

- *Reduce inventory buffers.* The typical production process is comprised of many separate steps that are required to transform raw materials into finished goods. Each of these steps, or workstations, operates separately from the workstations before and after them, so it is customary to build up a certain amount of inventory buffer between each of the workstations, so that no one has to wait for work to come in from an upstream workstation. A problem with these buffers is that an out-of-specification upstream machine could send quite a large number of units to the next downstream machine before anyone notices the problem. In addition, the buffers all involve an added investment in inventory, which increases the amount of working capital. Consequently, reduce or eliminate these buffers, so that defective parts are spotted more quickly.
- *Reduce container sizes.* In some applications, workstation operators are issued trays, bins, or boxes that they are told to fill up with processed parts before handing them off to the next scheduled work station. If these containers are large, it means that more work-in-process inventory is building up within the production area. Simply reducing the size of these containers reduces the amount of inventory buildup between workstations, which in turn reduces the investment in work-in-process inventory.
- *Terminate volume incentives.* When the production staff is paid a bonus based on the number of units it can churn out within a certain period of time, the focus is on unit totals, rather than the quality of what is produced. The inevitable result is an increase in the amount of scrap and rework, since employees will do whatever it takes to meet their goal, including producing goods that are on the edge of being out of specification. Also, a volume incentive can result in having too much finished goods inventory on hand, which increases the working capital investment in this area.

Additional inventory reduction concepts were addressed earlier, in the sub-sections related to manufacturing systems, production cells, and production lines.

Administrative Issues

- *Eliminate traditional cost accounting.* Traditional cost accounting spreads overhead costs across the number of units produced in a period, which gets management into the mindset that unit costs can be reduced by producing more units – even if there is no need for the additional units. Consequently, only use traditional cost accounting to derive inventory costs for financial reporting purposes, and ignore it for any actual decision making that might lead to a focus on producing in greater volumes.
- *Avoid production paperwork.* The intensely organized process that is implied by the preceding cost management suggestions should make it clear that the production staff cannot be interrupted by the need to fill out forms or deal with any other type of bureaucracy. Instead, simply count the output of the system, which is the number of finished goods units produced and the amount of scrap produced. All other reporting requirements should be kept away from the production staff, on the grounds that such activities do not add value to the production process.

In short, the best assistance that the administrative function can render to the production area is to stay away from it.

Summary

Of the preceding cost management possibilities, the greatest gains are likely to come from the adoption of a pull system that is combined with the creation of production cells, since doing so will yield a massive reduction in inventory. Of the remaining suggestions, close monitoring of the usage level of the bottleneck operation is most likely to increase overall company profitability. Many of the other changes support these two general concepts.

Maintenance Cost Reduction

This section contains a number of cost reduction concepts that address two key areas, which are the maintenance of equipment and the purchase of related parts and supplies. These areas mostly relate to production, but can be expanded to include the maintenance of equipment and facilities throughout a business, as well as the associated parts and supplies.

Equipment Maintenance

- *Standardize equipment.* It is much easier for the maintenance staff to maintain equipment when the company uses the same machine model throughout the production area. There are several reasons for this, including familiarity with the supplier's maintenance manuals, having the same preventive maintenance routines for all of the equipment, and acquiring a history of maintenance issues and how to fix them. In addition, the company can invest in a smaller amount of spare parts for these machines, since the same part is used in every machine. In addition, there is less chance that spare parts will never be used and end up being classified as obsolete, as would be the case if a stock of spare parts were to be maintained for a wide range of different machines from different suppliers. Thus, standardization is an excellent goal from the perspective of maintenance costs.

- *Shift routine maintenance.* The types of maintenance tasks conducted can vary from routine lubrication and similar tasks that require minimal skill to extremely difficult machine rebuilding projects. Since the maintenance staff is usually among the better-paid personnel in the production area, it may make sense to shift the more routine maintenance tasks to the machine operators, leaving the more difficult work for the maintenance department. This is an especially good idea when frequent lubrication is needed, since it can be handled on the spot, rather than requiring a maintenance person to continually travel to and from each machine. The main problem with this sort of offloading is that machine operators may forget to complete it, so the extra work must be included in their work instructions and rigorously enforced.

- *Plan for maintenance.* The typical maintenance manager must react to unexpected machine stoppages, requiring staff to race to machines and bring them back on-line, no matter what the expense. The cost of such an environment is likely to be lots of maintenance overtime pay, as well as overnight delivery charges for expedited spare parts. A vastly better approach is to plan for ongoing machine maintenance in an orderly manner, so that machine downtime is scheduled in conjunction with the production planning staff, and the maintenance staff is allowed sufficient time to engage in a thorough overhaul of each machine. Doing so greatly reduces the amount of unexpected machine downtime, results in a more orderly production flow, and shrinks the cost of maintenance.

- *Install equipment monitors.* Equipment monitors can be purchased that are emplaced on equipment, and which routinely send wireless signals back to a monitoring program the amount of vibration, temperature, and other factors emanating from a machine. These monitors can be used to predict when equipment is likely to break down, so that maintenance can be scheduled in advance. The monitors have their own battery power sources, which are intended to provide power for several years, after which the batteries are replaced.

The main point to remember with maintenance cost management is that costs cannot be reduced as long as the maintenance staff is reacting to unplanned machine downtime. Only after preventive maintenance has been implemented can a well-planned and effective maintenance management system be created.

Maintenance, Repair, and Operations Procurement

Part of the maintenance function that seems to defy cost reduction is expenditures on maintenance, repair, and operations (MRO) items. These can be comprised of a vast number of items that are frequently bought in very low volumes, and for which there may be only a small number of available distributors. Also, MRO items are usually charged to expense, rather than being recorded in a tracking database, so there is little usage information about them. Further, there is rarely any system in place for identifying or storing MRO items. All of these factors make MRO one of the more difficult areas in which to institute cost reduction concepts. Nonetheless, the following points could be of assistance:

- *Consolidate MRO items.* If there are multiple places within a company where MRO items are stored, consolidate them into one place. Doing so makes it easier to see if any items have been purchased in excessively large quantities. They can then be drawn down to a more reasonable level over time through ongoing usage.
- *Systematize storage.* Create a storage bin system, in which the same MRO items are stored in the same locations on a repetitive basis. This reduces the time required to locate items, and also makes it easier to conduct a visual inspection of the items on hand, to determine whether any items should be reordered.
- *Assign a responsible party.* Assign specific responsibility to a staff person for monitoring the MRO inventory and warning the procurement team when items must be restocked. Though this and the immediately preceding bullet point may seem like primitive enhancements, they are needed because computerized monitoring systems are usually not applied to MRO items, given that there is usually open access to the inventory that makes it more difficult to keep accurate records.
- *Ask the distributor.* Distributors have a very good knowledge of the availability of any substitute products, and can recommend whether the company should use these substitutes, rather than what is currently being purchased. To gain the cooperation of a distributor in this area, consider allocating the bulk of the company's MRO spend with a single distributor. This is an excellent improvement, since the bulk of the investigative labor is being provided by a third party for free.
- *Buy generic.* The parts sold by original equipment manufacturers are typically much more expensive than their generic equivalents, even though their quality is not noticeably different. Consequently, make it standard practice to always purchase generic equivalent parts and supplies, as long as the underlying quality meets the company's specifications.
- *Buy in economy sizes.* Many types of supplies are substantially less expensive on a per-unit basis when bought in large unit quantities, as specified by the manufacturer. If so, and there is a reasonable expectation of eventually using all of the goods ordered, it may be cost-effective to buy in the larger quantities and simply set aside more storage space for these items.

Conversely, buying in very small unit quantities may be inordinately expensive, and is not justified if there is a reasonable expectation for using more units over time.

- *Consolidate items.* It may be that slight variations on the same basic MRO item have been acquired over time. The result is greater risks of item obsolescence, lower purchasing volumes per item that reduce any chance for volume purchase discounts, and more manual tracking of more items. If this is the case, conduct an ongoing review of similar purchases, and pare away any extraneous items. Though an obvious cost management improvement, this suggestion can meet with resistance if employees prefer a specific brand of product.

- *Concentrate purchases.* Distributors do not earn large profits on an individual order basis, instead relying on large order volumes from their customers to generate reasonable profit levels over the long term. Consequently, a company can gain the favorable attention of a distributor by concentrating most of its purchases with just that one distributor. The distributor can return the favor by granting modest discounts, and providing advice about which MRO items are the most cost-effective purchases.

- *Match purchases to specifications.* A close examination of the requirements for certain MRO items may reveal that what is being purchased is of much higher quality or contains more features than what is actually needed. For example, the percentage of a solvent in a cleaning solution could be higher than required. If so, only buy in accordance with specifications, which can reduce costs.

- *Monitor costs only for high-volume items.* There are an enormous number of MRO items that are purchased in such small quantities that any type of cost reduction analysis is inherently not cost-effective. Instead, restrict all analysis to only the highest-volume MRO items. All other analysis is likely to be a waste of staff time.

- *Packaging credits.* When MRO items are delivered, they may be on pallets or contain spools, spindles, cores, or similar items that the distributor is interested in taking back in exchange for a credit against future purchases. If so, accumulate these items on an ongoing basis and hand them over to the delivery person whenever a new delivery arrives.

- *Reduce safety stocks.* One of the reasons why a business maintains significant amounts of MRO items on hand is because the delivery time from the distributor is excessively long, and there must be a sufficient number of these items on hand to fulfill the company's needs until the next delivery arrives. If a company can arrange with its distributor for faster delivery, it can reduce the amount of safety stock kept on hand, thereby reducing its overall investment in MRO inventory.

- *Shift ownership to a distributor.* Some distributors may be willing to own the MRO inventory positioned on the company premises, and to only charge the company for these items when they are actually used. This represents an additional inventory holding cost for the distributor, as well as a monitoring cost, so this approach will probably only be acceptable if the company agrees to sole source its MRO requirements, and has a large amount of MRO spend per year.

- *Tool checkout area.* Tools are among the most expensive of all MRO items, and are the most likely to be stolen, since they can be readily resold or used outside of the business. Accordingly, etch a serial number into each tool for tracking purposes, and store all tools in a central area. Employees must check out tools from this location, so that usage is tracked by person.
- *Tool replacement/refurbishment.* Many tools are sold with lifetime warranties. To take advantage of these warranties, have the tool crib staff routinely examine tools for damage and apply for free replacements as needed. Also, equip the tool crib with grinding and sharpening equipment, which can be used to refurbish tools that are becoming worn out. These steps are useful for avoiding or at least delaying the purchase of replacement tools.

A particular concern with many of the MRO suggestions just noted is that some of the items purchased will change, which may not go over well with employees at outlying locations who may be attached to particular brands. To mitigate these issues, allocate any resulting cost savings back to the locations, so the local staff can see that there is a benefit from accepting different MRO items.

Summary

The single most important issue in the maintenance area is to change the outlook of the department from a group that reacts to equipment failures to one that plans for maintenance in advance and so can conduct its activities in an orderly and well-planned manner. The next most critical issue is gaining control over MRO purchases by instituting a sufficient level of organization over these items to focus attention on the highest-usage items.

Summary

When engaged in cost management in the production and maintenance area, it is useful to think of the impact of specific cost reductions on the output of the *entire* area. For example, scaling back on staffing in the maintenance area might indeed lower maintenance costs, but will also reduce the availability of production equipment, which may reduce capacity to such an extent that the overall profitability of the company declines. Thus, a complete systems view is needed before shaving costs.

Cost management can be made especially effective by paying attention to the underlying production and maintenance systems, rather than just attempting to implement cost reductions on a spot basis. Thus, a prolonged effort to install a "pull" manufacturing system is likely to yield vastly greater benefits than an oppressive drive to squash labor rates or force suppliers to accept price reductions that destroy their profits.

The reduction of costs and improvement of overall profitability in the production area can be enhanced to a large extent by paying close attention to the constraints within the production area. While we have touched upon a few of these bottleneck-related issues in this chapter, we have not addressed the full range of constraint analysis. For that discussion, please refer to the Constraint Analysis chapter.

Chapter 15
Procurement Cost Reduction

Introduction

Procurement is the process used to obtain goods and services from outside parties. This can involve a byzantine process flow that requires an inordinate amount of staff time, and which unduly delays the time required to complete a purchasing transaction. It may also involve the use of an excessively large number of suppliers, or suppliers to which various company activities have been outsourced.

In this chapter, we begin with the details of the procurement process, and then move on to address a number of techniques related to the internal management of suppliers and the spending process, as well as relations with suppliers. We also describe the process used to aggregate expenditure information to more formally manage spending.

Purchase Requisition Procedure

There should be a formal process for ordering materials and services. Otherwise, there is no control over the amounts spent, and the purchasing department will be buried with purchase requests. To mitigate these issues, many companies require their employees to fill out purchase requisitions. A purchase requisition form details exactly what someone wants to buy, shows the purchasing staff where the indicated items might be bought, and requires at least one approval signature. Thus, it can be a useful tool for organizing the flow of purchasing requests into the purchasing department. A sample purchase requisition follows.

Sample Purchase Requisition

Requisition Number		**Purchase Requisition**
Requisition Date		

		Requisitioned By
Suggested Supplier	Ship to Address	Requisitioner contact information

Due Date	Item Description	Catalog Number	Charge Code	Quantity	Unit Price	Extended Price

Requisition Detail Block

Department Manager Approval Signature	Budget Approval Signature
Additional Approval Signature (as required)	
Additional Approval Signature (as required)	

The procedure for processing purchase requisitions is outlined below.

1. **Complete requisition form.** Obtain a two-part purchase requisition form and fill in the following information:

   - Item or service to obtain
   - Required delivery date
   - Shipping address
   - Account number to be charged
   - Recommended supplier and supplier part number

Control issues: It may be useful to use prenumbered purchase requisitions, so that the purchasing department can keep track of which requisitions are still open. This control is not needed in a computerized system, where the software assigns a unique number to each requisition.

2. **Obtain approval.** At a minimum, obtain the approval of the department manager, who signs the requisition. If the request is for a more expensive item, obtain additional approval signatures as per the company authorization table (see the next procedure).
   Control issues: It may be useful for the purchasing department to periodically route back to the department managers a listing of the requisitions that they have purportedly signed, which can be used to detect fraudulent requisitions. However, this can be a time-consuming control activity.

Tip: Include a field in the requisition form where the requesting person verifies that there is sufficient funding left in the budget for the requested item. Otherwise, there is a risk (especially towards the end of the budget year) that items will be inadvertently purchased for which there are no funds available.

---

3. **Forward to purchasing.** The requesting person should retain one copy of the requisition and forward the other copy to the purchasing department.
   Control issues: The purchasing department could send an acknowledging e-mail back to the requester, stating that they have received the requisition. However, given the extra work involved, this extra control is rarely used.

4. **Match to purchase order** (optional). If the purchasing department sends back a copy of the purchase order that was created from the requisition, compare it to the requisition to ensure that the correct items have been ordered. If not, contact the purchasing staff to have the purchase order revised or replaced.

The following exhibit shows a streamlined view of the purchase requisition procedure, including the optional matching step.

Purchase Requisition Process Flow

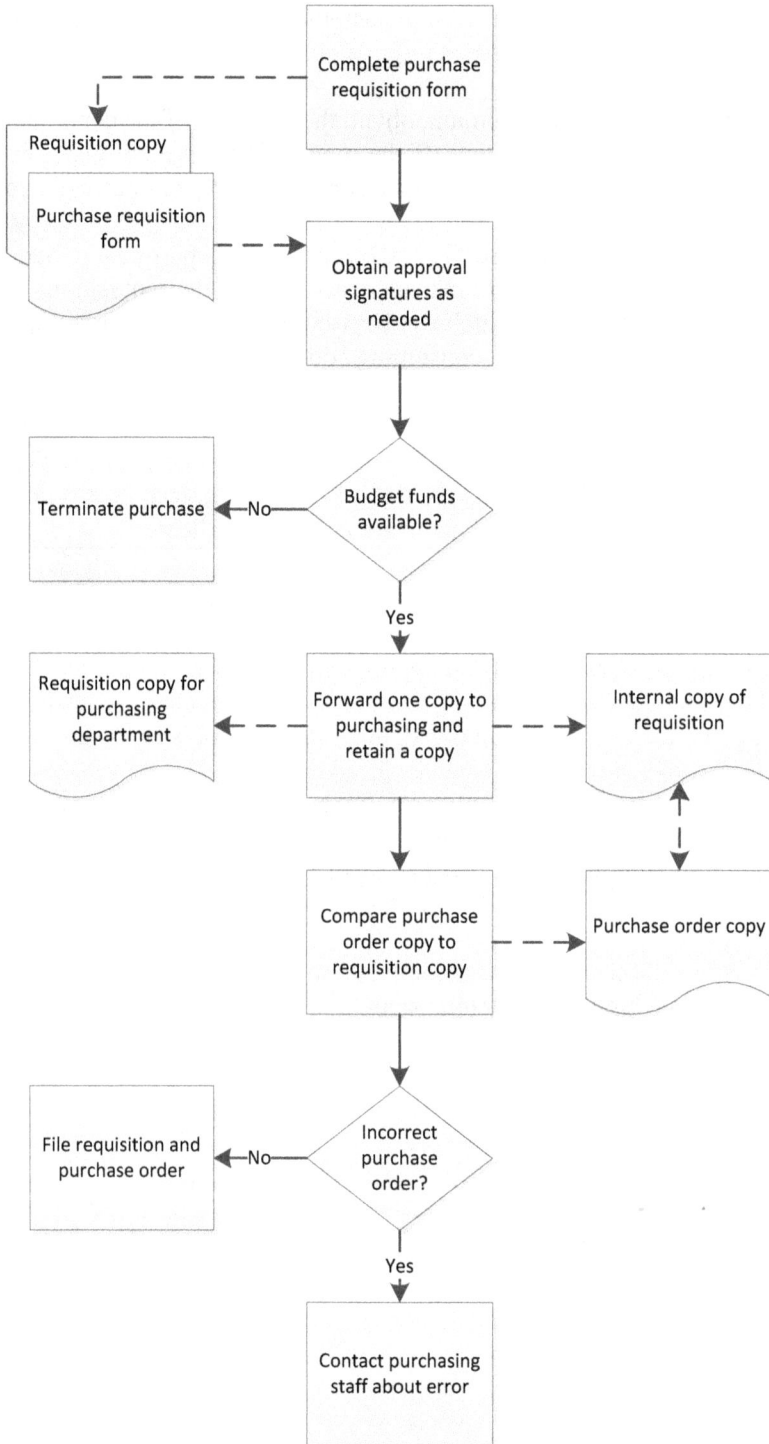

```
                                    Complete purchase
                                    requisition form

        Requisition copy

        Purchase requisition
              form                    Obtain approval
                                      signatures as
                                         needed


    Terminate purchase  ←No—    Budget funds
                                 available?

                                      Yes

  Requisition copy for          Forward one copy to       Internal copy of
      purchasing                   purchasing and           requisition
     department                    retain a copy


                                  Compare purchase
                                   order copy to          Purchase order copy
                                  requisition copy


  File requisition and            Incorrect
    purchase order    ←No—         purchase
                                    order?

                                      Yes

                                 Contact purchasing
                                 staff about error
```

Purchasing Procedure

The classic approach to ordered goods and services is to use a purchase order. It is a formal approach to buying that involves the issuance of a legal document, the purchase order, to a supplier. The purchase order identifies the items being ordered, as well as the price and other conditions under which a company is willing to make a purchase. A sample purchase order follows.

Sample Purchase Order

Bill To Address Block		Purchase Order	
Supplier Address Block	Ship To Address Block	Purchase Order Date	
		Purchase Order Number	
Payment Terms	Ship Via	Buyer Contact Information	
Freight Terms	Due Date	Confirm to Phone Number	

Item No.	Item Description	Quantity	Unit Price	Extended Price
	Purchase Order Detail Block			

	Subtotal
Comments	Sales Tax
	Grand Total

Authorized By: [signature]	Date

Though the issuance of purchase orders is usually well-controlled, it also requires time to complete. For this reason, it is generally restricted to more expensive purchases. The purchasing procedure is outlined next.

1. **Obtain pricing**. When the purchasing staff receives a purchase requisition, it needs to ascertain pricing in order to determine the level of authorization needed by the requesting party.
   Control issues: It is very time-consuming to obtain multiple prices for the items listed on every purchase requisition, so the purchasing manager should set rules for allowing purchases from a small number of designated suppliers, with multiple bids only needed for larger purchases.

2. **Match against authorization table.** Once the purchasing staff has obtained preliminary pricing estimates, compare the amounts requested to the company's authorization table. If the requesting person represents sufficient authorization to approve the purchase, then proceed with the ordering process. If not, retain a copy of the purchase requisition and send the original to the person whose approval is required. An example of an authorization table follows.

Sample Purchase Authorization Table

	Department Manager	Division Manager	Chief Operating Officer	Chief Executive Officer	Board of Directors
<$25,000	✓				
$25,000-100,000	✓	✓			
$100,001-250,000	✓	✓	✓		
$250,001-1,000,000	✓	✓	✓	✓	
$1,000,000+	✓	✓	✓	✓	✓

Control issues: The purchasing staff should routinely review its copies of unapproved purchase requisitions, and follow up with approvers regarding their status.

> **Tip:** It may be more efficient for the purchasing department to shift this task onto the requesting person, so that all purchase requisitions contain the required approvals. However, this approach may not work if the requesting person is not sure of the prices of items being requested.

3. **Obtain additional documentation** (optional). If the item being requested exceeds the company's capitalization limit, send the purchase requisition back to the requesting person with a request to complete a capital request form.
   Control issues: This step essentially terminates the purchasing process, so there is no need to retain a copy of the purchase requisition.

4. **Prepare purchase order.** Complete a purchase order, based on the information in the purchase requisition or bid results. Depending on the size of the order, it may be necessary for the purchasing manager to approve and sign the purchase order. Retain a copy of the purchase order in a pending file, stapled to the department's copy of the purchase requisition, and send the original to

the supplier. Additional copies go to the receiving department and accounts payable staff. Though not necessary, another copy could be sent to the person who placed the requisition, as evidence that the order was placed. If the purchasing system is computerized, then only a single copy is printed and sent to the supplier.

Control issues: If purchase orders are prepared manually, have them prenumbered, track all numbers used, and store unused purchase orders in a secure location. This is needed to keep someone from removing a purchase order and using it to order goods or services that have not been authorized.

5. **Obtain legal review** (optional). If the purchase order contains terms and conditions that are not the standard ones normally used in purchase orders, route the document to the legal staff for review.

Control issues: It can be difficult to determine what constitutes a reasonable exception from the normal terms and conditions, which would require legal review. Also, a legal review slows down the purchasing process. For both reasons, the purchasing staff may be reluctant to obtain a review. This issue can be detected after-the-fact with a periodic investigation by the internal audit team.

6. **Monitor change orders** (optional). If change orders are issued, keep track of the resulting change in the cumulative total authorized to be spent. If the cumulative total exceeds the original authorization level noted in the authorization table, obtain the higher authorization level needed for the new expenditure level.

Control issues: This step requires ongoing monitoring, which the purchasing staff will be reluctant to do. It can be made easier by modifying the purchase order form to include a field for the cumulative dollar total, which the purchasing staff updates for each successive change order.

7. **Monitor purchase acknowledgments** (optional). For the more important items being purchased, it may make sense to ensure that purchase orders have been received by suppliers and acknowledged. This can be a simple phone call to the supplier, or it may be a formal written acknowledgment. Another option is to include a "confirm to phone number" field in the purchase order, as was shown earlier in the sample purchase order template. If the company is issuing purchase orders by electronic means, the supplier's computer system may automatically send back an acknowledgment message.

Control issues: This step is probably of least use when dealing with long-term business partners, but could be of importance when ordering from new suppliers where the purchasing department has no idea of supplier performance levels.

8. **Monitor subsequent activity**. Following the due date of the purchase order, remove the department's copy from the pending file and verify with the

receiving department that the related goods were received. If not, contact the supplier to determine the status of the order. If complete, file the purchase order by supplier name. If the purchasing system is computerized, the receiving department will flag purchase orders on-line as having been fulfilled, which effectively eliminates this step.

Control issues: For more important items, the purchasing staff might consider contacting suppliers *in advance of* the due date to ensure that items were shipped on time.

Tip: If the purchasing staff finds that small residual balances were not fulfilled on a purchase order, and the company no longer requires the residual amount, they should issue a notification to the supplier that the order for the remaining amount has been cancelled.

---

9. **File documents**. When all activity associated with a purchase order has been completed, file the purchasing documents by supplier name for the current year. This will certainly include the purchase order and purchase requisition, and may also include a cancellation notice that terminates any residual unfulfilled balances on a purchase order, as well as any purchase order acknowledgments received from suppliers.

The following exhibit shows a streamlined view of the purchasing procedure, not including the optional steps to obtain additional documentation, conduct a legal review, or monitor change orders. It also does not include the bidding process.

Purchasing Process Flow

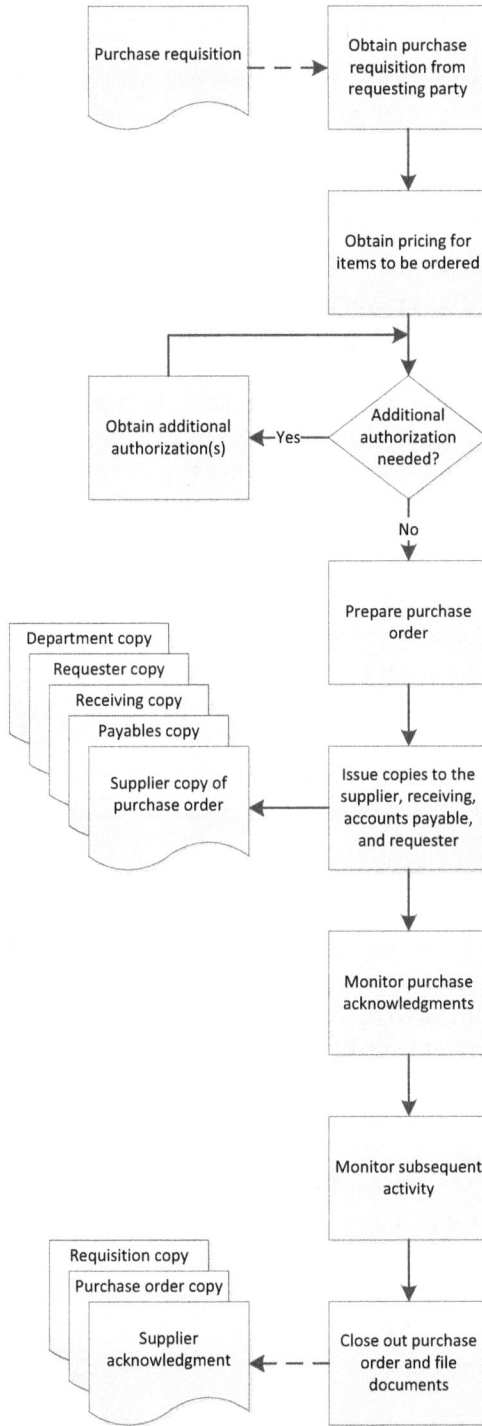

Procurement Process Changes

The preceding discussion of the procurement process flow should make it clear that the purchasing process can be a lengthy one, with many steps and a large amount of paperwork. The following points can be used to reduce the number of procurement transactions that go through the standard purchasing process, while also sidestepping some aspects of the process. Some of the points apply to the accounts payable function, rather than purchasing. The improvements are:

- *Issue procurement cards.* A large part of the administrative cost of the purchasing department involves issuing purchase orders to suppliers, while the accounts payable staff must then match these purchase orders to incoming supplier invoices. When purchase amounts are quite small, this added paperwork can be quite a burden, while providing little additional control over the procurement process. Instead, issue procurement cards (essentially company credit cards) to designated individuals throughout the company, and authorize them to use the cards for most purchases under a threshold amount. Doing so eliminates a vast amount of paperwork, while also eliminating the time delay normally involved in sourcing goods and authorizing a purchase. The purchasing staff can then spend more of its time attending to larger purchases, price negotiations, and other activities that are more likely to result in significant cost savings.

- *Automate ordering.* If a company has installed an enterprise resource planning system or material requirements planning system, either one can automatically review the need for materials in the production process and place orders with suppliers. Doing so takes a large chore away from the purchasing staff, and also improves the accuracy of orders for production materials.

- *Request aggregated invoices.* Have suppliers send a single invoice each month, containing all goods and services provided to the company for the past month. Doing so can considerably reduce the amount of invoicing volume that the accounts payable staff must deal with. However, the issuance of a single invoice departs from the standard invoicing procedure for most suppliers, where the shipment of goods automatically triggers the creation of an invoice. Also, there may be cash flow concerns when a supplier provides goods or services near the beginning of a month, but is not allowed to send an invoice until the end of the month. These concerns can be reduced by offering faster payment terms, or perhaps by offering to sole source with a supplier.

- *Minimize approvals*. Once an initial procurement has been approved, additional approvals should be avoided. There is a significant bottleneck involved in waiting for a manager to approve an invoice, so use as many other alternatives as possible. For example:

    o *Use purchase order as approval*. If the purchasing department has already issued a purchase order, then the purchase order itself should be sufficient evidence that an invoice can be paid.
    o *Eliminate approvals for small amounts*. Establish a threshold invoice amount, below which there is no need for an approval.
    o *Use negative approvals*. Send an invoice copy to an approver, with instructions to only respond if there is a problem with the invoice. The accounts payable staff will assume that all other invoices have been approved by default.

Procurement Centralization

The following points are intended to enhance the procurement processes of a business by placing spending activities under the control of a central group and forcing employees to buy only from certain suppliers. Doing so results in more spending volume with fewer suppliers, which can be used to negotiate for larger volume discounts with the remaining suppliers.

- *Centralize procurement*. When each subsidiary or location of a business is allowed to do its own purchasing, the company as a whole does not benefit from the concentration of purchases with a small number of suppliers that can generate volume discounts. The issue can be mitigated by centralizing the negotiation of purchasing contracts with a small number of suppliers, and then forcing local buyers to only use these designated suppliers. The purchasing of specific goods does not have to be centralized, as long as the local buyers only purchase from the designated suppliers. The company will need to aggregate the amount of its annual spend with each supplier across the entire company, to negotiate its volume discounts.
- *Monitor maverick spending*. There are typically a few people within an organization that step outside of the standard procurement process to buy whatever they want, from whichever supplier they want. These people are known as maverick spenders, and can get away with this behavior because they have positions of authority within the business. The trouble with this behavior is that maverick spenders do not always buy at the best price points and may not obtain the best payment terms. Consequently, it is useful for the purchasing staff to keep track of the amount of maverick spending going on with a business, and bring to the attention of senior management the cost caused by this behavior.
- *Centralize spending by commodity*. Suppliers tend to specialize in selling a certain category of commodity, so aggregate the company's spending in the same way, to obtain volume discounts. For example, have

representatives from each subsidiary agree on which supplier will be used for all purchases of fuel oil, and then approach that supplier about a volume purchasing discount. The arrangement is typically formalized in a master purchase agreement, which all parts of the company reference when ordering from a particular supplier. The master purchase order number is then tracked by both parties to aggregate the total amount of purchases made. This information is also used as the basis for the next round of volume discount negotiations. Purchases for a number of commodity groups can be arranged in this manner, usually starting with the largest-expenditure commodities and then working through the list of commodities in descending order by purchasing volume.

Supplier Relations

A large part of cost management for procurement costs results from the establishment of excellent relations with a core group of quality suppliers, funneling most purchases through them, and integrating their operations and systems with those of the company to the greatest extent possible. The following points illustrate how supplier relations should function.

Consolidation Activities

- *Reduce the number of suppliers.* When there are many suppliers, the purchasing staff must negotiate with more entities and issue more purchase orders. If there is a supplier certification system in place, the company must also send inspection teams to more suppliers. Further, the accounting department must maintain records on more suppliers, and issue a larger quantity of payments. These issues can be mitigated by gradually concentrating purchases with fewer suppliers, which has the added benefit of increasing the probability of obtaining volume purchase discounts. It is only possible to reduce the number of suppliers by centralizing control over which suppliers are used; otherwise, local buyers will choose their local favorites.
- *Consolidate suppliers by product family.* If the company buys a number of similar parts from multiple suppliers, consolidate these purchases with a single supplier. Suppliers are more likely to accommodate such requests for product families, where the underlying raw materials and production processes are quite similar. Since more orders are being concentrated with a smaller number of suppliers, this can result in volume discounts.
- *Examine switching costs.* A classic method used by suppliers to lock in their customers is to increase the cost of switching away from them. For example, a purchased machine may require the ongoing replacement of parts that can only be obtained from one supplier, or a certain raw material is only available from one supplier. In these cases, the purchasing staff should notify management of the risks of being unable to switch away

from that supplier. The result could be redesigned products or processes to avoid using a particular supplier.

Standardize Supplier Dealings

- *Mandate a single supplier contract.* If a company is big enough, it can force all of its suppliers to sign the same boilerplate supplier contract, which states the terms under which the company agrees to do business with them. This requirement eliminates the need for a large legal staff that might otherwise spend hours reviewing the terms of the agreements being required by suppliers. If the company does not have sufficient heft to enforce this level of contract rigor with its suppliers, it should at least attempt to have a specific set of standard clauses included in every contract, such as standard payment terms, the use of supplier certifications in order to avoid the receiving function, and requiring consistent labeling of incoming parts with bar codes.
- *Measure suppliers.* Set up a measurement program that monitors the timeliness of supplier deliveries to the company, any quality issues found, incorrect deliveries, and prices charged. Then incorporate the results into a comprehensive supplier ranking system. This information should be shared not only with management, but also with the suppliers, so that they know how they are performing. This information can spur suppliers to improve their performance, and can also be the basis for the replacement of a low-grade supplier.
- *Certify suppliers.* As part of the process of reducing the number of suppliers, the company can send out teams of engineers to key suppliers. The intent of these visits is to examine their procurement, production, quality assurance, and shipping processes to see if they comply with company standards. A certified supplier is much more likely to be retained over the long term, and may even be allowed to send shipments that bypass the company's receiving department and go straight to the company's production lines.

Integrate with Suppliers

- *Share production schedule.* Give suppliers access to the details of the company's production schedule. Suppliers can then integrate this information into their production schedules, so that goods ordered by the company can be delivered with great reliability. This approach works best if the company locks down its short-term production schedule, which prevents changes from rippling back into the production schedules of suppliers. Schedule sharing can be as primitive as a simple spreadsheet, but is vastly more informative if suppliers are given direct, read-only access to the real-time schedule in the company's computer system.
- *Look for duplicate tests and inspections.* A company may perform tests and inspections on purchased goods that have already been conducted by

the supplier. By making inquiries about a supplier's testing and inspection practices, a firm can strip these duplicate activities out of its own operations. If there is any concern about how well the supplier is conducting these activities, a supplier certification process may be a good idea, to ensure that suppliers are engaging in acceptable practices.

- *Integrate operations with suppliers.* It is entirely likely that a supplier is requiring a number of quality checks on goods before it ships them to the company, after which the company imposes similar checks at the receiving dock. Consider conducting a joint review of operations with suppliers to uncover these duplicate processes. The result may be the elimination of quality reviews at one business or the other, followed by a sharing of the related cost reduction.

- *Obtain a key account manager.* Ask the larger suppliers to designate one of their employees as a key account manager for the company. This person is the primary intermediary between the company and the supplier. The particular advantage of having a key account manager is that this person represents the company at the supplier (despite working for the supplier), and so can be of assistance in obtaining the best deals for the company.

- *Ask suppliers for advice.* Consider altering the relationship with key suppliers to an arrangement where both parties mutually work on new product designs and production processes. A knowledgeable supplier can assist with sourcing lower-cost components, and may offer advice on how a product should be designed to take advantage of different raw materials or components. Such relationships will only work if the company commits to sourcing more goods through these suppliers over long periods of time.

- *Offer suppliers financing.* Since the success of a business is in part based on the financial stability of its suppliers, it may make sense to offer financing to the suppliers. Under supply chain financing, a company sends its approved payables list to its bank, specifying the date on which invoice payments are to be made. The bank makes these payments on behalf of the company. The bank also contacts the company's suppliers with an offer of early payment in exchange for a financing charge for the period until maturity. If the supplier agrees with this arrangement and signs a receivables sale contract, then the bank delivers payment from its own funds to the supplier, less its fee. This approach works very well for suppliers, since they may be in need of early settlement. In addition, they receive a much higher percentage of an invoice's face value than would be the case if they opted for a factoring arrangement with a third party, where 80% of the invoice is typically the maximum amount that will be advanced. Also, the amount of the discount offered by the bank may be quite small, if the company is a large and well-funded entity that has excellent credit.

Other Cost Management Opportunities

- *Consider foreign suppliers.* The typical business only deals with domestic suppliers, which ignores the possibility of working with any number of excellent and low-cost foreign suppliers. This approach does include a certain amount of complexity, such as customs paperwork and possibly having to pay with letters of credit. Nonetheless, expanding into the international arena can result in a number of high-quality supplier relationships that could be highly profitable for a business.

- *Review supplier invoices.* Assign a staff person or third party to regularly review a selection of supplier invoices for errors, incorrect pricing, and other issues. This is a particularly common activity for freight and telecommunication billings. The intent is not just to claim credits on the few invoices selected for review, but to find pervasive issues for which larger claims can be made. Consequently, this type of review is usually restricted to billings from larger suppliers, where there is some prospect for obtaining a reasonable return from the time invested.

- *Match contract length to pricing trends.* If there is a long-term downward trend in the price of a particular commodity, expect suppliers to offer longer-term contracts, which allows them to garner larger profits over time as the company is locked into a fixed price while their costs decline. In such cases, it is better to steer clear of these offers. Alternatively, if there is a long-term upward trend in the price of a commodity, attempt to lock in the longest-term pricing arrangement possible. However, doing so may put a supplier at risk of becoming unprofitable, so consider including a cost-sharing clause in the contract that allows the supplier to continue to be financially viable.

- *Negotiate for alternative benefits.* The typical goal of a purchasing manager is to reduce the prices charged by suppliers. However, if this is an area in which a supplier is unwilling to provide additional discounts, consider shifting the focus to alternative benefits. For example, negotiations could center on faster deliveries, or allowing returns without a supplier authorization, or longer payment terms. Sometimes, a supplier that is unyielding on price may accept one or more of these alternatives.

It may seem that the central goal in supplier relations is to transfer as much of the supplier's profit as possible to the company by squeezing them for lower prices. While this is somewhat true, there is a limit to how aggressive a company should be in this area. A supplier that is regularly beaten up over its prices will have less interest in building a long-term relationship, and may even decide to "fire" the company and take its business elsewhere. A healthier view is to allow suppliers reasonable profits over the long term, so that they remain financially healthy and can reinvest in their infrastructure.

Total Cost Concept

When evaluating whether a company should deal with a supplier, it is useful to view the situation in terms of the total cost of the supplier. Much more than the cost per unit is involved in the total cost concept. Other costs that may arise include the following:

- *Unit cost.* This is the quoted price for goods or services. This amount should be adjusted for any full-year expected discounts from volume purchasing arrangements, or other types of discounts.
- *Freight in.* This is the charged cost of freight to ship goods from the supplier to the company. If the company uses its own freight service, then reduce the cost of freight by the projected amount of any volume discounts.
- *Setup fees.* If the supplier has to acquire molds or tooling in order to produce goods for the company, it may charge an up-front fee for these items, which should be amortized over the projected number of units to be purchased.
- *Hedging.* If goods must be purchased in a foreign currency, it may be necessary to enter into a hedging transaction to offset any possible changes in the exchange rate before the company issues payment. The cost of the hedge should be included in the total cost.
- *Holding costs.* Once goods have been acquired, the company may hold them in stock for a long period of time. If so, include the interest cost of the funds used to buy the inventory, as well as any projected costs for obsolescence, shrinkage, and damage to the inventory.
- *Warranty extension.* If the initial warranty period is too short, the company may have to purchase a warranty extension to cover the full usage period. This cost should be added to the price of the goods purchased.

Of the costs just noted, pay particular attention to the cost of freight. Many organizations have been lured by low labor costs to shift some or all of their production overseas; as energy costs have risen, this means that the cost of the freight needed to shift those goods to the company's customers will likely follow an ascending cost trend. Consequently, it is useful to continually re-evaluate the distance of suppliers from the company's core markets.

An additional issue related to the total cost of a supplier is the risk of a supply chain interruption. When a supplier is located in an area where production and shipping are at risk of interruption, there could be a pronounced risk that supplier difficulties could halt the company's operations. For example, a supplier may be located in a flood plain or in an area where citizen protests routinely shut down road access, or where the government is in danger of being overthrown. This may be a particular concern when a supplier is the sole source of a key part that cannot be easily sourced elsewhere. In such cases, integrate the risk of supply chain interruption into the total cost concept when evaluating a supplier.

Outsourcing Concepts

Outsourcing work to a supplier does not always yield the massive cost reductions that are claimed. Instead, a business may find itself embroiled in a quagmire of issues that either increases its costs, require additional management attention, or increase the risk of process failure. Consequently, consider the following issues before engaging in an outsourcing contract:

- *Layoff costs*. If the company intends to lay off the employees who used to work in the area intended for outsourcing, have the layoff costs been included in the decision model? These costs can include severance, retention bonuses, increased unemployment insurance rates, and even employee lawsuits for wrongful termination.
- *Initial transfer risks*. When a business initially outsources to a supplier, there is a significant risk that key employees that are to be terminated will leave the company before they have transferred their knowledge to the supplier. There is also a risk of service failures during the changeover period. If the company is shifting data to a new software system being operated by the supplier, there is an additional risk that the data transfer will be incorrect, resulting in further service failures.
- *Foreign business environments*. The low labor rates in foreign countries that may initially attract a business to an outsourcing deal may mask a number of other issues. Telecommunications or road systems may be unreliable, there may be a high level of graft, and local laws can make it difficult to back away from an outsourcing arrangement. Such an analysis may not stop management's determination to outsource, but it could shift the supplier to one located in a more amenable business environment.
- *Language barriers*. Before shifting work to a foreign location where a different language is the primary language, consider issues that a language barrier can cause when conducting business. This is a particular concern if customer service work is sent to such a location, since customers may become extremely frustrated and take their business elsewhere.
- *Supplier employee issues*. In a number of foreign locations, employee turnover rates are far higher than in developed countries. This means that the supplier must incur higher training costs for replacement employees, and also that productivity levels could be low. Also, if many companies are outsourcing to a particular low-wage location, expect that the pool of available employees will rapidly shrink, leading to spiraling wage costs that offset the original reason why the company chose to outsource.
- *Shipping from foreign locations*. If outsourcing involves production activities, factor in the added cost of shipping through foreign ports, dealing with customs inspections, and transport on local road systems that may be substandard. Also, take note of the additional time required to transport goods from distant locations to the company's customers.

- *Travel costs*. Factor into an outsourcing arrangement the amount of staff time and costs related to traveling to the supplier location, to monitor the work being done. If a large amount of outsourcing work has been given to a supplier, this may mean that the company must pay several of its employees to live near the supplier and establish a permanent presence on the supplier's premises. These costs can be substantial, and must be subtracted from the potential gains expected from the arrangement.
- *Switching costs*. Once work has been outsourced to a supplier, it may be inordinately difficult to switch away from that supplier without incurring substantial costs. Accordingly, review several worst-case scenarios where the company must terminate a supplier, and decide whether the associated costs and risks are really worthwhile.

Having pointed out the problems that can be caused by outsourcing, there are situations where costs can be effectively managed through the careful use of outsourcing. Consider the following possibilities:

- *Overflow situations*. When a company's capacity is maxed out at current demand levels and there is no certainty regarding the amount of additional demand that will arise, shift any excess demand to suppliers, but only under short-term contracts. If demand subsequently stays at a higher level, the company can consider bringing the work back in-house. If demand subsequently falls, the outsourcing arrangement can be terminated.
- *Low-volume situations*. When a company deals with certain activities at very low volume levels, it can make sense to switch the work to a supplier that deals with very high transaction volumes, and which can therefore achieve higher efficiency levels. For example, if testing equipment has a high fixed cost and is only needed occasionally for testing, shift this work to a supplier that already owns the equipment and who can spread the cost of testing over a large number of tested units.
- *Cash-strapped situations*. When a company has little available cash, it may be forced into outsourcing any activities that might otherwise require a large up-front cash investment, such as the construction of a production facility. In this case, the company shifts all capital-intensive activities to a supplier. This is a common situation for a start-up company that only has small amounts of invested funds.
- *Core focus*. When management wants to focus on just a few core elements of its business, it can deliberately outsource most other functions. For example, a company that focuses on innovative product designs could place most of its attention on a high-quality in-house design group, while outsourcing the production function.
- *Low staff quality*. A company may be dealing with a department where the overall quality of staff expertise is relatively low, perhaps due to recent departures of the best staff. If so, one way to achieve an instant upgrade in

staffing is to shift the work to an organization that has made a practice of hiring high-grade personnel.

- *Additional shifts.* A business may have a well-staffed function, but only during one eight-hour portion of the work day. If so, it may be reasonable to hand off to a supplier during the second and third shifts or during weekends. This scenario most commonly arises for customer service functions, where different work shifts may be based in different parts of the world, to take advantage of daytime working hours. Similarly, a company dealing with around-the-clock programming projects can hand off its work to a design team several time zones away, where the day shift is just beginning.

Any of these scenarios can be applied to a broad range of outsourcing possibilities. The areas stated in the following exhibit are commonly outsourced.

Commonly Outsourced Business Functions

Accounting	Data storage	Payroll
Application hosting	Disaster recovery	Product design
Benefits administration	Human resources	Production
Claims administration	Internal auditing	Software development
Customer support	Network management	Training

In short, there are any number of situations in which outsourcing can be employed as an effective cost management tool. However, each of these situations must also be evaluated in light of the concerns raised earlier in this section.

Spend Management

Spend management involves the aggregation of information about a company's expenditures into a database, which can then be sorted in a variety of ways to uncover opportunities for cost reductions, primarily through the concentration of purchases with a smaller number of suppliers.

The spend management database lies at the center of the spend management system. Information from the company's purchasing departments in all of its subsidiaries is pulled into the database. Once the information is assembled, it must be cleaned up with the following techniques:

- *Name linkages.* It is extremely likely that each subsidiary uses a different supplier identification code for its suppliers, so the aggregated information probably contains information about purchases from a single supplier that are listed under several different names. A table must be constructed for the database that links all of these name variations to a single supplier name. Thus, purchases from ATT, AT&T, and AT&TWIRELESS would all be linked to the same phone company.

- *Description linkages.* As was the case for supplier names, the descriptions of items purchased may vary wildly from each other at the subsidiary level, and so must be standardized in the spend database. To do so, have the suppliers always load the official supplier part number for each item into their purchasing software, so that this can be ported into the spend database. Then attach a file to the database that contains all supplier part numbers and part descriptions. Once supplier part numbers are identified in the data feeds from subsidiaries, they can be linked to the supplier descriptions.
- *Commodity code linkages.* Every purchase made should have attached to it a standard commodity code, which assigns a spend category to the purchase. This information is useful for aggregating purchases by commodity type, which can then be used to concentrate purchases with preferred suppliers for volume discounts. It is best to have all subsidiaries record purchases using the same standard commodity code system, such as the North American Industry Classification System (NAICS). If commodity codes are not being entered, then there should be a feedback loop to the subsidiary purchasing departments to remind them to do so.
- *Credit rating linkages.* The database should include a data feed from a third party credit rating service, which contains the credit rating for each supplier. This information is useful for determining which suppliers may be in financial difficulty, so that spending can be shifted to more reliable suppliers.

A spend database can be enormous, which means that all of the preceding data cleansing and enhancement activities must be performed through automated routines. It is not even remotely cost-effective to engage in these activities manually.

Tip: Have the company's purchasing staff review the information resulting from the various automated routines just described, and recommend additional automated routines to further clean up the information.

Once information has been fully aggregated into the spend database, sort the information by commodity code to determine spend levels for all of the various types of commodities. The resulting reports can be used to drive down costs by any of the following means:

- *Consolidate suppliers.* While each subsidiary may proudly point out that it has already consolidated its supplier base, each one may have consolidated around a different group of suppliers. The database can reveal that the subsidiaries have few suppliers in common at the commodity code level, which represents an opportunity for *all* of the subsidiaries to consolidate their purchases with the same group of suppliers. The net result can be a remarkable decline in the overall number of suppliers from which purchases are made. For example, if there are five subsidiaries and each one purchases from five suppliers, of which only 20% are commonly used by all subsidiaries, this means a total of 20 suppliers could potentially be stripped away from a pool of 25 suppliers, which is an 80% reduction.

- *Source through distributors.* The spend report may reveal that the company is spending a relatively small amount with a large number of suppliers in certain commodity code categories. When this is the case, the easiest solution may be to locate a single distributor through which all of the items can be purchased. The result could be a massive reduction in the number of suppliers, which reduces the administrative and accounting burden of the purchasing and accounting departments.
- *Source overseas.* If certain commodities have high labor content, there may be an opportunity to source them from overseas locations where labor rates are extremely low, which can yield significant cost reductions. However, this choice is subject to the concerns raised earlier in the Outsourcing Concepts section.

It can take a long time to gradually work through the information provided by a spend database, shifting purchases to a smaller and smaller pool of suppliers. Over time, the categories of unaddressed commodity codes will shrink, in which case the emphasis should always be on the next largest remaining spend by commodity code. It is possible that the lowest-spend commodity codes will never be addressed, because the potential savings are so small that they are not worth investigating.

Once purchases have been shifted to a small group of preferred suppliers, the company must ensure that it is obtaining the full amount of volume discounts from these suppliers. Accordingly, monitor the amount spent with each supplier and compare the aggregate spend with the contractual trigger points at which volume discounts will be achieved. The company should remind suppliers whenever volume discounts have been earned.

This level of spend analysis is made easier if the database contains a listing of the trigger points at which volume discounts and other rebates will be earned, by supplier. This listing is essentially a summarization of the key elements of each supplier contract. The primary data items to include in the listing for discount tracking purposes are:

- Contract start and stop dates
- Discount thresholds and amount of discounts
- Rebate thresholds and amount of rebates

When this contract information is matched against the spend database, one may find that suppliers are not following the terms of their own contracts, and that the company is entitled to volume discounts right now, before any supplier consolidation activities have commenced. Consequently, matching contract terms against the spend database should be one of the earlier activities to engage in, once the database has been created.

The following points relate to additional spend management concepts that can be used to drive down costs further:

- *Standardize parts.* The spend database may indicate that subsidiaries are purchasing slight variations on the same parts. If so, there may be an opportunity to redesign products so that exactly the same parts are used in multiple locations. Though such redesigns can drive down costs through bulk purchases, they also involve years of redesign work, and so may not be worth the effort.
- *New supplier additions.* Compare the approved supplier list to the most recent additions to the spend database, to see if any new suppliers have been added that were not approved. Use of these new suppliers should be curtailed, so that purchases are more heavily concentrated with preferred suppliers.
- *Purchase order receiving requirement.* Have the receiving staff reject any deliveries for which there is no authorizing purchase order. If the purchasing system is configured to only issue purchase orders to suppliers on the preferred supplier list, this means that all other purchases not being acquired with procurement cards are effectively blocked. However, it can also result in annoyed employees who are wondering why their purchases were turned away at the receiving dock.
- *Audit billed prices.* The sales staff of suppliers may not route new contracts with the company to their billing departments, which means that the company will be billed at old price points. This issue can be detected by conducting regular audits of supplier invoices, where billed prices are matched against contract prices. If the audit reveals continuing pricing issues for a supplier, designate that supplier for more frequent audits.

The construction of a spend management system is one of the more expensive database projects that a company can engage in. To accelerate the payback period, consider the following ways in which to roll out the system:

- Initially include in the database the purchasing information for just the largest subsidiaries. Doing so accumulates the bulk of the information needed for the database, without wasting an undue amount of time creating interfaces to the smaller purchasing systems.
- Estimate which commodity codes comprise most of the company's spending activity, and focus all of the data cleanup efforts on purchases within these codes. Doing so allows the purchasing staff to take more immediate action to engage in volume purchasing in these areas.

These actions should yield relatively rapid results, which may encourage management to provide additional funding for a more complete rollout of the system.

Summary

There are a multitude of opportunities for cost management within the general area of procurement. We have advocated following a specific procedure for channeling purchase requisitions into the purchasing department, as well as another procedure that yields an orderly flow of purchase orders from that department. The purchasing staff should also be supported in its cost management efforts by a spend database, which reveals exactly where funds are being spent. There are also many ways to improve relations with suppliers. However, the premier method for managing procurement costs is to concentrate purchases with a small number of suppliers. This is not easy, for there is a natural tendency for a business to constantly expand its supplier base. Consequently, be ready for employee resistance not only in the initial reduction of suppliers down to a core group, but also on an ongoing basis, as they attempt to add unauthorized suppliers. Thus, supplier consolidation requires a surprising amount of employee relations activity.

Chapter 16
Administration Cost Reduction

Introduction

The administration area encompasses most company activities outside of production and sales. These costs tend to be fixed, and so require particularly aggressive efforts to reduce. In this chapter, we describe a number of general cost reduction concepts in the areas of accounting, human resources, legal services, information technology, and travel and entertainment. The concepts discussed here do not begin to cover the full range of possible cost reductions. For greater detail, consult the author's other publications in this area, including the *Lean Accounting Guidebook*, *Closing the Books*, *Payroll Management*, and the *Credit & Collection Guidebook*.

General Administration Cost Reduction

This section addresses several general cost management concepts that can be applied to any administrative area. The primary emphasis of these suggestions is to closely monitor how expenditures are being made at the local level, and avoiding any bureaucracy that prevents employees from engaging in the central mission of the business. We also reserve a special place for taking a company private, which avoids the burdens of a publicly held company. The recommendations are:

- *Centralize services*. If there are any services that are duplicated within business units or departments, consider consolidating these services into centralized groups. Doing so eliminates any overlaps in staffing and fixed assets. For example, if there is a separate data center for each business unit, consider merging them.
- *Reduce forms*. Many forms creep into a company through an excessive focus on bureaucratic processes. While a form may be useful for standardizing the information required for a process, this does not mean that the form should subsequently be retained, since doing so requires filing time and storage space for the forms. There are a number of ways to deal with the plague of forms, including:
    - Reduce the number of form copies to be retained
    - Reduce the amount of information collected on a form
    - Once the information on a form has been entered into a computer, scrap the form
    - Digitize a completed form, and then scrap the form

- *Eliminate special initiatives.* A larger business may have accumulated a number of "special initiatives" that require ongoing staff time, such as a company donations committee, or a manager of corporate sports teams. None of these initiatives build upon the strategic direction of the business, so if they soak up too much employee time, remove them entirely. Also, be watchful for the introduction of replacement initiatives, and cut them off when first suggested.
- *Go private.* If a company is currently a publicly held entity, consider the alternative of taking it private. There are a number of major costs associated with being publicly held, including higher audit and legal fees, the cost to prepare filings with the Securities and Exchange Commission, higher directors and officers insurance costs, additional controls, and so on. If a company is not obtaining additional funding through its public offerings of securities, or if its investors are not gaining much additional liquidity for their share holdings, then these added costs may outweigh the benefits of being publicly held.

Energy Cost Reduction

A firm can shift the task of controlling energy costs to its employees, rather than focusing on creating specific initiatives in a particular area. The general concept is to keep monitoring costs low by merely pointing out to employees that energy costs are being tracked at the department level. This monitoring message can be combined with periodic feedback reports, perhaps coupled with bonus payments for exceptional cost reductions. At this point, it is up to the employees to figure out how energy costs can be reduced. An administration person can conduct interviews in any departments where significant cost improvements have been experienced, to see if any best practices have been uncovered. If so, management can decide whether these best practices should be rolled out more extensively within the company.

Accounting Cost Reduction

The accounting function is the crossroads for most of the processes in a business, and as such is an excellent area in which to implement cost management concepts. In this section, we suggest a number of ways to reduce work and/or be more effective in the areas of accounts payable, auditing, collections, cost accounting, customer billings, fixed assets, payroll, reporting, and systems.

Accounts Payable

The processing and payment of supplier invoices is perhaps the single most con-voluted of all accounting processes, and is highly amenable to efficiency improve-ments. Most of the following bullet points emphasize ways to simplify the accounts payable process, so that much less staff time is required to pay suppliers. The sug-gestions are:

- *Avoid three-way matching.* A classic payable control is to compare a sup-plier's invoice to the authorizing purchase order and receiving document, to ensure that the price is approved and that the goods have arrived. How-ever, matching is very slow and subject to error. Instead, set a threshold for supplier invoices, below which matching is not required. Also, skip matching for suppliers that have been certified as reliable.

- *Approve at the receiving dock.* Have suppliers mark the authorizing pur-chase order number prominently on the outside of each delivery made to the company. Upon receipt, the receiving staff calls up the indicated pur-chase order number in the accounting system and flags the order as being received. The computer system can then pull in the purchase order prices to automatically derive the payment to be made to the supplier. This ap-proach requires the use of purchase orders for all items ordered, but avoids the need for a three-way matching process, as well as the need for supplier invoices.

- *Install evaluated receipts.* If the company sole sources parts from its sup-pliers and has them deliver the parts directly to the production line, then there is an opportunity to employ an evaluated receipts system. This sys-tem compiles the number of units produced by the production system, cal-culates the number of parts that must have been used to produce that many finished units, adds in any scrapped parts, and issues a payment to the sup-plier based on this information and the price stated in the underlying pur-chase order. Clearly, a large amount of just-in-time systems analysis is required to make an evaluated receipts system work properly, but it also eliminates the need for supplier invoices, approvals, and three-way match-ing.

- *Centralize accounts payable.* A larger organization likely has a number of divisions, and may have allowed each one to process its own accounts payable. Doing so results in the duplication of management staff, facilities, and accounting software licenses. It may be possible to achieve a reduction in the overall amount of resources assigned to accounts payable by cen-tralizing these operations in a single location. This can eliminate several types of expenses, while the increased transaction volume may justify the acquisition of more expensive improvements, such as invoice scanning systems.

- *Create an online invoicing form.* Create an online form into which suppli-ers can enter their invoices. Doing so shifts the data entry task to suppliers, after which the invoices are fully loaded into the company's accounts payable system. This approach will be more acceptable to suppliers if they are also given online access to payment status information – which in turn means that they are less likely to call the payables staff to inquire about payments.

- *Require a W-9 with first payment.* A Form W-9 should be completed by every supplier, so that a company can reliably issue Form 1099s following the end of the calendar year. To ensure that the 1099 issuance process goes smoothly, insist on a completed Form W-9 before the company issues its first payment to a supplier. This approach works well, because the company can threaten to withhold payment up-front, but has less power to enforce compliance after the year is over.

- *Flag early payment discounts.* Suppliers sometimes offer early payment discounts, which typically have very high effective interest rates. If the company has enough cash to take advantage of these offers, it should certainly do so. The most effective method for taking discounts is to flag suppliers in the vendor master file and include the terms offered, so that the system automatically schedules the payments early and takes the discounts.

- *Use negative approvals.* If supplier invoices are routed to managers for approval, there is a good chance that the invoices will be lost, and payment will therefore be delayed. Instead, record all invoices in the payables system first and then route a copy of each invoice to the responsible manager, with a note that no response equals approval. This approach means that only a specific directive *not* to pay a supplier will prevent the payables staff from issuing a payment.

- *Audit expense reports.* Employee expense reports are highly detailed, contain many line items and attachments, and so are time-consuming to review in detail. Given the relatively small number of errors or fraudulent claims made in expense reports, a detailed review is not a cost-effective activity. Instead, audit a sampling of the expense reports submitted in each reporting period. If errors or fraudulent claims are found, flag the submitting employee for more frequent reviews, and possibly backtrack through earlier submissions to see if the same issues occurred in the past.

- *Review recurring charges.* Over time, a business may accumulate any number of ongoing service or rental contracts that require an ongoing series of payments. The staff becomes used to making these recurring payments on a regular basis, and may not investigate them so thoroughly. Consequently, consider a periodic review of all recurring charges. For example, look for equipment rentals that are no longer needed, cell phone contracts for phones that are no longer in use, and parking space rentals for too many employees. In essence, this concept represents a general questioning of whether expenses are truly necessary.

- *Pay by ACH.* The normal process for paying suppliers is to cut checks, stuff them in envelopes, and mail them, which means that costs are incurred for the check stock, envelopes, and stamps. A less-expensive alternative is to make electronic Automated Clearing House (ACH) payments directly into the bank accounts of suppliers. While there is some setup time required for an ACH payment and a small fee, it is still less expensive than a mailed check. The savings can be significant, when multiplied over a large number of payments.

- *Recover credits.* Suppliers may have granted the company credits for various reasons. Contact suppliers to see if they will reimburse the company for these credits in cash. If not, contact the purchasing manager to see if any purchases can be directed toward these suppliers in order to use up the credits.
- *Clean the vendor master file.* It is quite likely that a supplier has been set up multiple times in the vendor master file, which is the file used to process payments to suppliers. The result can be payments to old addresses, or what appear to be missing payments that have actually been recorded under another name. The amount of time required to investigate and correct these issues can be epic. Accordingly, conduct a periodic analysis of the vendor master file to locate duplicate files, and flag the duplicates as inactive.

Auditing

The comments noted below are designed to reduce the fees charged by a company's outside auditors. The suggestions are not easy ones to implement, but can yield notable cost reductions.

- *Adjust audit timing.* Work with the company's outside auditors to schedule as much audit work as possible outside of their busiest parts of the year, in exchange for a discount. The auditor work load is especially heavy in February and March, so a business with a calendar year end could have control reviews done in November or December, and push for a fast close that allows for an early audit in January.
- *Alter fiscal year end.* If the company's audit fees are substantial, consider shifting to a fiscal year that ends near a slow period for the company's auditors. By shifting the audit to a period when the audit firm does not have sufficient work for its staff, the company should be able to negotiate lower fees.
- *Follow up on fraud notifications.* If there is even a hint of possible fraud, always follow up on it at once. Fraud tends to be a high-expense item, so terminating such activities can represent a significant cost reduction. Also, any controls implemented as a result of the fraud can keep the fraud expense from being incurred again, and can result in a more robust control environment that can reduce subsequent audit testing.

Collections

The emphasis in collecting from customers is not really on cost reduction, since cutting back on the collection staff may amplify a company's bad debt problems. Instead, we note a number of ways to focus the efforts of the collection staff and avoid some collection problems from arising in the first place. The result should be cost reduction by shrinking the amount of bad debt incurred.

- *Install a collections database*. There are several software packages available that are specifically designed to make the work of the collections person more effective. They use a custom-built interface to the accounting system to access information about unpaid customer invoices, as well as store information about customer contact information and prior promises to pay, and can even link to an auto-dialer. The collections staff can rapidly work through their call lists with the aid of this software, which presents all relevant information to them as they talk to customers. Ideally, this should result in a massive increase in the number of calls that a collections person can make. The downside is that the software and its installation is expensive, and so may only be cost-effective for a larger collections department.

- *Collect largest invoices first*. In many organizations, the vast majority of the cash tied up in accounts receivable is concentrated in a small number of large invoices. It is quite common for 80 percent of the cash to be tied up in approximately 20 percent of the invoices. In this situation, the collections staff should focus most of its efforts on collecting the large-dollar invoices, and doing so as quickly as possible.

- *Collect by ACH debit*. In a small number of markets, it has become acceptable for customers to pay by ACH debit. This means that the seller triggers a debit transaction from customer bank accounts. Doing so virtually guarantees that funds will be collected on time, and eliminates the need for a collection function. However, it is usually only acceptable to customers when these debits are for small amounts and are on a recurring basis. A typical use of the ACH debit is a recurring monthly payment for a parking space.

- *Require payment in advance*. It may be possible to obtain payment in advance from customers. This can be accomplished by offering a small discount for payment in advance, and may also be encouraged by offering a somewhat higher commission to the sales staff if they can obtain these kinds of sales. All risks of incurring a bad debt are thereby eliminated.

- *Resolve internal issues*. Any experienced collections person will point out that many collection issues originate within a business, not its customers. These issues may involve incorrect invoices, shoddy products, damaged deliveries, incorrect order taking, and so forth. Because of these problems, customers refuse to pay for invoices without some prior problem resolution, which the collections staff can ameliorate only by granting a large number of credits. A fine solution to these internal errors is to form a working group within the company that meets regularly to discuss and resolve the issues found by the collections staff. The members of this group should include representatives from those departments that are causing the problems, as well as those being impacted by the problems.

Cost Accounting

We note several traditional cost accounting activities that have no place in a modern organization, since they provide no value, and which can be safely eliminated or scaled back.

- *Terminate labor tracking.* The production staff can spend an inordinate amount of time recording the hours they spend on specific production jobs, as can the accounting staff that transcribes this information into a database. Once recorded, management usually finds that the information changes little from period to period, and so ignores it. A reasonable solution is to terminate all labor tracking. This means that the production line workers, administrative staff, maintenance personnel, and so on can immediately stop tracing their hours worked to specific products or services. The only labor tracking they should be doing is clocking in and out of work each day, for compensation calculation purposes (and only if they are paid on an hourly basis). The only exception to this recommendation is when hours worked are being billed to customers. If so, the billing function is a key aspect of revenue generation, and therefore must be maintained.
- *Terminate variance reporting.* A large part of the cost accountant's time is spent reporting on variances from various budgets or standards, usually involving either prices paid or the efficiency of resource usage. We advocate the elimination of all variance reporting, for several reasons. First, variance reports are issued too late to be of any meaningful assistance to management. Second, the standards from which variances are derived are themselves subject to manipulation. Third, variances are useless in a just-in-time environment, where the whole point of the system is to *not* use resources if there are no customer orders to fill.
- *Minimize overhead allocations.* Incredibly elaborate overhead allocation methodologies have been derived to assign the cost of overhead to inventory. Since the result is only being used to report the ending balance of finished goods inventory and the period's cost of goods sold, it is much more efficient to implement a simple allocation methodology that requires less time to complete.

Customer Billing

Cost management in the customer billing area is mostly about error prevention, so that customers will not find billing issues that could cause them to delay payments to the company. Since delayed payments can severely impact cash flows, the following points should be considered mandatory.

- *Improve the invoice layout.* It may be possible to make several modifications to the invoice template to reduce the time required to receive payments from customers, as well as to reduce the number of customer payment errors. The goal in creating an invoice format is to present the minimum amount of information to the customer in order to prevent confusion, while presenting the required information as clearly as possible. Consider implementing the adjustments noted in the following table.

Invoice Format Changes

Credit card contact information	If customers want to pay with a credit card, include a telephone number to call to pay by this means.
Early payment discount	State the exact amount of the early payment discount and the exact date by which the customer must pay in order to qualify for the discount.
General contact information	If customers have a question about the invoice, there should be a contact information block that states the telephone number and e-mail address they should contact.
Payment due date	Rather than entering payment terms on the invoice (such as "net 30"), state the exact date on which payment is due. This should be stated prominently.

- *Integrate related systems.* Consider installing a computer system where the transactions generated by the order entry, shipping, and accounting departments are fully integrated. Under such a system, the billing clerk is notified by the system as soon as a shipment has been made, and can generate an invoice from an on-line copy of the sales order. An integrated system mitigates the risk of not issuing invoices, while also requiring minimal re-typing of information for each billing – which reduces the incidence of invoice errors.
- *Proofread invoices.* Some billings are extremely complicated. The billing clerk must assemble many line items of information, as well as account for an array of adjustments and discounts. There is a strong likelihood that these invoices will be rejected due to errors, which means that even more time must then be spent to create a revised invoice. The possible payment delay associated with invoice errors makes it nearly mandatory to have an experienced person review these invoices prior to issuance. The best reviewer is the person in charge of the business relationship with a specific customer, since they are deeply involved in the work being done for the customer. In addition, consider having an experienced clerk review these invoices for clerical-level errors that might also lead to invoice rejection.

Fixed Assets

The accounting for fixed assets is much more complex and long-term than the accounting for expenses, so the following points are primarily intended to treat more purchases as expenses, rather than fixed assets. We also note how to simplify some of the accounting for fixed assets.

- *Mandate a high capitalization limit.* It requires significant effort to properly record and account for a fixed asset over its life span. The simplest way to eliminate fixed asset accounting activities is to impose the highest possible capitalization limit on fixed assets. This means setting the capitalization threshold at a large number, so that all smaller expenditures will be written off as expenses in the period incurred.
- *Minimize base unit aggregation.* A base unit is a company's concept of what constitutes a fixed asset. For example, a group of desks may be considered a single fixed asset. However, a group of items designated as a fixed asset means that items individually falling beneath the capitalization limit (see the last suggestion) can now be classified as fixed assets, which increases the amount of long-term record keeping. Consequently, it is best not to aggregate items into a single base unit.
- *Simplify depreciation.* There are a number of advanced depreciation methods that can be applied to fixed assets, usually to emphasize either accelerated depreciation or to tie depreciation to the exact usage of an asset. These methods are excessively complicated, and present the risk of an incorrect depreciation balance that will require time to repair. Instead, adopt the extremely simple straight-line method for all fixed assets, preferably without incorporating any salvage value estimates that might clutter up the calculations.

Payroll

Payroll is one of the few accounting areas in which nearly the entire process can be automated, so that the accounting staff only has a monitoring role. The following points emphasize the use of simplified systems and more automation in order to achieve this goal.

- *Minimize payroll cycles.* One of the more important cost management issues is how long to set the payroll cycle. Each payroll requires a great deal of effort by the payroll staff to collect information about time worked, locate and correct errors, process wage rate and deduction changes, calculate pay, and issue payments. Consequently, it makes a great deal of sense to extend the duration of payroll cycles. If payrolls are spaced at short intervals, such as weekly, then the payroll staff has to prepare 52 payrolls per year. Conversely, paying employees once a month reduces the payroll staff's payroll preparation activities by approximately three-quarters. Since paying just once a month can be a burden on employees, companies frequently adopt a half-way measure, paying employees either twice a month (the semimonthly payroll) or once every two weeks (the biweekly payroll). The semimonthly payroll cycle results in processing 24 payrolls per year, while the biweekly payroll cycle requires the processing of 26 payrolls per year.

- *Eliminate off-cycle payrolls.* Whenever the payroll staff must complete a payroll, it has to enter any necessary documentation, review preliminary payroll registers, print checks, finalize the payroll cycle, and so forth. Despite the extra workload, some managers insist on having additional off-cycle payrolls in order to make special bonus payments to their employees. Given the high labor cost involved, the payroll manager should insist on a large interdepartmental charge to run extra payrolls, or at least the approval of the chief financial officer. If an off-cycle payroll is needed to correct errors in a prior payroll, try to push the error corrections forward into the next regularly-scheduled payroll.

- *Install automated timekeeping.* The single largest amount of time spent in a manual payroll environment is in the tabulation and verification of hours worked by employees. Rather than engaging in this highly clerical and error-prone work, install computerized time clocks that allow hourly employees to scan a badge through the machine, which then records their start and stop times, while also recording the information in a central database. Variations on this approach are a website through which time can be entered by employees, and a smart phone app that performs the same function.

- *Minimize data collection.* A time tracking system is a data collection system, and so can be used to collect information about *anything*. However, do not be tempted to overuse this capability, since collecting additional data requires more data entry time by employees. Instead, question the need for any additional data collection above the bare minimum amount. Ideally, this means the identification number of each employee and his time worked are being collected – and nothing else.

- *Simplify the commission plan.* Many commission plans require complex calculations to derive commissions, splits, overrides, bonuses, and so forth. These calculations require a large amount of staff time to complete, and are also highly subject to error. The best way to avoid this work is to minimize the commission plan by offering the sales staff a simple commission percentage on sales generated. However, the sales manager may oppose this approach on the grounds that he or she then has less control over the selling behavior of the sales staff.

- *Pay by direct deposit.* Direct deposit involves the electronic transfer of funds from the company to the bank accounts of its employees, using the Automated Clearing House (ACH) system. The payment process is to calculate pay in the same manner as for check payments, but to then send the payment information to a direct deposit processing service, which initiates electronic payments to the bank accounts of those employees being paid in this manner. Direct deposit is more efficient than payments by check, because it does not require a signature on each payment, there are no checks to be delivered, and employees do not have to waste time depositing them at a bank. Direct deposit can also be more efficient from the perspective of the remittance advice. A number of payroll suppliers offer an option to notify employees by e-mail when their pay has been sent to them, after which employees can access a secure website to view their remittance advice information.

Reporting

The accounting staff can spend an inordinate amount of time reporting information in various formats to the rest of the company. We note several ways to speed up the reporting process, while cutting back on the number of reports issued.

- *Conduct a fast close.* The total amount of time required by the accounting staff to create financial statements is minimized when it completes the closing process within a very short period of time. Otherwise, the process drags on for weeks, while the staff multi-tasks between closing work and other activities. A short closing period also puts a company's financial results in the hands of management very quickly, which is useful for feedback purposes. See the author's *Closing the Books* book for more information about this topic.
- *Terminate reports.* Managers may ask that a certain report be created by the accounting staff, in order to deal with a specific situation that may last a short period of time. If not notified to stop, the accounting department may continue to issue the report long past the point when it was needed. Accordingly, conduct an ongoing review of all reports issued to see if they are still needed. Further, examine each line item in the reports that *are* needed, to see if those requiring the most labor to accumulate can be terminated.

Systems

If a company has a number of subsidiaries that report their information to corporate headquarters for consolidation, it is quite possible that the headquarters accounting staff will spend an inordinate amount of time trying to consolidate the disparate results that it has received. Further, if the corporate staff detects a possible error in the results forwarded from a division, it must make inquiries with that division, which may take a long time to respond. Also, some subsidiaries may use different procedures that require more time to forward closing information to headquarters. The result of these issues is a slower close and a great deal of inefficiency.

The solution is a high degree of standardization throughout the accounting operations of a business. Standardization can be applied in a number of areas, including:

- *Software.* It is very useful to have a single company-wide enterprise resources planning (ERP) system, but that solution is so expensive that it may not be cost-effective. Instead, consider installing the same accounting software in all locations, so that common procedures can be designed around them.

- *Chart of accounts*. Use an identical chart of accounts in all locations. This makes it much easier to map the results of the subsidiaries to the general ledger of the parent company.
- *Procedures*. Use an identical set of procedures for all accounting transactions. This can be difficult if some transactions are based on non-standard systems elsewhere in the company, so there will likely be some variability in procedures.
- *Policies*. Accounting policies should be the same in all locations, so that business transactions are treated in the same way. For example, different capitalization policies would mean that an expenditure would be recorded as a fixed asset in one location and as an expense in another location.
- *Journal entries*. There should be a standard set of journal entries that are used in all locations, and which use the same accounts. Thus, journal entry templates are standardized.
- *Calendars*. The same activity schedules are used everywhere, so that the managers of all accounting operations know when they are supposed to complete assigned deliverables.

Human Resources Cost Reduction

The need for or even the existence of a human resources department may be one of the more hotly-debated issues in a company. This function can be extremely useful in certain circumstances, but in other cases can devolve into a bureaucratic group that does not appear to present much value. Thus, the recommendations noted in this section should be considered in light of management's stated positions regarding the existence of human resources. Our recommendations are:

If Human Resources is Supported

If the department is to be supported, the following points emphasize how it can be operated most cost-effectively, especially in regard to handling recruitment activities on behalf of other departments.

- *Centralize recruiting*. When a company is recruiting, use the human resources staff as a filter that actively pares down the number of applicants and pre-screens anyone who submits a resume. As long as the human resources staff is properly informed regarding the skill sets that are needed in new recruits, the result should be a massive reduction in the number of resumes that are forwarded to department managers. This approach keeps local managers from being buried under piles of resumes.
- *Pre-screen with video conference calls*. Have the human resources staff use video conferencing to pre-screen initial candidates for a position. This is particularly useful when a candidate is located relatively far from the company, and the business would otherwise have to offer travel

201

reimbursement to the candidate. This approach can also be useful for initial interviews, just to see if a candidate possesses the relevant interviewing skills to succeed in the contemplated position.

- *Forward recorded interviews to managers.* To further reduce the time that managers spend selecting finalists for positions, consider videotaping the preliminary screening interviews conducted by the human resources staff, and forwarding selections from these interviews to the hiring managers. A few minutes reviewing these videos may allow a manager to avoid an in-person interview, thereby reducing the amount of his or her time required for recruiting.

- *Note drug screening requirement.* Note on all company notices of new job postings that a drug screening will be part of the selection process. Doing so will likely keep a number of applicants from ever applying for the posted positions, which reduces the number of applications that must be reviewed.

- *Centralize temporary staffing.* If department managers currently hire their own temporary staff, consider shifting the oversight of these hires to the human resources department. By doing so, all temporary hires can be sourced from a single temp agency, which gives the company the ability to demand volume discounts. Department managers can still conduct their own temp hires, but must use the preferred temp agency.

- *Set compensation boundaries.* Department managers are more likely to approve outsized compensation increases for their employees in order to ensure their retention. However, doing so can also result in massive increases in long-term compensation costs. Instead, use the human resources department as the compensation enforcer that must review and approval all compensation requests. By giving this group a fixed amount by which total corporate compensation can be increased, as well as the power to enforce it, costs can be significantly mitigated.

- *Employee and manager self-service.* See if the company's payroll service provider offers an add-on module that allows employees to make on-line changes to their human resources and payroll information. Similarly, there may be a module for managers, through which they can update employee status and compensation information. This approach shifts the data entry task away from the human resources and payroll departments, and is usually cost-effective if there are a large number of employees.

If Human Resources is Not Supported

If there is to be no human resources department, the following points illustrate how this can be achieved.

- *Shift work to department managers.* The need for a human resources function is closely tied to the recruiting requirements of a business. A rapidly-growing company will find that a human resources team that can effectively hire large numbers of new employees may be the key to its success.

However, if a business has relatively stable staffing needs and little turnover, it is entirely possible that human resources can be shifted into the payroll function, resulting in no department at all.

- *Outsource benefits management.* Consider shifting the management and administration of all company benefit plans to a third party. By doing so, the company eliminates a largely administrative task and gives it to a supplier that is likely to be more efficient and knowledgeable about available benefit plans. This approach works best for smaller companies, where there are fewer employees who require assistance about benefit issues.

Legal Services Cost Reduction

A typical approach to legal services is to obtain all of it from a nearby law firm, probably one that has long-standing ties to the company. Such a relationship can be quite expensive, and is not necessarily the most effective way to deal with legal concerns. The following points illustrate alternative ways to address legal issues.

- *Avoid one-stop shops.* The legal profession is subdivided into a multitude of specialty areas, where no one has a complete, in-depth knowledge of all legal issues. Consequently, if a company is relying upon a single law firm for all of its needs, it is likely that a portion of the legal fees paid will pay for research into issues that the law firm's staff needs to educate itself about. Further, because the law firm's staff will not be expert in all areas, the company may not obtain the best legal advice. An alternative is to use several law firms, each one specializing in a different area that impacts the company. Thus, one firm may deal with acquisition issues, another with shareholder lawsuits, another with public company filings, and yet another with employee relations issues.
- *Outsource lower-value services.* A number of legal documents are of the boilerplate variety and have little risk associated with them. Examples are non-disclosure agreements and trademark registrations. In these cases, consider shifting the work to low-cost third parties, possibly in other countries where labor costs are lower.
- *Evaluate value gained.* In many situations, a company manager may be intent on pursuing an adversary to the ends of the earth. The ultimate conclusion of such a chase might be quite gratifying, but may also incur legal fees far in excess of the value gained. Consequently, put emotions aside and evaluate all legal situations to determine which ones are most likely to return a good value to the business, net of all legal fees. The outcome of this discussion is likely to be far fewer legal actions being taken.
- *Communicate expectations.* When a large project is handed to a law firm, it may be worthwhile to communicate to the engagement partner the company's expectations for which level of attorney will be assigned the work. For example, the company expects that the partner will not be involved in depositions or in the review of documents, which means that the billing

rates for these items should be reduced. This approach is different from negotiating a discount after the fact, without being excessively intrusive in regard to how the partner plans to manage the assignment.

- *Match actions to legal goals.* Before embarking on any type of legal action, define the precise goal that the company wants to attain, such as securing a valuable patent or obtaining reimbursement from a customer. All legal costs expended should be in pursuit of these goals. All too frequently, a company's legal advisors are asked to pursue topics that drift away from these goals, resulting in excessive legal fees. To curtail these additional topics, channel all legal requests through one person, who decides which ones are worthy of qualified legal attention. This individual should possess considerable backbone, since many irrelevant requests are likely to come from senior management.

- *Monitor excessive legal work.* Some attorneys will pursue every conceivable lead in a project, tracking down information that is only peripherally necessary to the outcome of the project. In essence, they are working in areas that have marginal value (if any) to the company. This additional work can yield large additional billings to the company. To combat this problem, communicate to the law firm the company's expectations for when a project is considered to be complete, and peruse billings to spot instances of excessive work. This level of detailed examination is only possible if legal billings are submitted in detail, noting exactly which tasks were pursued. If the problem persists, shift legal work to a different firm.

- *Match legal work to potential risks.* Keep track of the more significant risks to which the business is subjected, and target legal work at these areas. Doing so means that costs are being incurred in areas where there is a good payback in the reduction of risks. For example, it makes sense to spend a large amount on legal fees for the investigation of a prospective acquisition target, but not to pursue customers for small outstanding balances.

- *Hire temporary legal staff.* Legal activities do not tend to follow a smooth and predictable path, where there is a consistent flow of work. Instead, there tend to be large projects at irregular intervals, such as a shareholder lawsuit that must be addressed. In cases where the amount of work suddenly increases, do not automatically shift this work to the company's law firm (thereby incurring the attendant high fees). Instead, there are temporary agencies that can provide qualified legal assistance for substantially lower rates.

- *Handle some tasks internally.* When a legal issue could threaten the competitive advantage of a business, this is extremely high-risk from the perspective of the company, and so should be managed internally, perhaps in close association with an outside firm that has in-depth knowledge in this area. Other types of legal issues that are of a more routine nature require less in-house staff work, and can instead be shifted to low-cost providers.

Legal services is one of the few areas in which concentrating purchases with a single supplier in order to obtain volume discounts is not a good idea. Since the service provided is knowledge-based, and a single supplier is not likely to have the full range of required knowledge, there is no way to achieve a valid cost-benefit from volume purchases. Instead, the focus should be on paying top-dollar for the most competent legal advice in targeted areas, while also shifting lower-risk work to lower-cost providers.

Information Technology Cost Reduction

Information technology (IT) encompasses a broad area of services and equipment that can devour a large part of a company's resources. The following points are only intended to address the more high-level IT concepts in relation to cost management. Engaging in an IT audit would likely uncover a number of additional opportunities.

- *Limit bleeding edge applications.* When a company installs computer applications, there may be a temptation to acquire the latest and greatest of every kind of application. The trouble is that these applications tend to be more expensive, and are also more likely to contain residual bugs that have not yet been worked out. These systems also may not interface easily with older installed applications. The net result is a more expensive investment. Instead, limit such purchases to those areas of the business that will experience a noticeable competitive advantage from the installation. In all other cases, it is entirely sufficient to acquire commercial, off-the-shelf applications that offer a standard set of features, and which have proven to be entirely reliable. This approach limits a company's exposure to inordinately high IT expenditures.

- *Clean up processes prior to automation.* There may be a management mandate to install information technology in areas that have previously been operated manually. This may not be a good idea if there are deep inefficiencies in the underlying processes. Automating this type of system merely creates a computerized system that is also inefficient. Instead, conduct a thorough analysis of each system scheduled for computerization, and see if it can be upgraded with a cleaner process flow, fewer reports, less processing time, fewer approvals, and so forth. Only after this analysis has been conducted should a system be handed over to the IT staff for computerization.

- *Avoid custom programming.* To build upon the last point, custom-designed systems are to be avoided unless they confer a key strategic advantage on a business. In most cases, commercially-available systems are sufficient for the operational needs of an entity. Avoiding custom programming also means that the business will not be tied to legacy systems for many years, or to particular programming languages. Not using custom programming also means that the company does not need to retain a core group of system designers and programmers to support these systems.

- *Use software as a service.* The cost of commercially available software includes the initial purchase price, ongoing maintenance fees, on-site hardware on which to store the software, and personnel to operate the equipment and software. All of these costs can be swept away by renting the software on a monthly basis and accessing it at a remotely-managed data center. The software provider owns the software and updates it regularly, so that the company also avoids any expensive internal upgrade cycles. However, do not use this option if the company has irregular Internet access. It also may be a dubious option if the supplier has questionable finances, and so may not remain in business.

- *Invest in commoditized equipment.* Computer equipment has become a commodity, so treat it like a commodity and buy in bulk to obtain the best prices. It is not necessary to obtain electronics for employees that contain the fastest processors, highest definition displays, and largest amounts of memory, unless employees are engaged in computer-generated graphics modeling or similar applications that require high-end equipment. In the vast majority of situations, employees are simply accessing standard database packages, word processing software, and electronic spreadsheets – none of which require exceptional computer equipment. In short, buy computer equipment that matches the needs of users.

- *Stretch replacement cycles.* Extend the time period over which desktop and laptop computers are retained by employees before requiring replacement. This may be less of an option for laptop computers, which are inherently subject to more damage, but could be a valid option for desktops. This is an especially enticing alternative if employees are using computers for less computing-intense applications, and so do not need the latest and greatest computers with the highest processing speeds.

- *Consolidate data centers.* If the company operates in an environment where it must store vast amounts of data, it has probably built up several data centers. Each of these facilities represents a large fixed cost investment that increases the breakeven point of the business. Consider consolidating these facilities to the greatest extent possible, in order to strip away duplicate overhead costs. However, only do so to the extent that the company is not placed at risk by storing all of its data in a single location that may be impacted by a natural disaster.

- *Obtain national-level service contracts.* If the company has multiple locations, hire a national-level service provider to attend to the company's IT needs in such areas as network support, equipment maintenance, and security monitoring. Doing so gives the company more purchasing volume with a single supplier, and so can be used to drive down the price paid.

- *Monitor cell phone issuances.* Cell phones have essentially taken over as the primary form of telecommunications, and so are demanded by large numbers of employees as an essential benefit. However, if an employee works in the office most of the time, and so has access to the company's land line phone system, is there really a need to provide a cell phone? Each phone requires a monthly fee, which can add up quickly when cell phones are provided to a large number of employees. Consequently, an approval process should be required before a cell phone is issued.

- *Monitor data plans*. There is a basic fee for unlimited phone calls and texting on a cell phone, but the data plan cost for a smart phone can be substantially higher. An employee who is accessing videos on a company-owned smart phone can pile up substantial charges in short order. Consequently, have someone review the monthly cell phone bill and make inquiries of department managers whenever unusual data plan usage is detected.

- *Aggregate cell phone plans*. A company can realize the largest cell phone cost reductions by concentrating its cell phone purchases with a single national carrier. This may not be popular with employees at all, if they want a particular phone that is not offered by the company's preferred carrier, or if cell phone coverage is spotty in areas where they travel. Consequently, it may be necessary to aggregate cell phone plans with a primary carrier, and allow other purchases through a secondary carrier.

- *Shift password resets to employees*. The IT staff is typically involved in password resets for employees. This issue regularly arises for employees who have forgotten their login information, and must be dealt with at once because users are locked out. However, this is hardly a value-added application for the IT staff. Instead, install a self-help application that users can access by themselves, so that password resets are removed from the work list of the IT department.

- *Buy voice-activated systems*. Customer service systems that require customers to punch their keypads through an endless series of decision trees are intensely annoying to customers, especially when they use the small, mistake-prone keypads on their cell phones. To improve customer retention, invest in voice-activated systems that interpret customer questions and route them straight to the customer service personnel or applications they need. This approach avoids the use of decision trees.

Travel and Entertainment Cost Reduction

Entire books have been written about the management of travel and entertainment expenses, and we do not intend to reduce their contents to a single page. Instead, we note several general concepts that can be effective in driving down an expense that can be considered one of the most difficult cost categories to control.

- *Reduce travel in aggregate*. The cost of travel is one of the largest spend categories in many businesses. If so, the key factor is the aggregate amount of total travel being engaged in by employees. Rather than focusing on the cost of travel, place the main controls on why someone is traveling at all. This means that only certain classes of employees, such as the sales staff and field service employees, are allowed to travel, and even then only within certain guidelines. Outside of this group, require the approval of a senior manager for all travel that will incur more than a certain amount of expense.

- *Encourage teleconferencing.* There has been a trend toward teleconferencing for some time, and now the cost of doing so is minimal, if not free. Accordingly, engage in an ongoing campaign to encourage the use of teleconferencing as a replacement for travel. At a minimum, only allow initial face-to-face meetings with third parties to establish relations, after which teleconferencing is to be used.

- *Centralize bookings.* Route all travel bookings through a single travel agency, so that the company can concentrate its travel with the smallest possible number of airlines, hotels, and rental car agencies. By doing so, the company increases its purchasing volume with targeted suppliers, and can use this information to obtain the best rates. This approach requires an increased level of cooperation from employees who may be accustomed to making their own travel arrangements. An alternative is to allow employees to make their own travel arrangements, but to book their travel using a list of pre-authorized suppliers, and only using company credit cards. This latter approach still traces all purchases back to the company, which can aggregate the information for volume discount negotiation purposes.

- *Adopt a travel policy.* Unless boundaries are placed around employee expenditures, there is a high likelihood that employees will make travel expenditures that are not in their employer's best interests, such as always flying first class. These concerns can be reduced by issuing a comprehensive travel policy to employees that clearly states allowable types of expenditures. If an employee chooses to buy something outside of this policy, then the company will not issue a reimbursement for that item.

Summary

The administration area is one of the most fruitful ones in which to manage costs. As noted in this chapter, there are dozens of methods available for limiting or even eliminating certain types of these costs.

Of particular concern in administration is the tendency for costs to continue unchecked from period to period, unless specific steps are taken to investigate and mitigate expenditures. Consequently, above all other techniques used, we recommend an ongoing audit of *all* costs that questions why expenditures are being made. These audits must be repeated over the long-term, and even for costs that were previously considered necessary, since later changes in the circumstances of a business may indicate that such costs can now be eliminated or reduced.

Chapter 17
Facilities Cost Reduction

Introduction

The amount of cost associated with a company facility can be enormous, and typically represents a long-term fixed cost commitment. Given the amount of these costs and the inability to avoid them once a lease agreement is signed, a company should give thought to where its employees will be housed. Issues to consider include the location of the building, lease rates and other facility costs, and how the building is to be used. These and other matters are discussed in the following sections.

Facility Location

The precise location of a company facility can have dramatic effects on profitability and even employee turnover. Consequently, consider the following points before committing to a specific location:

- *Customer focused.* If the company sells an inordinate amount of goods to a major customer, consider the convenience of the company location from the perspective of the customer. If a new location especially close to a customer has a reasonable chance of increasing or maintaining sales to that customer, then conduct a cost-benefit analysis to see if constructing the facility will have an overall positive effect on profits. However, this approach can only be taken a few times to accommodate the largest customers.
- *Employee focused.* If employee homes are clustered within a short distance of the current company location, switching to a location further away from them could be a serious mistake, since there may be a surge of employee turnover if they find that their commuting times suddenly lengthen. In many cases, they cannot move to a new company location for any number of family-related reasons, and so must choose between an annoying commute and finding work with a different company. A good technique when considering a new location is to create a map of all employee homes, and to find a location that will be the least bothersome to the largest number of employees.
- *Mass transit focused.* Real estate located near mass transit terminals tends to be more expensive than facilities located further away. However, the increased cost may be more than offset by the reduced cost of parking facilities, since more employees are likely to use mass transit to commute to the company, and so will not require any parking spaces.

- *Local taxes.* Some local governments charge unusually high personal property taxes, and some even impose a tax on headcount. When a company has determined the approximate area within which it wants to have a facility, do not forget to examine these tax rates to see if situating the facility on one side or the other of a government border might have a noticeable impact on costs.

Lease Rates

The lease rates paid by a business for facilities can vary dramatically, depending on supply and demand at any given point in time. In this section, we address how to achieve lower lease rates despite the vagaries of market dynamics. Several options are:

- *Bargain early.* Landlords will bargain for the highest possible prices when they know that a company has only a short time in which to settle upon a new facility location. Also, rental rates vary dramatically, depending on the amount of available square footage in a region. For these reasons, management should constantly monitor the state of the real estate market, and be willing to negotiate a lease well in advance of the expiration of the company's current lease, if circumstances warrant such action. Obtaining a new lease well in advance can be cost-effective, even if the company still has an obligation to make some remaining payments under its old lease. It may still be possible to sublease the old facility, which mitigates the cost of paying for two leases at once.
- *Delay in a peaking market.* If the current market conditions involve a very small amount of available square footage, the cost to lease a facility is likely to be much higher than would normally be the case. If so, do not conclude a new, long-term lease at stratospheric rates. Instead, negotiate the shortest-term lease possible for the existing facility, and wait for prices to subside. If the company is looking for a new location, then find a sublease with a relatively short duration. Eventually, market prices will decline, and a more favorable leasing deal can be concluded.
- *Swap rate reductions for longer term.* Even if an existing lease has several years to run, it may make sense to offer the landlord a commitment to a longer lease term in exchange for lower lease rates through the remainder of the lease. Landlords always want to maintain a high occupancy rate, and so might find such an offer to be quite acceptable, especially if the company has consistently paid its bills on time.

Facility Costs

Once a business moves into a facility, most of the costs it will incur are relatively fixed. However, there are some options for expense mitigation, which are outlined in the following bullet points:

- *Review facility costs in advance.* When first contemplating a leased facility, conduct an energy audit to estimate the approximate utility cost of the facility. It is entirely possible that a cheaply constructed and inadequately insulated building will have a greater net cost than a higher-grade facility that has a higher lease rate.
- *Reduce energy costs.* There are a number of ways to reduce the amount of energy used by a building. For example, cover windows with blinds or solar window film. Also, install computer-controlled thermostats that automatically change the temperature based on the time of day. Install LED lighting to reduce electricity costs. Review the heating and ventilation systems for leaks that can be mitigated. A good feedback loop is to see how these changes impact the cost of utilities on a month-to-month basis. Also, if the remaining lease term is relatively short, it may not make sense to install the more expensive energy reduction devices, since their cost will not be paid back by the end of the lease.
- *Stagger multiple shifts.* In a production environment, it is fairly common to have multiple shifts operating. If there is some overlap in the ending time for one shift and the start of the next shift, then the number of vehicles in the parking lot will double for the period of this overlap, which requires a much larger parking lot to accommodate the extra vehicles. If possible, schedule a short gap between the shifts for at least some of the employees, so that departing employees have enough time to clear out of the parking area before the next shift arrives. The result can be a much smaller parking facility that still accommodates all employees.
- *Offer bus passes.* If a facility is located in an urban area where the cost of parking is high, consider offering free bus passes to employees. Doing so may be far less expensive than paying fees for a large number of parking spaces.

Facility Usage

A great deal of thought should be expended on the layout of a new facility, so that both work flows and every cubic inch of space are optimized. The following points address different techniques for arriving at the best possible configuration:

- *Optimize traffic flows.* Before any other cost management issues are addressed, plan for the shortest possible traffic flows within the floor plan of the facility. The reduction of employee travel time within the facility can generate efficiencies that comfortably outweigh any cost reductions that may be contemplated. It may be useful to hire a consultant to examine existing traffic flows, and use this information to create an optimized traffic flow for the new facility. For example, the industrial engineering staff should be located adjacent to the production floor, while the billing clerk could be positioned near the shipping dock.

- *Compress space*. While it is certainly pleasant to operate a facility with generous office space and wide aisles, the associated lease cost for this added space is not pleasant at all. Instead, plan for a more compressed facility that maximizes the use of office space. This does not mean that working in the facility should be annoying, since productivity will then decline. A good way to develop the proper amount of square footage per person is to bring in a consultant to design the facility to maximize space usage, based on comparisons to other companies in the same industry.
- *Eliminate offices*. An office can be a pleasant place to work, but it is not space efficient. Instead, consider minimizing the number of offices in the facility, in favor of cubicles. If a number of private meetings are needed, then increase the number of meeting rooms, and encourage their use by the people working in cubicles. If employees need to concentrate, then provide them with cubicles that have additional sound proofing and higher walls. The net result should be an extremely small number of offices in comparison to the total floor space in use.
- *Shift employees offsite*. Where possible, encourage employees to work from home. This may require a small investment in local computer equipment and smart phones, but pays off by reducing the amount of office space. This approach works best when combined with hoteling (see next), so that the office space usually used by these employees is no longer reserved for their use. It may be necessary to schedule occasional in-person gatherings to promote teamwork.
- *Institute hoteling*. Many employees, such as salespeople, are rarely in the office. If so, have them store their office materials in mobile carts, and assign them a free office or cubicle on those rare occasions when they are in the office. This can result in a massive reduction in the amount of office space, though it can also generate complaints from employees about the impersonal nature of the work environment.
- *Shift storage offsite*. Office space is designed for people, not storage. Items requiring storage can be moved offsite to much less expensive warehousing facilities. This means that only the most necessary documents are kept near the staff. Where possible, consider digitizing documents and making them available to the staff on a corporate intranet, thereby allowing for the offsite storage of essentially *all* documents.
- *Sublease space*. When compressing the amount of space used, attempt to shift employees completely out of isolated blocks of office space, which can then be partitioned off and subleased. Simply compressing the amount of space used makes little sense unless there is a plan to derive revenue from the space that is no longer in use. At a minimum, create a plan to

block off unused space and minimize temperatures and lighting in that area, to reduce utility costs.

The deliberate compression of office space per person can be taken to an extreme. In some companies, it is essential that employees have sufficient space in which to design products, collaborate, and just think in peace. In these environments, tight quarters may equate to intense employee dissatisfaction, as well as reduced productivity. Consequently, do not consider the image of employees packed in like sardines as the ultimate goal of effective space utilization.

Furniture and Office Equipment

A business may expend substantial sums on the purchase of furniture and fixtures and office equipment. By following the guidelines presented in this section, a modest amount of planning can result in a substantial reduction in costs in this area. The points are:

- *Reduce cubicle walls.* We noted earlier that some people work best in sound-insulated environments, which calls for the use of higher cubicle walls. However, the reverse may also be the case, where collaboration requires direct line-of-sight contact. If so, reduce the cost of cubicles by obtaining low-wall configurations.
- *Acquire refurbished cubicles.* While some cubicles are extremely high-end, such fancy surroundings are not needed in the typical office environment. Accordingly, do not feel that it is necessary to purchase new cubicles when it may be possible to buy reasonable-quality cubicles that only require minor cleaning or other refurbishing.
- *Standardize purchases.* Where possible, standardize on the same office equipment, cubicles, and furniture for the entire company. By doing so, and not catering to the demands of employees for more personalized configurations, the company can negotiate lower prices with its suppliers for these items. Also, having large numbers of the same make and model of office equipment makes it easier to stock supplies and spare parts for these items.
- *Favor local printing and copying.* It may seem more cost-effective to buy a high-grade printer for an entire department. However, this does not take into account the employee travel time to and from the printer. Instead, consider providing most employees with their own printer, so that they do not have to leave their desks to print a document. Printers are so inexpensive that they are essentially throw-away devices, which makes this a cost-effective option. Further, consider buying combination printer-scanner-copier devices for local use, which also reduces the need for centrally-located copiers. While these steps may not quite eliminate the need for a central printer or copier, they can reduce the volume requirements for these

machines, allowing a company to acquire lower-volume and lower-cost equipment.

This section has been focused on reducing the cost of furniture and office equipment, but that does not have to be the case when it comes to seating and other ergonomic arrangements. When the entire cost of employee workplace injuries and comfort are combined with the cost of (for example) a more expensive ergonomically-correct chair, the extra cost of the chair may prove to be worthwhile.

Projecting Future Usage

When it is time to renew a lease or find new facilities, the most difficult part of the process is not necessarily negotiating the right price, but rather how much space to lease. An all-too-common occurrence is for an overly optimistic president to assume massive growth, resulting in the incurrence of an excessively large and long-term set of lease payments. Even in the absence of such a person, it is still hard to estimate space requirements over the usual five-year lease period. Here are several considerations that can assist with the projections:

- *Market share.* It is extremely difficult to gain market share in most industries, so assume a baseline headcount level that is derived from the current market share. The market itself may expand, resulting in a certain amount of growth. However, unless the company is actively budgeting for more marketing and product development expenditures, a large increase in market share is not likely to arise.
- *Staffing relationships.* The market share assumption just noted should lead to a rough estimate of revenues through the leasing period. It is likely that the current relationships of headcount to revenues will roughly hold steady, so estimate additional headcount in the same proportions to revenue that now exist. The relationship issue does not hold true for all positions (for example, only one president is needed), but is likely in most departments. Also, the relationship between staffing and revenue is more likely to hold true unless management is considering a major revision in how the company is structured.
- *Plateau effect.* If the company has been experiencing rapid growth, do not assume that this growth will continue. At some point, sales will plateau, as will the need for more facilities. It is extraordinarily difficult to determine when the plateau will be reached. One possible prediction method is to look at product life cycles in adjacent industries, and decide whether the same pattern may carry over into the company's industry.
- *Contract-level changes.* If a large proportion of company business is associated with a specific customer contract, concentrate management attention on predicting whether that contract will be renewed, since the outcome strongly affects headcount. If it is not possible to estimate the

outcome at this time, attempt to obtain a lease extension that lasts until the fate of the contract can be resolved.

- *Changing workplace patterns.* If there are incipient patterns emerging for how people work, extrapolate these changes forward to see how they will impact headcount and square footage per person. For example, any experiments with remote work and/or hoteling can be used to estimate reduced square footage requirements in the future. However, it only makes sense to adjust estimates for these changes if there is a commitment by management to follow through.

The main point with staffing projections is to assume that the current state of affairs will continue, in terms of market share, square footage per person, and headcount to revenue ratios, unless there is a significant and prolonged management effort to change the structure and expenditure pattern of the business. Such change is extremely rare, and usually only happens when an entirely new senior management team takes over control of the business. In all other cases, carrying forward historical information for projection purposes is probably the best approach.

Summary

Though the focus of this chapter has been on reducing the cost of facilities, it does not mean that a company should relocate to a Quonset hut. There are valid reasons why an investment in top-notch facilities makes sense, such as when a high-end consulting business wants to project a certain image to its clients. Similarly, more expensive facilities can make it easier to recruit top-notch employees. However, expenditures at this level should not be contemplated unless they are a stated part of the company's strategy. If they are not part of the strategy, then facility upgrades should be considered unnecessary upgrades that only reduce company profitability. In most cases, the best approach is to continue with the current grade of office space and furnishings.

Chapter 18
Finance Cost Reduction

Introduction

An area in which companies tend to manage costs poorly is in finance, probably because it is non-operational in nature, and so escapes the notice of most managers. Nonetheless, there are opportunities for significant cost reductions in this area, especially if a business can consolidate its banking operations to wield more influence over its banking partners. In this chapter, we describe a number of ways to manage the costs of banking, cash management, leasing, and insurance. In addition, we address how to maximize returns from investment, and several related topics.

> **Related Podcast Episodes:** Episodes 38, 41, 125, and 137 of the Accounting Best Practices Podcast discuss automatic cash application, remote deposit capture, debt refinancing, and lean cash receipts, respectively. They are available at: **accountingtools.com/podcasts** or **iTunes**

Banking Cost Management

The essential characteristics of good management in banking are to consolidate banking activities as much as possible in order to negotiate from a position of strength, and to closely examine bank fees to see which ones are actually needed. More specifically:

- *Consolidate banking relationships.* A company has more power to negotiate lower rates with its bank when it is concentrating its business activities with fewer banks. This means closing down as many incidental banking relationships as possible and moving accounts and other transactions to a core set of banks. Further, consider setting up a comparison matrix to view the fees charged by each one. This information can be used to negotiate for standardization at the lowest fee level.
- *Consolidate debt.* If the company has several loans outstanding, consider consolidating them into one loan, which may result in a lower interest rate. This is especially useful if each of the loans was with different banks, and the company is seeking to concentrate its business with a single lender.
- *Consolidate accounts.* Review accounts having extremely low transaction volumes to see if the transaction activity can be shifted into a more active account. This can eliminate account servicing fees, and makes it easier to concentrate cash for investment purposes.

- *Consolidate procurement card programs.* If the company has several procurement card programs, consolidate all of them with a favored bank, thereby concentrating the fees paid and giving the company more leverage over the bank in regard to lending arrangements and other fees.
- *Note international credit card transactions.* Many credit card providers charge a large foreign transaction fee for purchases made in other countries, usually in the vicinity of 3%. If so, search for a card provider that does not charge this fee, or use a separate card just for international transactions that does not charge the fee.
- *Pay from local accounts.* To avoid payment delays and reduce wiring fees, consider funding an account within any country where the company routinely issues payments, and eliminate wire transfers in favor of in-country payment systems that are paid from that account.
- *Plan payments.* If payments can be scheduled two days early for what would normally have required a wire transfer, the expensive wiring charge can be replaced with an ACH payment that costs a few cents.
- *Review acquired accounts.* Include on the company's acquisition checklist a reminder to review the bank accounts of every acquired business. There are likely to be opportunities for account reduction within these inherited accounts.
- *Restructure debt.* It may be possible to restructure the terms of existing debt to take advantage of lower market interest rates, or improved company performance that may lead to a fixed interest rate. Such a restructuring is heavily dependent on timing, and so requires monitoring over a long period of time to decide when conditions are optimal to begin negotiations.
- *Terminate unused lines of credit.* If the company has arranged for a line of credit and then not used it, consider shutting down the arrangement to avoid the annual fee associated with maintaining it. This situation most commonly arises when a company acquires another business, along with the banking relationships of the acquiree. However, first consider whether the cost of the arrangement may be offset by having extra funds available through the line of credit.
- *Negotiate the value date.* The value date is the bank-imposed period of time that a company must wait before a deposited check is converted into available funds. Some banks unreasonably extend the value date in order to earn interest on funds that they are not yet releasing to their customers. If a company does a large amount of business with such a bank, it may be able to negotiate a more immediate value date for its deposited checks.

Debt Management

The following cost management topics are primarily targeted at reducing the cost of debt. This can be accomplished by reducing the aggregate amount of debt and pursuing lower-cost debt arrangements. Consider the following options:

- *Roll over debt early.* If there is a loan with a large balloon payment, begin watching trends in interest rates and credit availability well before the payment is due, and roll over the loan into a new debt instrument early, if reduced interest rates warrant such action.
- *Supplier loans.* It may be possible to shift some of the financing burden to the company's suppliers by offering to pay interest for a longer payment interval on outstanding invoices. This can be a good deal for the company even if the interest rate offered is somewhat higher than the rate available through a bank's line of credit, since there is no collateral associated with a supplier loan, and this approach leaves the line of credit untouched.
- *Sell assets.* Pay close attention to which assets are being utilized, and sell off those that have fallen into disuse. Before doing so, however, ensure that these assets are not being held as reserve capacity for situations when demand spikes. Also, routinely review all business units and see if any can be sold off that no longer fit within the strategic direction of the business. The cash produced by these activities can be used to pay down company debt.
- *Restrict dividend payments.* Once the board of directors begins to authorize the payment of dividends to investors, the continuance of such payments tends to be viewed by investors as an ongoing obligation of the company. Consequently, it may be prudent to minimize increases in the dividend, and instead redirect the cash toward paying off any company loans or building up a cash reserve. Reducing dividends can be hazardous to the stock price of a company, since those investors attracted to the dividend are more likely to sell their shares when the dividend is reduced, thereby leading to a price decline.
- *Replace debt with equity.* If the cost and burden of debt exceeds the ability of the company to repay it, consider selling shares in the company and using the proceeds to pay down the debt. This approach tends to be resisted by existing shareholders, since their ownership percentage in the business will be reduced. Also, selling shares when the company is in financial trouble will result in a low share price, so many shares must be sold to make a meaningful dent in the amount of debt outstanding.
- *Invoice discounting.* Invoice discounting is the practice of using a company's unpaid accounts receivable as collateral for a loan, which is issued by a finance company. This approach essentially accelerates cash flow from customers, so that instead of waiting for customers to pay within their normal credit terms, cash is received almost as soon as the invoice is issued. The amount of debt issued by the finance company will be less than

the total amount of outstanding receivables, with a typical limit of 80% of all invoices less than 90 days old. This form of financing is expensive, but can work when a business needs the cash to fund rapid growth in its operations, and has the margins to absorb the high interest cost of this arrangement.

- *Tighten early payment discount offers.* When a business offers customers a discount in exchange for early payment, the implicit interest rates on these offers can be enormous. For example, a 2% discount if a customer pays in 10 days, rather than the usual 30 days (also known as "2/10 net 30" terms) equates to an annualized interest rate of 36.5%. Instead, offer a very low implicit interest rate, and see if there are any takers.
- *Focus on faster cash-to-cash transactions.* In some industries, the time required to spend cash on raw materials, convert the materials to finished goods, and obtain cash from their sale is extremely long. If you are in such an industry, consider whether there are adjacent markets where similar types of products require shorter cash-to-cash conversion periods, and see if it may be possible to enter these markets. Doing so reduces the need for working capital, and therefore for the debt that pays for the working capital.

Cash Management Cost Reduction

There are a number of ways to reduce the cost of handling incoming cash, as well as to increase the speed with which cash is deposited, which can then result in more interest income. The following options are available:

- *Bank lockbox.* Contract with a bank to set up a lockbox, and instruct all customers to mail their payments directly to the lockbox. The bank then opens all incoming mail, deposits checks, and posts images of the checks and related materials on-line, which the company can use to apply cash to open accounts receivable. By doing so, a company can typically reduce the amount of mail float by at least one day, especially if it sets up a network of lockboxes throughout the areas where customers are located. Accelerated cash receipts can then earn interest for a longer period of time. Of course, this benefit must be weighed against the cost of maintaining a network of lockboxes.
- *Remote deposit capture.* When a business receives checks, it typically processes the payments and then hands them off to a courier, who hand-delivers them to the local bank. However, late mail deliveries and delayed processing can easily result in the arrival of checks at the bank after the bank has closed, which delays depositing by a day. To avoid this problem, obtain remote deposit capture equipment from the bank. This equipment is essentially a check scanner and related software that allows for the digitization of check images and their electronic forwarding to the bank for immediate deposit. The paper checks are retained by the company, and

eventually shredded. Some banks offer remote deposit capture equipment for free, to encourage their customers to stay away from bank locations and reduce the work load on bank tellers. A further advantage of this approach is that a company can do business with a bank that is not located nearby, but which may offer better pricing.

- *Automatic cash application.* When a company receives a large number of customer payments every day, it can be quite difficult to apply the receipts against open accounts receivable in a timely manner, which means that there may be a delay in the depositing of these checks. An alternative to manual cash application is automatic cash application, where software uses a set of decision tables to apply check payments against accounts receivable. For example, the software matches the bank account number on the check to the correct customer, and then matches payments to individual invoices where the payment amount exactly matches the invoice amount. Next, cash application may be made for clusters of invoices that are coming due for payment, if the clusters match the amount paid. Other variations can also be applied, after which all remaining payment amounts are kicked out for manual review. Over time, the decision tables can be tweaked based on actual experience to arrive at quite a high rate of automatic application.

- *Cash sweeping.* A business may have a large number of bank accounts, which means that its cash holdings are scattered far and wide. If so, consider entering into a cash sweeping arrangement where a single bank controls all of the accounts, and automatically shifts all excess cash into a central account from which investments can then be made. This system also pushes cash out to those accounts that are about to have a debit balance, to prevent bank overdraft charges. This approach concentrates cash for investment purposes, so the company can earn a higher return on investment. However, some local tax jurisdictions may take exception if a business recognizes all of its interest income at the corporate level, since the cash that generated the income is located at the subsidiary level. To offset this problem, all interest earned should be allocated back to the subsidiaries based on the amount of their cash that was used to generate the income. Also, the bank fees for cash sweeping are rather high, so it is only cost-effective when there is a large amount of unused cash located in a company's bank accounts.

- *Notional pooling.* Cash sweeping can be considered an intrusive cash concentration system, since it moves cash among accounts. Local managers may complain that they do not have control over their cash, since it is being moved out from under their control. An alternative is to allow cash to remain where it is and under local control, but to record it at the bank as though the cash has been centralized. This is called notional pooling. The bank simply adds up the balances in all accounts and automatically invests the funds on behalf of the company. Some banks can even allocate interest income back to the accounts where cash is stored, based on the actual amount of interest earned and the relative proportions of cash in the accounts included in the pooling arrangement. The primary restrictions on the use of notional pooling are that it is outlawed in some countries, may not be allowed for partially-owned subsidiaries, and only works within the account network of a single bank.

In the next section, we turn to a discussion of how to take advantage of the extra cash made available through the points noted in this section.

Investment Strategy

What strategy should a treasury department follow when investing cash? Several possibilities are noted in the following bullet points. When considering the options, please note that the more active ones require accurate cash forecasts, which may not be available.

- *Earnings credit*. The simplest investment option of all is to do nothing. Cash balances are left in the various bank accounts, where they accrue an earnings credit that is offset against the fees charged by the bank for use of the accounts. If cash balances are low, this can be an entirely acceptable strategy, since more active management of a small amount of cash will probably not glean a significantly larger return.

EXAMPLE

Suture Corporation has an African division that is in startup mode, and so has little excess cash. Currently, the division maintains an average of only $20,000 in its sole bank account. Its bank offers a 1.5% earnings credit on retained cash balances, which is $25 per month that can be offset against account fees. The best alternative is a money market fund that earns 2%, but which requires the manual transfer of funds several times per month.

Given the minor amount of the balance and the low return on other investment alternatives, the treasurer elects to accept an earnings credit, rather than taking any more aggressive investment actions.

- *Automated sweeps*. Sweep all excess cash into a central account, and shift the funds in that account to an overnight investment account. This strategy requires no staff time, but yields a low return on investment, since banks charge significant fees to manage this process.
- *Laddering*. The laddering strategy involves making investments of staggered duration, so that the company can take advantage of the higher interest rates typically associated with somewhat longer-term investments. For example, a treasury department can reasonably forecast three months into the future, so it invests in a rolling set of investments that mature in

three months. To begin this strategy, it invests a block of funds in an investment having a one-month maturity, another block in an investment with a two-month maturity, and yet another block in an investment with a three-month maturity. As each of the shorter investments matures, they are rolled into new investments having three-month maturities. The result is an ongoing series of investments where a portion of the cash is made available for operational use at one-month intervals, while taking advantage of the higher yields on three-month investments.

- *Match maturities*. An option requiring manual tracking is to match the maturities of investments to when the cash will be needed for operational purposes. This method calls for a highly accurate cash forecast, both in terms of the amounts and timing of cash flows. To be safe, maturities can be planned for several days prior to a forecasted cash need, though this reduces the return on investment.
- *Tiered investments*. If a business has more cash than it needs for ongoing operational requirements, the treasury staff can conduct an analysis to determine how much cash is never or rarely required for operations, and use this cash in a more aggressive investment strategy. For example:
  - *Continual cash usage*. Cash usage levels routinely flow within a certain range, so there must be sufficient cash available to always meet these cash requirements. The investment strategy for the amount included in this investment tier should be concentrated in highly liquid investments that can be readily accessed, with less attention to achieving a high rate of return.
  - *Occasional cash usage*. In addition to cash usage for daily operating events, there are usually a small number of higher-cash usage events that can be readily predicted, such as a periodic income tax or dividend payment. The strategy for this investment tier should focus on maturity dates just prior to the scheduled usage of cash, along with a somewhat greater emphasis on the return on investment. There should be a secondary market for these types of investments.
  - *No planned cash usage*. If cash usage levels have never exceeded a certain amount, all cash above this maximum usage level can be invested in longer-term instruments that have higher returns on investment, and perhaps with more limited secondary markets.

EXAMPLE

The treasurer of Suture Corporation wants to adopt a tiered investment strategy. He finds that the company routinely requires a maximum of $200,000 of cash for various expenditures on a weekly basis. In addition, there are scheduled quarterly dividend payments of $50,000 per quarter, and quarterly income tax payments of $100,000, which fall on the same date. There have not been any instances in the past three years where cash requirements exceeded these amounts. Currently, Suture maintains cash reserves of $850,000 on a weekly basis.

Based on the preceding information, the company could invest the cash in the following ways:

Investment Tier	Amount	Investment Type
Continual cash usage	$200,000	Money market
Occasional cash usage	150,000	Certificates of deposit, commercial paper
No planned cash usage	500,000	Bonds
Total	$850,000	

The tiered investment strategy requires close attention to the cash forecast, particularly in regard to the timing and amount of the occasional cash usage items. Otherwise, there is a risk of being caught with too much cash in an illiquid investment when there is an immediate need for the cash.

- *Ride the yield curve.* An active treasury staff can buy investments that have higher interest rates and longer maturity dates, and then sell these investments when the cash is needed for operational purposes. Thus, a company is deliberately buying investments that it knows it cannot hold until their maturity dates. If the yield curve is inverted (that is, interest rates are lower on longer-maturity investments), you would instead continually re-invest in very short-term instruments, no matter how far in the future the cash is actually needed again by the company.

EXAMPLE

The treasurer of Suture Corporation has $300,000 available to invest for the next 90 days. He notes that the interest rate on 3-month T-Bills is 2.0%, while the rate on 6-month T-Bills is 2.25%. He elects to take advantage of this 0.25% difference in interest rates by investing the $300,000 in 6-month-T-Bills, and then selling them on a secondary market in 90 days, when he needs the cash for operational purposes.

The following investment strategies require investing expertise and the incurrence of more risk, in exchange for the possibility of higher investment returns. These strategies should not be followed unless the treasury staff has specialized expertise in the indicated areas, and spends enough time modeling probable outcomes to understand the risks being undertaken. The strategies are:

- *Credit rating anticipation.* If the treasurer expects that the credit rating of a debt issuer is about to be revised upward, it may make sense to acquire those debt securities to which the rating change would apply. If anticipated correctly, this means that the company buys securities at a reduced price and later sells them at the higher price associated with the higher credit rating. This is a difficult game to play, since it is not easy to anticipate a credit upgrade, much less the timing of the upgrade. Also, an investment in the securities of a low-grade entity is at greater risk of suffering from a default, where the company loses its entire investment. Credit rating anticipation also requires a notable amount of analysis time, which is usually not available in smaller treasury departments.
- *Leveraged investing.* A larger organization may be able to issue debt at quite a low interest rate, and then invest the borrowed funds in higher-yielding investments, resulting in an incremental financing gain to the business. This behavior is not recommended, since it diverts attention from the management of operations. It is particularly risky when the maturities of the company's investments are shorter than those of its borrowings, since the return on investment may suddenly decline below the cost of its borrowings, resulting in losses.

A variation on all of the preceding strategies is to outsource the investment task to an experienced third party money manager. This option works well if a company is too small or has too few cash reserves to actively manage its own cash. If outsourcing is chosen, be sure to set up guidelines with the money manager for exactly how cash is to be invested, primarily through the use of lower-risk investments that mitigate the possibility of losing cash. A variation on the outsourcing concept is to invest primarily in money market funds, which are professionally managed.

Leasing Cost Reduction

There is an undeniable attraction to acquiring assets with a lease, since it replaces a large up-front cash outflow with a series of monthly payments. However, before signing a lease agreement, be aware of the following issues that can increase the cost of the arrangement:

- *Buyout price.* Many leases include an end-of-lease buyout price that is inordinately high. If the lessee wants to continue using a leased asset, the buyout price may be so outrageous that the only realistic alternative is to continue making lease payments, which generates outsized profits for the lessor. Therefore, always negotiate the size of the buyout payment before signing a lease agreement. If the buyout is stated as the "fair market value" of the asset at the end of the lease term, the amount can be subject to interpretation, so include a clause that allows for arbitration to determine the amount of fair market value.

- *Deposit usage.* The terms of a lease may allow the lessor to charge any number of fees against the up-front deposit made by the lessee, resulting in little of the deposit being returned at the end of the lease.
- *Rate changes.* The lessor may offer a low lease rate during the beginning periods of a lease, and then escalate the rates later in the lease term. Be sure to calculate the average lease rate to see if the implicit interest rate is reasonable. In these sorts of arrangements, a rate ramp-up usually indicates an average interest rate that is too high.
- *Return fees.* When the lease term is over, the lessor may require that the leased asset be shipped at the lessee's cost to a distant location, and sometimes even in the original packaging.
- *Termination notification.* The lease agreement may require the lessee to notify the lessor in writing that it intends to terminate the lease as of the termination date stated in the contract. If the lessee does not issue this notification in a timely manner, it is obligated to continue leasing the asset, or to pay a large termination fee. Whenever this clause appears in a lease agreement, always negotiate it down to the smallest possible termination notification period.
- *Wear-and-tear standards.* A lease agreement may contain unreasonable standards for assigning a high rate of wear-and-tear to leased assets when they have been returned to the lessor, resulting in additional fees being charged to the lessee.

In short, many lessors rely upon obfuscation of the lease terms to generate a profit, so it makes sense to delve into every clause in a lease agreement, and to be willing to bargain hard for changes to the terms. Also, have a well-managed system in place for retaining lease agreements and monitoring when the key dates associated with each lease will arise. Finally, conduct a cost review after each lease agreement has been terminated, to determine the total out-of-pocket cost and implicit interest rate; the result may be the discovery that certain lessors routinely gouge the company, and should not be used again.

Insurance Cost Reduction

The main thrust of this chapter is to manage the cost of the finance area. Since insurance is sometimes placed within the responsibility of the treasurer, we include the following pointers regarding the management of insurance:

- *Consider self-insurance.* Review the company's claims history and real risk exposure, and see if it makes sense to self-insure some risks. Doing so eliminates the profit component of the fees charged by insurance companies. The amount of risk incurred in a self-insurance arrangement can be mitigated by purchasing an umbrella policy that is only triggered after a certain amount of claims have already been paid out by the company.

- *Self-insure shipping insurance.* Offer customers shipping insurance for deliveries made to them, and provide the coverage internally. This means that the company builds up a cash reserve from the insurance payments made, and pays out claims from this fund, keeping all residual cash as profit. If properly priced, this type of insurance can yield substantial profits, and usually with only a moderate amount of risk.
- *Investigate covered items.* Review existing insurance contracts to see if the company is still paying for coverage of assets that no longer exist, or for inconsequential risks. Of course, a result of this review could well be an increase in insurance costs, if you discover that some assets are not being covered, or major risks are not being addressed.
- *Terminate double coverage.* Compare the coverage of all insurance policies to see if the company is paying for different insurance contracts that provide overlapping coverage of the same asset or risk. If so, eliminate the overlap when the contracts are up for renewal.

Please note that we do not advocate the outright reduction of insurance, since doing so may expose a business to an unwarranted amount of risk. However, we *do* advocate paying close attention to the cost of shifting risk to an insurance company, and of closely tailoring the insurance purchased to the precise needs of a business.

How to Operate with Zero Working Capital

Working capital is the net difference between current assets and current liabilities, and is primarily comprised of accounts receivable, inventory, and accounts payable. The amount of working capital that a company must invest is usually considerable, and may even exceed its investment in fixed assets. The amount of working capital will increase as a business increases its credit sales, since accounts receivable will expand. In addition, inventory levels also increase with sales growth, as management elects to keep more inventory in stock to support ongoing sales, usually in the form of additional stock keeping units to meet the needs of customers.

A typical business is short of capital, and so may have an interest in operating with zero working capital in order to reduce its financing costs. Doing so requires the following two items:

- *Demand-based production.* It is nearly impossible to avoid increases in working capital if management insists on keeping stocks of inventory on hand to meet projected customer needs. To reduce capital requirements, set up a just-in-time production system that only builds units when they are ordered by customers. Doing so eliminates all stocks of finished goods. In addition, install a just-in-time procurement system that only buys raw materials to support the exact amount of demand-based units that must be produced. This approach essentially eliminates the investment in inventory. An alternative approach is to outsource all production, and have the supplier ship goods directly to the company's customers (known as drop shipping).

- *Receivable and payable terms.* The terms under which credit is granted to customers must be curtailed, while payment terms to suppliers must be extended. Ideally, cash should be received from customers before it is due for payment to suppliers. This essentially means that customer payments are directly funding the payments to suppliers.

For example, a computer manufacturer can insist upon cash in advance credit card payments from its customers, orders component parts from suppliers on credit, assembles them under a just-in-time system, and then pay its suppliers. The result can be not only zero working capital, but even negative working capital.

While the concept of zero working capital may initially appear enticing, it is extremely difficult to implement, for the following reasons:

- Customers are not willing to pay in advance, except for consumer goods. Larger customers will not only be unwilling to pay early, but may even demand delayed payment.
- Suppliers typically offer industry-standard credit terms to their customers, and will only be willing to accept longer payment terms in exchange for higher product prices.
- A just-in-time, demand-based production system can be a difficult concept for customers to accept in those industries where competition is based on immediate order fulfillment (which requires a certain amount of on-hand inventory).
- In a services industry, there is no inventory, but there are plenty of employees, who are typically paid faster than customers are willing to pay. Thus, payroll essentially takes the place of inventory in the working capital concept, and must be paid at frequent intervals.

In short, zero working capital is an interesting concept, but is usually not a practical implementation. Still, if a company can improve upon its working capital in any of the key areas indicated, it can at least reduce its investment in working capital, which is certainly a worthy goal.

Summary

As indicated by the large number of issues described in this chapter, the finance area can yield a treasure trove of cost reductions for a business. However, these are not items that will be apparent to anyone outside of the accounting and treasury departments, so it is imperative that the controller and treasurer pay particular attention to this topic.

The finance area requires constant attention, for there is no ultimate level of cost reduction to be achieved; instead, a company must continually adapt to its changing finance needs, and revise its methods for reducing costs within the boundaries set by its need for funds.

Chapter 19
Accounts Receivable Reduction

Introduction

A business may have invested in a large amount of accounts receivable, primarily to encourage orders from its customers. However, too large an investment in receivables presents a risk of nonpayment, which will result in the recognition of bad debt expenses. To manage the cost of bad debts, we present in this chapter a number of techniques for reducing credit risk, as well as for collecting overdue receivables from customers.

Related Podcast Episode: Episode 86 of the Accounting Best Practices Podcast discusses credit best practices. It is available at: **accountingtools.com/podcasts** or **iTunes**

Credit Risk Reduction

Every time a company grants credit to a customer, it is at full risk of not collecting the entire billed amount from the customer. In some industries, a remarkably high percentage of these receivables are at risk of default, so there is a potentially massive amount of bad debt associated with credit sales that could bankrupt a company.

There are a variety of ways to deal with the prospect of bad debts. Some businesses grant credit only to the most financially stable customers. Other businesses use credit risk as a competitive weapon, scooping up those customers that no one else wants in exchange for bearing a higher risk of default. Both of these strategies can be improved upon through the judicious use of credit risk reduction. By using the tools described in this section, an excessively conservative business can grant credit to more customers, while an aggressive company can reduce its bad debts on credit sales to higher-risk customers.

The suggestions in this section can generally be aggregated into the following classifications of risk reduction:

- *Find alternate payer*. Someone besides the customer agrees to also be liable for payments, or to pay insurance claims for bad debts.
- *Retain ownership*. There are a variety of ways to retain a legal interest in goods sold, so that the goods can be recovered.
- *Offload ownership*. Once an invoice is issued, transfer ownership of the invoice to a third party in exchange for cash, so that the new owner bears the risk of default.

- *Pay early.* Require the acceleration of payment by customers, so that only smaller payments are at risk of default, and for shorter periods.

By using a mix of these tools, it is possible to achieve a significant reduction in the amount of bad debt risk that may be incurred, even while extending credit to customers that are not entirely financially sound.

Payment Guarantees

The owner of a small business may be willing to personally guarantee that a payment owed by his or her company will be paid, if necessary out of personal assets. While this approach may initially appear satisfactory to the seller, there are actually several problems with it. First, the owner's net worth may be closely tied to the fortunes of the business, so there will be no personal assets left if the business fails. Also, the owner may have issued personal guarantees to many suppliers, so a failure of the business will lead to a scramble by this group to attach the owner's personal assets. And finally, demanding a personal guarantee is hardly a way to obtain the long-term loyalty of a customer. Given these issues, a common path to follow is a personal guarantee requirement when a customer is a new business, followed by its revocation after several years of reliable payment history have been achieved.

If a business is a subsidiary, it can be useful to obtain a payment guarantee from the parent company. Depending on the structure of the organization, the parent entity may have more assets than the subsidiary, and so may be an excellent backup payer. However, some parent companies are essentially shell organizations that contain minimal assets. Accordingly, request the financial statements of the parent company to determine the amount of available assets. If the parent does not appear to be an adequate guarantor, consider demanding a guarantee from another subsidiary that owns more assets.

It is sometimes possible to obtain a guarantee from a third party. This may be a related party that has an interest in the operations of the buyer, such as a member of its board of directors, a key supplier, a manager, or a family member. This type of guarantee can be quite valuable, since the assets of the third party may not be so closely tied to the fortunes of the buyer, and can survive the demise of the business. When researching the possibility of a third party guarantee, be sure to request documentation of the net assets of the third party, as well as any guarantees that may take precedence over the guarantee being negotiated.

Title Retention

It is possible to retain title to goods that are shipped to customers, and only transfer the title to buyers once payment has been made. This can be an effective risk reduction tool, but only if capital goods are being sold – the option is not practical for small-value items, with the exception of a consignment arrangement, as noted below. There are three alternatives for title retention described in this section, which are the UCC-1 financing statement, the purchase money security interest, and the inventory consignment arrangement.

If title retention is selected for risk reduction, the seller creates a security agreement between the buyer and seller that states the rights of each party in regard to the asset. The seller then files a UCC-1 financing statement with the required government office (usually the secretary of state) to publicly reveal the presence of a lien on the asset. Doing so gives the seller seniority over other creditors who might also file liens against the asset at a later date; this is known as *perfecting* the lien.

When a seller files a UCC-1 financing statement, it may find that it has done so after several other creditors, which means that its claim is junior to the claims of those entities that preceded it in making their claims. It is possible to leapfrog ahead of these other creditors by obtaining a *purchase money security interest* (PMSI). Obtaining a PMSI is not simple. The seller must send notice of the arrangement to all other secured parties, so that they are fully briefed on the proposed PMSI arrangement. A PMSI statement and UCC-1 must then be filed at the office of the secretary of state for the state in which the company's primary office is located. Also, the customer should sign the PMSI. The PMSI is only available to those sellers whose goods are readily identifiable in the buyer's inventory.

There may be situations where a distributor or retailer wants to sell a company's products, but does not have sufficiently robust finances to purchase the goods outright. If so, the distributor or retailer can act as an agent for the seller, rather than a buyer, and hold the goods on behalf of the seller. Under this consignment arrangement, the "seller" retains ownership of the goods and cannot recognize a sale until the distributor or retailer actually sells the goods to a third party. At that point, the agent notifies the seller of the sale transaction, and remits payment to the seller, while retaining its profit.

Credit Insurance

A seller may find that it can shift some of the risk associated with its accounts receivable to a firm that provides credit insurance. Under a credit insurance policy, the insurer protects the seller against customer nonpayment. The insurer should be willing to provide coverage against customer nonpayment if a proposed customer clears its internal review process. Credit insurance offers the following benefits:

- *Increased credit.* A company may be able to increase the credit levels offered to its customers, thereby potentially increasing revenue.
- *Faster international deals.* An international sale might normally be delayed while the parties arrange a letter of credit, but can be completed faster with credit insurance.
- *Custom product coverage.* The insurance can cover the shipment of custom-made products, in case customers cancel their orders prior to delivery.
- *Reduced credit staff.* Credit insurance essentially shifts risk away from a business, so it is especially beneficial in companies that have an understaffed credit department that cannot adequately keep track of customer credit levels.

- *Knowledge*. A credit insurance firm specializes in the risk characteristics of various industries, and so may have deep knowledge about the risk profiles of individual customers, as well as aggregations of customers by region. This information is a useful supplement to other sources of information about customers.
- *Tax deductibility*. Credit insurance premiums are immediately deductible for tax purposes, whereas the allowance for doubtful accounts is only deductible when specific bad debts are recognized.

Insurers are more willing to provide coverage of accounts receivable if the seller is willing to take on a small part of the bad debt risk itself. This typically means that a customer default will result in the insurer reimbursing the seller, minus the amount of a 5% to 20% deductible. There may also be an annual aggregate deductible that requires the company to absorb a certain fixed amount of losses in a year before the insurer begins to pay reimbursements. Requiring a deductible means that the company continues to have an interest in only selling to credit-worthy customers.

Factoring

Under a factoring arrangement, a finance company agrees to take over a company's accounts receivable collections and keep the money from these collections in exchange for an immediate cash payment to the company. This process typically involves having customers mail their payments to a lockbox that appears to be operated by the company, but which is actually controlled by the finance company. Under a true factoring arrangement, the finance company takes over the risk of loss on any bad debts, though it will have the right to pick which types of receivables it will accept in order to reduce its risk of loss. A finance company is more interested in this type of deal when the size of each receivable is fairly large, since this reduces its per-transaction cost of collection.

Letters of Credit

A letter of credit is a useful tool for essentially eliminating credit risk, by having the buyer escrow funds in advance of a sale with a reliable third party (its bank). Doing so ensures that the funds will be available when payment is due. The letter of credit is most commonly used for international trade, where the importer's bank (known as the issuing bank) recognizes an obligation to pay the bank of the exporter, which in turn credits the funds to the account of the exporter. To obtain these funds, the exporter must present an invoice and proof of delivery to one of the banks (depending on the circumstances), sometimes accompanied by a certificate of insurance.

The issuing bank guarantees payment under a letter of credit arrangement, and so bears the risk of payment. The issuing bank offsets this risk by either paying the funds from the line of credit of the importer, or by blocking a sufficient amount of funds in the importer's bank account. In effect, this means that the importer is paying in advance for an order, even though the exporter will not receive the funds until all terms and conditions of the letter of credit arrangement have been met.

Export-Import Guarantees

If it is not possible or practical to obtain a letter of credit for an international sale, an alternative may be to obtain a credit guarantee from the Export-Import Bank (Ex-Im Bank) of the United States. This guarantee is available to any entity shipping domestic goods to a customer in a foreign location. The Ex-Im Bank offers guarantees for a variety of situations, including:

- Preshipment coverage, to protect against the cancellation of an order for customized goods
- Coverage of sales to multiple buyers on open account terms
- Sales to individual customers

It is not always easy to obtain a guarantee from the Ex-Im Bank. Depending on the size of the proposed sale transaction, it may be necessary to submit the audited financial statements of the buyer, a credit report, and trade references. Further, the customer must have at least a three-year history of being in the same line of business. Also, it may be necessary to meet certain minimum financial ratios.

Outside Financing

When the goods being sold are high-cost fixed assets, it may be possible to arrange with a third-party lender to provide financing to the buyer to either buy or lease the items being sold. This type of arrangement shifts the credit risk to the lender. Of course, the lender will apply its own credit granting standards to buyers, and may not provide financing to those customers it considers being at an elevated risk of default.

Distributor Sales

When the credit department decides not to extend credit to a prospective customer, it may still be possible to refer the proposed transaction to a distributor of the company's products. If the distributor has more relaxed credit standards, the sale may still go through, and the distributor takes on the risk of the deal. However, if the customer reneges on payment to the distributor, the distributor may have trouble paying the seller for the goods that the distributor is reselling. Consequently, this type of arrangement does not entirely eliminate credit risk – it only means that the distributor is now liable to the seller for payment, rather than the ultimate customer.

A further consideration when shifting customer orders to a distributor is that the seller is giving up what may be a substantial margin on the sale of its goods, since the distributor is buying from the company at a reduced price.

Adjustment of Days to Pay

A customer may request credit for an amount that the credit department decides is too risky for the company to allow, based on the normal number of days during which the receivable will be outstanding. However, the risk profile of the situation can be improved upon by shortening the number of days over which the customer is allowed to have credit. This approach only works when a customer order can be subdivided into several pieces, and the customer has sufficient cash on hand to pay on shorter terms.

Collection Tactics

There is no tried-and-true collection methodology that works for all overdue invoices, all of the time. Instead, the collection staff must choose from an array of collection tactics, depending on such issues as the amount of the invoice, the intransigence of the customer, and common collection practice in the industry. Accordingly, we do not present a collection methodology in this section, but rather a series of possible collection options. These options are listed in order from the most innocuous to the most severe.

Dunning Letters

A dunning letter is a notification sent to a customer, stating that the customer is overdue in paying an account receivable to the sender. Dunning letters typically follow a progression from polite reminders to more strident demands for payment, if the customer continues to be non-responsive in paying. The first few letters that are sent should be polite, on the theory that the customer has simply overlooked payment, and the company wants to retain its goodwill for future business.

However, as more time passes, the company begins to change its assumption of doing further business with the customer, and so tends to downplay the amount of customer goodwill that it wants to retain in favor of being paid now. Irrespective of the tone of the letter, it always states the amount due, the date of the unpaid invoice, the number of the invoice, and any late payment fines or interest penalties.

Dunning letters are frequently generated by a computer, with no human input at all. The system is configured to use a particular text if payment has not been made within a certain number of days, and to then use a different text for letters generated after a longer time period has passed without payment.

The collections staff may periodically change the timing or content of these automatically-generated letters, if they feel that some variation will improve the rate of collection. This can be accomplished with *A-B testing*, where two versions of a dunning letter are issued, and the effectiveness of each one monitored; if one version results in more customer payments, that version becomes the new default letter format to be used.

Take Back Merchandise

If a company is selling goods, the buyer usually finds a use for or resells the goods in short order, leaving no asset that the company can take back in the event of nonpayment. This is particularly likely when the terms of payment are relatively long, giving the buyer more time in which to disposition the goods. However, if this is not the case and the customer still retains the goods in unused condition, a reasonable option is to take back the goods if the customer is unable to pay.

Taking back merchandise is a better option when the goods have long-term value and can be readily resold at roughly the same as the original price. If the goods decline rapidly in value, as is the case with fashion goods and some consumer electronics, the decision to cancel a receivable in exchange for taking back merchandise may be a more difficult one.

Hold Orders

A similar concept to taking back merchandise from a customer is blocking any additional shipments to the customer. To do so, the collections staff must have access to the customer orders database, and the authority to halt shipment of a pending customer order. This can be a highly effective way to dislodge a payment, especially if the seller is in the enviable position of selling goods that no other suppliers offer for sale. The company's computer system can even be set to trigger a warning message to the collections staff when a forthcoming customer order will cause a customer's actual receivable amount outstanding to exceed the amount of its credit limit.

While the order holding concept may initially sound ideal, here are two cautionary items to consider:

- When the goods on order can be commonly found elsewhere, a customer may simply cancel the order as soon as it receives an order hold notification, and take its business elsewhere.
- Holding an order may not be possible if the order is already in the production process, since doing so would throw the production schedule into disarray. If this is the case, the goods will have to be produced, and then a hold is placed on the shipment. This can be a problem when goods are customized, since the company may have no other way to dispose of the goods.

Split Payments

If a customer claims that it cannot pay an invoice right now, offer to split the invoice into several payments over the short term. Better yet, ask for part of these split payments immediately over the phone, using a credit card. By doing so, a pattern of payment is immediately established, which the collector can follow up on at regular intervals. This may result in a series of credit card payments over the phone, but at least results in payments.

The split payments approach varies from the following promissory note concept in that split payments are intended to cover a relatively short period of time, and do not have an associated guarantee or assets used as collateral. There may or may not be an interest charge associated with split payments.

Postdated Checks

It may be possible to obtain from a customer one or more postdated checks, which the collector promises not to cash until the date listed on each check. If so, the collector notes on a calendar when each check is to be cashed, and does so on the specified dates. If a postdated check is from a commercial customer, no further notifications to the customer need to be made. If a check is from an individual, the collector must send a written notification to the customer within three to ten business days of the date when the check will be cashed.

Promissory Note

There will be times when a customer does not have sufficient cash to pay for an overdue invoice, but is willing to work with the seller to pay off the amount over a longer time period. If so, an option may be to convert the invoice into a promissory note that contains a series of specific payment dates, an interest component, and a guarantee or collateral. The key element of this note is that the company is either given a guarantee of payment by a third party, or collateral that can be accessed if the customer defaults on payments. This approach improves the ability of the seller to obtain some form of payment, even if it may take some time to do so.

> **Tip:** The key element in a promissory note is a guarantee or collateral; to obtain it, consider such inducements as a low interest rate, a slight reduction in principal, or allowing a restricted amount of credit for continuing purchases from the seller.

It is much easier to win a lawsuit over nonpayment of a promissory note than over nonpayment of an account receivable, since the customer has signed the note, and therefore has agreed to its specific terms.

Arbitration

There may be cases where the customer feels that it has a legitimate complaint against the seller. For example, the customer may believe that it ordered goods with certain specifications, and received goods that did not meet the specifications. If the seller is not willing to negotiate the issue, then consider shifting the claim to arbitration. Under arbitration, the parties select a presumably impartial third party to review the claims of both sides, and then issue a judgment that the parties agree to respect. The arbitration process tends to be fairly short, but it does require time to prepare a presentation to the arbitrator, and the arbitrator's fee must be paid. Also, the resulting decision may go against the seller.

Attorney Letters

It is entirely possible that a series of dunning letters will not convince a customer to make an overdue payment, possibly because a mere letter from the seller is not sufficient to provoke real action. A possible option at this point is to have an attorney send a letter, written on the attorney's letterhead and structured as a final reminder before legal action commences.

The fact that the matter has now been turned over to an attorney is a good way of telling a customer that the seller is now extremely serious about the unpaid receivable, and is not willing to tolerate any further delays. Consequently, the probability of payment is higher following an attorney letter than it is following a dunning letter. However, sending such a letter alters the relationship between the parties, since the seller is now making the assumption that it may not want to do business with the customer on an extended basis, and simply wants the account paid off now.

Issue Small Claims Court Complaint

After all manner of threats have been exhausted, one last option that may result in payment from an intransigent customer is to fill out a small claims court complaint form and send a copy of it to the customer, with a note stating that the complaint form will be filed at a specific date and time, unless payment is received before then. Doing so makes it extremely clear that a judgment against the customer is likely to be made in the near future, and that the seller is willing to proceed down this path.

This option has the additional advantage of being inexpensive, since there are no attorney fees involved, nor any court costs. The only downside is that the seller clearly signals no further interest in an ongoing business relationship with the customer.

Collection Agency

When a company's in-house collections program has difficulty collecting from an account, it can be worthwhile to shift the collection effort to a collection agency. This is an independent group of collection specialists who may succeed where the company has failed. Though their fees are high, paying the fee in exchange for collecting an invoice is much better than writing off the invoice.

Having a collection agency can itself be used as a threat, somewhat like keeping an attack dog on a leash. In some cases, the mere threat of referring an invoice to a collection agency can be sufficient to cause a recalcitrant customer to issue a payment. This approach can even be used to save a relationship, where the in-house staff acts as the good cop and the collection agency as the bad cop, thereby shifting any customer anger to the agency and away from the company. Doing so may allow the customer and seller to continue doing business in the future on a reasonably cordial basis.

Money Judgment Collection Activities

If the seller obtains a favorable judgment against a debtor in court, it still faces the task of obtaining payment from the debtor. The court is not responsible for obtaining payment from the debtor – the company must do so.

Obtaining payment may require seizing debtor assets in payment of the debt, so the first task is to determine where the assets are located. One option is to conduct a *judgment debtor examination*, where the debtor is asked under oath about the locations and amounts of all assets. The debtor must appear in court for this examination, or else the court will issue a warrant for their arrest.

Once the company knows where personal property assets are located, it can contact the sheriff having jurisdiction over the county in which the assets are located, and request that they be seized and sold at a public auction.

If not sufficient funds have been raised through the seizure of personal property, another option is to place a lien on the real property of the debtor, which can be accomplished with a notice of judgment filing through the secretary of state. *Real property* is defined as land and any property attached to the land (such as buildings). This approach does not result in immediate payment, but makes it more difficult for the debtor to sell its assets to third parties, since clear title cannot be transferred until the lien is settled. It may be possible to request a judicial foreclosure of the property, in which case the company can be paid from the proceeds of the asset sale (assuming there are no senior liens on the property that must be settled first).

In cases where the company is pursuing payment from an individual, it can apply to the court to issue a *garnishment*. A garnishment requires the employer of an individual to withhold a portion of the person's wages and remit them to the company. Wage garnishments may yield little cash if the company has a low priority after other garnishment claims on the person's wages, such as for child support payments and tax liens. A garnishment can also be repeatedly applied to the bank account of a debtor, which can be used to extract any funds that have been deposited into the account.

Summary

The risk reduction techniques described in this chapter do not entirely eliminate risk, and may even introduce additional costs and delays. For example, the use of a personal guarantee to mitigate risk may result in a lengthy lawsuit against the guarantor, only to find that the guarantor does not have sufficient assets to pay the guaranteed amount. Similarly, a credit insurance policy may be invalid for a specific claim because the customer disputes the invoice. Consequently, do not assume that risk reduction strategies will always work. It may be necessary to instead adopt layers of risk reduction strategies, so that a backup strategy will still provide protection if the primary approach fails. Also, there will still be bad debts even if all of the risk reduction and collection tactics noted in this chapter are employed; the amounts will be reduced, but be prepared to incur some losses on an ongoing basis.

For a more detailed analysis of the credit and collection issues described in this chapter, see the author's *Credit & Collection Guidebook*. The book also addresses credit policy, credit ratings, payment deductions, skip tracing, litigation tactics, and other issues related to accounts receivable.

Chapter 20
Inventory Reduction

Introduction

Inventory is recorded in a company's balance sheet as an asset. However, it is a dangerous asset to possess, for its value is constantly declining, it is expensive to store, and can be difficult to convert to cash. Consequently, from the viewpoint of cost management, inventory should be minimized to the greatest extent possible. This chapter is organized around the concept of reducing inventory in order to reduce cost. We do so by first examining the various costs incurred to store inventory, and then proceed to a number of areas in which inventory reduction can be accomplished – product planning, purchasing and receiving, storage, production, fulfillment, inventory disposition, and inventory management.

The Cost of Inventory

Before embarking on a discussion of the many ways in which inventory can be reduced, it is useful to make note of just how much inventory can cost a company. Consider the following costs:

- *Facility costs*. This is the cost of the warehouse, which includes depreciation on the building and interior racks, utilities, building insurance, and warehouse staff. There are also utility costs, such as electricity and heating fuel for the building. Also, if the company stores overflow stock in trailers near the warehouse, this includes the rental cost of the trailers. The cost of a facility is largely fixed, and so can only be allocated generally to items inventoried within the warehouse; there is no way to directly associate this cost with an individual unit of inventory.

- *Cost of funds*. This is the interest cost of any funds that a company borrows in order to purchase inventory (or, conversely, the foregone interest income). This can be tied to a specific unit of inventory, since selling a single unit immediately frees up funds which can then be used to pay down debt.

- *Risk mitigation*. This is not only the cost of insuring inventory, but also of installing any risk-management items needed to protect the inventory, such as fire suppression systems, fences, security staff, and burglar alarms. As was the case with facility costs, this is largely a fixed cost.

- *Taxes*. The business district in which the inventory is stored may charge some form of property tax on the inventory. This cost can be reduced by selling off inventory just prior to the date on which it is measured for tax purposes.

- *Obsolescence*. Inventory may become unusable over time (especially for perishable items), or it may be superseded by technological advances. In either case, it may only be disposed of at a large discount, or have no value at all. This tends to be an incremental cost that is more likely to be associated with low turnover goods.

Tip: Be particularly careful to consider the cost of inventory obsolescence when determining the most appropriate quantities of raw materials to order. If there is not a clear need for certain items, it is likely that any excess quantities purchased will eventually be written off as obsolete inventory.

As noted in many of these points, a large proportion of inventory storage costs are fixed; thus, a company with an empty warehouse will find that the incremental cost associated with one extra unit of inventory is quite small, whereas a company operating a filled warehouse must deal with large step costs to accommodate additional units of inventory.

Product Planning

There are a number of methods that can be employed by the engineering department to design products that require the smallest possible amount of investment in inventory. For example:

- *Minimize parts*. Product designers can develop products that share many of the same component parts. This is particularly likely across product families, where the same basic design is being used as the foundation for a cluster of products. By doing so, a business can eliminate a number of parts from raw materials inventory. This concept also tends to result in less obsolete inventory, since so few parts are solely linked to a single product. However, it typically requires at least one product cycle to build the parts minimization concept into the product design philosophy, so it can take years to implement this approach.
- *Design for broad tolerance*. Some products are designed to work only with parts whose dimensions are very precisely defined. If a part does not exactly match the planned characteristics, it is designated as scrap and thrown away. This scrap cost can be reduced by designing products to operate with components whose characteristics can vary somewhat from specifications. A side benefit of this approach is that it may be less expensive to construct or purchase parts that have a broad tolerance range.
- *Match materials quality to design specifications*. A company may obtain raw materials that are of too high a quality level in comparison to the design specifications of a product. Doing so means that customers may not even notice the difference, while the company incurs a higher cost than it should. For example, a part may be built from titanium to save a small amount of weight, while less-expensive stainless steel would be suitable

241

from the perspective of the customer. Ideally, the procurement staff should only buy raw materials and components that meet the expectations of customers.

- *Incorporate supplier recommendations.* Suppliers know more about raw materials than the company's design team, so include suppliers in the design process. They may be able to recommend the use of less-expensive or more easily sourced parts that will reduce the overall inventory investment, reduce sourcing risk, and/or mitigate product failures.

- *Review the bill of materials.* The engineering staff delivers a bill of materials (BOM) along with each new product design. The BOM precisely defines the parts and unit quantities that go into the construction of a product, and is an essential tool used for ordering raw materials. If the BOM is incorrect, a business may use it to buy the wrong quantities of certain parts, or perhaps the wrong parts. To avoid this cost, have a second person review each BOM before it is released for ordering purposes, and lock down access to the BOM file in the computer system. It may also be necessary to monitor changes to the BOM file over time, since engineering change orders may require that the file be altered.

- *Employ risk pooling.* When products share a large number of component parts, fluctuations in demand for the products may offset, so that demand for the component parts does not vary that much. With a reduced demand deviation, it is possible to maintain a smaller safety stock for these commonly-used items. This technique is only possible when parts sharing is used, as advocated in a preceding point.

- *Minimize the number of product variations.* The marketing department typically pushes for the production and subsequent stocking of a broad array of variations on a basic product design. By doing so, they feel that sales can be maximized by addressing all possible product niches. However, only a few of these product variations are likely to sell in any volume, so the inventory used to support the remaining product variations can represent not only a large inventory investment, but also a substantial risk of inventory obsolescence. Consequently, be sure to examine the cost of all product variations, and consider cancelling those for which there is a large inventory cost.

- *Schedule change orders.* If the engineering department wants to alter a product, it usually issues an engineering change order that stops the use of one component and substitutes another. If these change orders are issued without regard to the component parts currently in stock, the result could be a significant amount of obsolete inventory (especially if a part is unique to the product being modified). Instead, all change orders should be scheduled to coincide with the draw-down of any affected raw materials.

- *Enhanced product life cycle planning.* This item encompasses several of the preceding points. The engineering and materials management teams should jointly plan the time period over which a product will be offered for sale, after which a replacement version will be released. This level of planning allows the materials management department to draw down inventory levels towards the end of the planned life cycle, so that all types of inventory are reduced in expectation of the next product launch. Ideally, there should be only a minimal amount of residual inventory on hand that relates to an old product when its replacement is introduced to the market.

Purchasing and Receiving

There are several methods available for reducing the inventory investment by modifying the manner in which purchasing and receiving are conducted. The following concepts apply to this area:

- *Consolidate suppliers*. Concentrate orders with the smallest number of suppliers, in order to take advantage of volume discounts. This approach is easier to implement when procurement is centralized, and requires ongoing auditing to ensure compliance with the consolidation policy. It is usually necessary to conduct a certification review of those suppliers that are to be retained, to ensure that the quality, timeliness, and accuracy of their deliveries meet the company's standards.
- *Move production to raw materials*. There may be cases where a product is largely comprised of just a small number of raw materials. If so, and the transportation costs for these items are high, it may make sense to relocate the production facility closer to the source of supply. This technique is most applicable when local markets are served by local production facilities, rather than from a small number of central production locations.
- *Reduce order size*. Reduce the number of units ordered per purchase, which means that the total number of orders will be increased. By doing so, the average amount of inventory on hand at any time is lower than would be the case if a single large order had been placed. This approach works best when delivery costs are low, which usually means that suppliers must be located nearby.
- *Give suppliers access to production schedule*. Give suppliers direct access to the company's production scheduling system. By doing so, suppliers are better able to make timely deliveries, which reduces the company's need to maintain a buffer of safety stock to guard against supplier stockout conditions.
- *Split deliveries*. A supplier may require that a certain quantity be ordered at one time in order to take advantage of a specific pricing deal. However, despite the need for a single order, it may still be possible to split the order into multiple deliveries, so that some items are delivered later. Doing so reduces the overall investment in inventory at one time.
- *Review open orders*. The production schedule may change over time, and the purchasing staff may not keep pace with these changes by altering the contents of outstanding purchase orders. The result may be the receipt of raw materials that are no longer needed. Consequently, there should be an

ongoing review process for open purchase orders. Better yet, create a report that flags purchase orders for review whenever the items being ordered have been altered by a production schedule alteration.

- *Reduce safety stock.* A company may maintain a large amount of safety stock, which is inventory kept on hand to guard against stockout conditions. The amount of safety stock can be reduced when suppliers are located nearby, since replacement components can be reordered and delivered within a short period of time.

- *Suppliers own inventory.* Have suppliers own their inventory in the company's warehouse until the moment when it is used or sold. This eliminates the holding period for inventory, thereby shifting the cost of the inventory to suppliers until the inventory is needed. This approach is usually only possible if inventory is sole sourced to certain suppliers, so that they can be assured of more sales in exchange for taking on the inventory holding cost.

- *Certify suppliers.* Have the purchasing and engineering staff visit customers and certify their production and shipping methods. By doing so, there is no need for receiving inspections, so that suppliers can deliver goods directly to the company's production lines. The result is the complete elimination of inventory in the receiving area.

Inventory Storage

A warehouse can require a large amount of funds to construct and operate, so it is worthwhile to consider a number of options for reducing its overall cost. Here are several suggestions for doing so:

- *Configure storage space.* Review the cubic storage area of the warehouse to see if the inventory planned for it will maximize the storage space. In many cases, there will be unused cubic space in the building. This may call for the use of higher storage racks, adjusting the size of cases to fit better on pallets, storage cabinets for smaller items, altered aisle widths, and/or double-deep racks. Other options include the use of wheeled storage racks in order to further compress the storage area, and open lanes in which large quantities of the same inventory item can be stacked. The emphasis here is on safely packing the largest amount of inventory into the smallest possible space.

- *Rent temporary storage.* Many businesses are subject to variable amounts of inventory storage requirements, due to such factors as seasonal demand and production ramp-ups for product launches. There may be a temptation to construct a storage facility that will handle the maximum amount of this inventory, but doing so will also result in the incurrence of the maximum possible storage expense. A more prudent approach may be to maintain a warehouse that is large enough to store the average amount of inventory, while renting temporary storage space to accommodate any overflow needs. Once the peak storage period has passed, the company can shift all remaining residual inventories at outside locations back to its main storage facility and terminate its temporary storage rentals.

> **Tip:** Only retain low-usage items in rented storage facilities, to minimize the warehouse staff's time in moving goods to and from these locations.

- *Employ cross-docking.* The most common approach to handling merchandise inventory is to receive and then store it in a designated storage facility, after which the goods are picked from stock and shipped to customers. The seller must invest in inventory for the period during which it is sitting in the storage facility. To reduce this investment, as well as the size of the storage facility, use cross-docking, which involves shifting inventory from an incoming truck to an outgoing truck for immediate delivery to the customer. Not only is the inventory holding period greatly reduced, but there are also no putaway or picking transactions that might damage inventory. Cross-docking only works effectively when the warehouse staff has excellent knowledge of the timing of incoming and outgoing deliveries. Also, the transshipment area must be larger than normal, and the loading area should contain many loading docks to accommodate the extra trucks that will be required.
- *Configure to use oldest items first.* Some types of inventory, such as produce, have very limited shelf lives, and so represent a heightened risk of inventory obsolescence. This risk can be mitigated by configuring the storage area to include gravity-flow racking, where goods are loaded onto the back of a shelf and roll to the front, from which picking is conducted. This approach is also available for entire pallets of goods.

Production

There are a large number of techniques available for reducing the amount of inventory being used within the production process. The following list addresses several of the more effective techniques:

- *Use the pull system.* Only produce goods when there is a customer order. This means that an actual customer order triggers the production of goods, rather than a sales forecast. By doing so, there should be little or no finished goods inventory on hand. The alternative (called a push system) schedules production based on *estimates* of customer demand, which frequently results in large amounts of unsold goods that may become obsolete.
- *Access customer planning systems.* The best use of the pull system just described can be attained by gaining direct access to the planning systems of key customers. Doing so allows the company to base its production planning on the actual requirements of customers, rather than guesstimates

of what they may order. The result should be a reduction in the amount of finished goods inventory.

- *Concentrate machinery.* Reconfigure the production area so that machines are as close together as possible. Doing so reduces the amount of work-in-process inventory that is in transit between the machines. Ideally, the equipment layout can be configured into production cells, so that a worker can walk a single unit of production through multiple work stations for processing, thereby eliminating the bulk of all inventory used in the production area.

- *Install conveyors.* Once production equipment has been placed close together, install conveyor belts between them. By doing so, there is no need to let outgoing inventory pile up next to each machine and then be transported on a pallet to the next machine. Instead, inventory flows in units of one, which reduces the overall inventory requirement.

- *Minimize production runs.* Schedule very small production runs, preferably only large enough to accommodate existing customer orders. Otherwise, excessive production will result in finished goods that may sit in the warehouse for some time before being sold (which also increases the risk of obsolescence).

- *Minimize machine setup times.* It is much easier to have the short production runs just described if it takes only a few moments to reconfigure a machine to manufacture a different product. Setup time reduction involves videotaping the current setup process and then examining the process to see which steps can be eliminated, reduced, or performed in parallel with other tasks. Some setup time can be eliminated just by storing materials and tools adjacent to machines.

Fulfillment

There are many methods in use for fulfilling customer orders that can minimize the total amount of inventory kept on hand. Consider the following alternatives:

- *Allow backorders.* The senior management of a company may want to provide superior customer service by always maintaining large stocks of merchandise. Doing so likely increases sales and customer satisfaction, but at the cost of maintaining a large investment in inventory and absorbing significant obsolete inventory charges. Instead, consider a careful reduction of merchandise levels to reduce the cost of inventory, balanced against a reasonable amount of backorders. This decision hinges on how the company treats its customers, and is not to be taken lightly.

- *Delay final assembly.* If a company has many products that are slight variations on each other, build inventory only to the point at which the variations are added to the products, and then complete the products once customer orders arrive. By doing so, one can avoid having committed too much of an investment in finished goods for very specific product variations that then sit in the warehouse until an order arrives.

- *Concentrate slow-order items in storage.* If there are a large number of warehouses, only store high-turnover finished goods in them, while retaining slow-moving items in a central location. This is a balancing act of minimizing the inventory of slow-moving items by storing a small number of them in one place, while also paying more for overnight deliveries to continue to deliver them to customers in a timely manner.
- *Use drop shipping.* If a company is selling goods to customers that are made entirely by its suppliers, pass the customer orders to the suppliers and ask them to ship the goods directly to the customers. Some suppliers that only deal with bulk orders will not consent to drop shipping, so this approach may not work in all situations.
- *Impose a restocking fee.* Customers may want to return goods to the company. If so, the company may have to test and repackage the goods, or possibly re-sell them as used goods at a lower price. To mitigate these costs, impose a restocking fee on customers, which usually takes the form of a reduced credit allowed on their returns.

Distribution

The manner in which inventory is delivered to customers can have a significant impact on the amount of distribution costs incurred. Here are several alternatives:

- *Fill trucks on return.* If the company makes deliveries using its own trucks, consider arranging with other businesses to pick up their goods for the return trip. Doing so allows the company to generate revenue from its truck fleet, rather than moving empty trailers around the country after delivering to customers. This approach requires additional overhead for the staff needed to arrange for the return truckloads, and so is not normally cost-effective unless there are a number of trucks on long-haul routes that can generate a sufficient amount of revenue.
- *Improve fleet mileage.* Pay attention to all possible enhancements to the mileage costs of the company fleet. Slightly better miles per gallon or lower engine maintenance costs can make a substantial difference when the fleet is driving over long distances. This is less of an issue for short-haul or local deliveries.
- *Ship slow.* If a customer does not care about the delivery date, there is no need to exceed expectations by using an overnight delivery service. Instead, use the delivery service that most closely matches the delivery date expected by the customer. However, do not use delivery services that have unusually variable delivery times; in these cases, customers may be unpleasantly surprised by an occasional extremely long delivery.
- *Use regional warehousing.* If the company is spending an inordinate amount shipping to all parts of the country from a central warehouse

location, it could make more sense to selectively stock some items from regional warehouses. Doing so cuts the cost of transportation, but increases the cost of facilities and inventory holding costs. Consequently, this concept should be modeled regularly to position warehouses in relation to the locations and ordering patterns of customers.

- *Wait to fill truckloads.* If customers are not especially picky about when they need to receive goods from the company, hold off on delivering shipments until a full truckload can be achieved. Doing so greatly reduces the total number of truckloads leaving the warehouse. Conversely, if customers are picky about delivery dates, then be sure to charge extra for this service.

Inventory Disposition

Some inventory items will inevitably become obsolete, in which case the main objective is to dispose of the goods at the highest possible price. The following techniques can be used to properly dispose of inventory:

- *Ongoing review process.* Obtaining a high price usually requires that obsolete items be identified as soon as possible, since prices decline over time. To assure rapid identification of these items, install a procedure for reviewing the inventory at regular intervals to see if any items are not being used. Also, assign responsibility for their disposition, and install a reporting system for verifying the amounts at which goods were dispositioned.

- *Donate inventory.* There may be cases where inventory cannot be dispositioned for a reasonable price. If so, donate the inventory to a charity and take a tax deduction for the value of the donated items. This is a particularly useful option when inventory items have a short life span. This is only an option when there is taxable income against which the tax deduction can be used.

- *Waste review.* The typical production and warehousing staff is allowed to throw all scrapped, broken, or otherwise unusable inventory items in the dumpster. An alternative is to require that these items first be placed in a review area, and only dropped in the dumpster after a review team has examined the items to determine why they can no longer be used. A result of this review may be process changes that keep waste from occurring, thereby reducing the cost of inventory consumed.

- *Designate service parts.* A company may be tempted to dispose of all units of an inventory item that has been declared obsolete. However, it is possible that customers may have service requests in the future, for which the inventory is needed. If so, it is better to designate an appropriate number of the parts as service parts and retain them in stock. Otherwise, it may be more expensive to procure or build the parts at a later date, and at much greater expense, when requested by a customer.

Inventory Management Practices

An additional consideration is the type and level of management to be applied to inventory. The essential issues are the types of monitoring to be applied to inventory, and the intensity of hands-on inventory management. The key management issues are:

- *Perpetual inventory system.* All inventory items should be tracked using a perpetual inventory system. This approach means that the current unit count is always being updated to reflect every inventory-related transaction, such as receipts, picks, removals due to obsolescence, and so forth. This system provides the basic database of information needed to install the other management improvements noted next.
- *Cycle counting.* Have the warehouse staff count a small portion of the inventory every day, on a rolling basis. The intent of this count is to compare the database record of unit quantities and locations to their actual amounts and locations, so that the inventory records can be corrected. An essential part of this process is an investigation of why each error occurred, which may lead to a procedural improvement to keep an error from arising again.
- *Warehouse management system.* The records derived from the perpetual inventory system just described should be incorporated into a warehouse management system (WMS). A WMS tells the warehouse staff where inventory is located for cycle counting and picking purposes, as well as where empty bins are available for storage purposes. It can also be used to reconfigure inventory storage locations to minimize travel times to and from the most frequently used inventory items. A WMS does not necessarily reduce the investment in inventory, but it does improve the ability of the warehouse staff to monitor and access inventory.
- *Material requirements planning* (MRP). A company may use a "push" system to schedule production (where production planners schedule production based on a forecast). If so, install MRP software to calculate the exact amount of inventory that will be required to produce items. An MRP system incorporates the production schedule, existing inventory on hand, and bill of materials information for the items to be produced to determine which raw materials to order. The system also incorporates supplier lead times to place orders far enough in advance to assure the delivery of raw materials just before production is scheduled to commence. This system can yield a notable decline in on-hand inventory.
- *Review management criteria.* When inventory items are originally set up in the warehouse management system, initial estimates of the ordering lead time and safety stock level are commonly loaded into the warehouse management or MRP system. There should be a scheduled periodic review of these management criteria, to see if the original estimates were correct, or require some adjustment to ensure that inventory levels are appropriate.

Such reviews should be made on an ongoing basis, even for older inventory items, in case supplier delivery times or unit costs have changed.

- *Inventory stratification.* In many organizations, there are far too many different inventory items in stock to give each one a reasonable amount of monitoring attention. Instead, consider stratifying certain segments of the inventory for more or less review. For example, inventory items that have high rates of turnover, or which are planned to be used in the near future, or which are the most expensive can be highlighted at the top of an inventory report and targeted for more intense review than other inventory items that do not fall into these more critical groupings. By doing so, inventory shortfalls can be avoided, as well as excessively large inventory investments.

Summary

The benefits of reducing the investment in inventory are substantial, and can result in remarkable declines in the working capital required by a business. However, many of the recommendations in this chapter involve ongoing staff training, building reconfigurations, new product designs, new procedures, and/or the installation of various types of software – all of which take time. Consequently, inventory reduction should be considered a long-term proposition.

It is also possible to pare away too much inventory. When this happens, any unanticipated disruption to the flow of materials can bring operations to a halt almost immediately, as well as drive away customers. Consequently, be prudent in reducing inventory costs, since there is a lower limit on how far inventory reductions can be taken.

Chapter 21
Capital Budgeting Decisions

Introduction

The decision to purchase a fixed asset is a key part of cost management, since some fixed assets may absorb the bulk of a company's available cash. Given the importance of this decision, a methodology for analyzing fixed asset purchases, called capital budgeting, has been developed.

Capital budgeting is a series of analysis steps followed to justify the decision to purchase an asset, usually including an analysis of the costs, related benefits, and impact on capacity levels of the prospective purchase. In this chapter, we will address the issues to consider when deciding whether to purchase a fixed asset, including constraint analysis, the lease versus buy decision, and post-acquisition auditing.

> **Related Podcast Episodes:** Episodes 45, 144, 145, and 147 of the Accounting Best Practices Podcast discuss throughput analysis, evaluating capital budgeting proposals, capital budgeting with minimal cash, and net present value analysis, respectively. They are available at: **accountingtools.com/podcasts** or **iTunes**

Overview of Capital Budgeting

The normal capital budgeting process is for the management team to request proposals to acquire fixed assets from all parts of the company. Managers respond by filling out a standard request form, outlining what they want to buy and how it will benefit the company. The financial analyst or accountant then assists in reviewing these proposals to determine which are worthy of an investment. Any proposals that are accepted are included in the annual budget, and will be purchased during the next budget year. Fixed assets purchased in this manner also require a certain number of approvals, with more approvals required by increasingly senior levels of management if the sums involved are substantial.

These proposals come from all over the company, and so are likely not related to each other in any way. Also, the number of proposals usually far exceeds the amount of funding available. Consequently, management needs a method for ranking the priority of projects, with the possible result that some proposals are not accepted at all. The traditional method for doing so is net present value (NPV) analysis, which focuses on picking proposals with the largest amount of discounted cash flows.

The trouble with NPV analysis is that it does not account for how an investment might impact the profit generated by the entire system of production; instead, it tends to favor the optimization of specific work centers, which may have no particular impact on overall profitability. Also, the results of NPV are based on the future projections of cash flows, which may be wildly inaccurate. Managers may even tweak their cash flow estimates upward in order to gain project approval, when they know that actual cash flows are likely to be lower. Given these issues, we favor constraint analysis over NPV, though NPV is also discussed later in this chapter.

A better method for judging capital budget proposals is constraint analysis, which focuses on how to maximize use of the bottleneck operation. The bottleneck operation is the most constricted operation in a company; to improve the overall profitability of the company, concentrate all attention on management of that bottleneck. This has a profound impact on capital budgeting, since a proposal should have some favorable impact on that operation in order to be approved.

There are two scenarios under which certain project proposals may avoid any kind of bottleneck or cash flow analysis. The first is a legal requirement to install an item. The prime example is environmental equipment, such as smokestack scrubbers, that are mandated by the government. In such cases, there may be some analysis to see if costs can be lowered, but the proposal *must* be accepted, so it will sidestep the normal analysis process.

The second scenario is when a company wants to mitigate a high-risk situation that could imperil the company. In this case, the emphasis is not on profitability at all, but rather on the avoidance of a situation. If so, the mandate likely comes from top management, so there is little additional need for analysis, other than a review to ensure that the lowest-cost alternative is selected.

A final scenario is when there is a sudden need for a fixed asset, perhaps due to the catastrophic failure of existing equipment, or due to a sudden strategic shift. These purchases can happen at any time, and so usually fall outside of the capital budget's annual planning cycle. It is generally best to require more than the normal number of approvals for these items, so that management is made fully aware of the situation. Also, if there is time to do so, they are worthy of an unusually intense analysis, to see if they really must be purchased at once, or if they can be delayed until the next capital budgeting approval period arrives.

Once all items are properly approved and inserted into the annual budget, this does not end the capital budgeting process. There is a final review just prior to actually making each purchase, with appropriate approval, to ensure that the company still needs each fixed asset.

The last step in the capital budgeting process is to conduct a post-implementation review, in which the actual costs and benefits of each fixed asset are summarized and then compared to the initial projections included in the original application. If the results are worse than expected, this may result in a more in-depth review, with particular attention being paid to avoiding any faulty aspects of the original proposal in future proposals.

Bottleneck Analysis

Under constraint analysis, the key concept is that an entire company acts as a single system, which generates a profit. Under this concept, capital budgeting revolves around the following logic:

1. Nearly all of the costs of the production system do not vary with individual sales; that is, nearly every cost is an operating expense; therefore,
2. Maximize the throughput of the *entire* system in order to pay for the operating expense; and
3. The only way to increase throughput is to maximize the throughput passing through the bottleneck operation.

Consequently, a business should give primary consideration to those capital budgeting proposals that favorably impact the throughput passing through the bottleneck operation. The concept is addressed in greater detail in the Constraint Analysis chapter.

This does not mean that all other capital budgeting proposals will be rejected, since there are a multitude of possible investments that can reduce costs elsewhere in a company, and which are therefore worthy of consideration. However, throughput is more important than cost reduction, since throughput has no theoretical upper limit, whereas costs can only be reduced to zero. Given the greater ultimate impact on profits of throughput over cost reduction, any non-bottleneck proposal is simply not as important.

Net Present Value Analysis

Any capital investment involves an initial cash outflow to pay for it, followed by a mix of cash inflows in the form of revenue, or a decline in existing cash flows that are caused by expense reductions. We can lay out this information in a spreadsheet to show all expected cash flows over the useful life of an investment, and then apply a discount rate that reduces the cash flows to what they would be worth at the present date. This calculation is known as *net present value*.

Net present value is the traditional approach to evaluating capital proposals, since it is based on a single factor – cash flows – that can be used to judge any proposal arriving from anywhere in a company.

EXAMPLE

Milford Sound, a manufacturer of audio equipment, is planning to acquire an asset that it expects will yield positive cash flows for the next five years. Its cost of capital is 10%, which it uses as the discount rate to construct the net present value of the project. The following table shows the calculation:

Year	Cash Flow	10% Discount Factor	Present Value
0	-$500,000	1.0000	-$500,000
1	+130,000	0.9091	+118,183
2	+130,000	0.8265	+107,445
3	+130,000	0.7513	+97,669
4	+130,000	0.6830	+88,790
5	+130,000	0.6209	+80,717
		Net Present Value	-$7,196

The net present value of the proposed project is negative at the 10% discount rate, so Milford should not invest in the project.

In the "10% Discount Factor" column, the factor becomes smaller for periods further in the future, because the discounted value of cash flows are reduced as they progress further from the present day. The discount factor is widely available in textbooks, or can be derived from the following formula:

$$\text{Present value of a future cash flow} = \frac{\text{Future cash flow}}{(1 + \text{Discount rate})^{\text{squared by the number of periods of discounting}}}$$

To use the formula for an example, if we forecast the receipt of $100,000 in one year, and are using a discount rate of 10 percent, then the calculation is:

$$\text{Present value} = \frac{\$100,000}{(1+.10)^1} = \$90,909$$

254

A net present value calculation that truly reflects the reality of cash flows will likely be more complex than the one shown in the preceding example. It is best to break down the analysis into a number of sub-categories, to see exactly when cash flows are occurring and with what activities they are associated. Here are the more common contents of a net present value analysis:

- *Asset purchases.* All of the expenditures associated with the purchase, delivery, installation, and testing of the asset being purchased.
- *Asset-linked expenses.* Any ongoing expenses, such as warranty agreements, property taxes, and maintenance, that are associated with the asset.
- *Contribution margin.* Any incremental cash flows resulting from sales that can be attributed to the project.
- *Depreciation effect.* The asset will be depreciated, and this depreciation shelters a portion of any net income from income taxes, so note the income tax reduction caused by depreciation.
- *Expense reductions.* Any incremental expense reductions caused by the project, such as automation that eliminates direct labor hours.
- *Tax credits.* If an asset purchase triggers a tax credit (such as for a purchase of energy-reduction equipment), then note the credit.
- *Taxes.* Any income tax payments associated with net income expected to be derived from the asset.
- *Working capital changes.* Any net changes in inventory, accounts receivable, or accounts payable associated with the asset. Also, when the asset is eventually sold off, this may trigger a reversal of the initial working capital changes.

By itemizing the preceding factors in a net present value analysis, you can more easily review and revise individual line items.

We have given priority to bottleneck analysis over net present value as the preferred method for analyzing capital proposals, because bottleneck analysis focuses on throughput. The key improvement factor is throughput, since there is no upper limit on the amount of throughput that can be generated, whereas there are only so many operating expenses that can be reduced. This does not mean that net present value should be eliminated as a management tool. It is still quite useful for operating expense reduction analysis, where throughput issues are not involved.

The Payback Method

The simplest and least accurate evaluation technique is the payback method. This approach is still heavily used, because it provides a very fast "back of the envelope" calculation of how soon a company will earn back its investment. This means that it provides a rough measure of how long a company will have its investment at risk, before earning back the original amount expended. There are two ways to calculate the payback period, which are:

1. *Simplified.* Divide the total amount of an investment by the average resulting cash flow. This approach can yield an incorrect assessment, because a proposal with cash flows skewed far into the future can yield a payback period that differs substantially from when actual payback occurs.
2. *Manual calculation.* Manually deduct the forecasted positive cash flows from the initial investment amount, from Year 1 forward, until the investment is paid back. This method is slower, but ensures a higher degree of accuracy.

EXAMPLE

Milford Sound has received a proposal from a manager, asking to spend $1,500,000 on equipment that will result in cash inflows in accordance with the following table:

Year	Cash Flow
1	+$150,000
2	+150,000
3	+200,000
4	+600,000
5	+900,000

The total cash flows over the five-year period are projected to be $2,000,000, which is an average of $400,000 per year. When divided into the $1,500,000 original investment, this results in a payback period of 3.75 years. However, the briefest perusal of the projected cash flows reveals that the flows are heavily weighted toward the far end of the time period, so the results of this calculation cannot be correct.

Instead, run the calculation year by year, deducting the cash flows in each successive year from the remaining investment. The results of this calculation are:

Year	Cash Flow	Net Invested Cash
0		-$1,500,000
1	+$150,000	-1,350,000
2	+150,000	-1,200,000
3	+200,000	-1,000,000
4	+600,000	-400,000
5	+900,000	0

The table indicates that the real payback period is located somewhere between Year 4 and Year 5. There is $400,000 of investment yet to be paid back at the end of Year 4, and there is $900,000 of cash flow projected for Year 5. If the same monthly amount of cash flow is assumed in Year 5, the final payback should be just short of 4.5 years.

The payback method is not overly accurate, does not provide any estimate of how profitable a project may be, and does not take account of the time value of money. Nonetheless, its extreme simplicity makes it a perennial favorite in many companies.

Capital Budget Proposal Analysis

Reviewing a capital budget proposal does not necessarily mean passing judgment on it exactly as presented. A variety of suggestions can be attached to the analysis of the proposal, which management may incorporate into a revised proposal. Here are some examples:

- *Asset capacity*. Does the asset have more capacity than is actually needed under the circumstances? Is there a history of usage spikes that call for extra capacity? Depending on the answers to these questions, consider using smaller assets with less capacity. If the asset is powered, this may also lead to reductions in utility costs, installation costs, and floor space requirements.
- *Asset commoditization*. Wherever possible, avoid custom-designed machinery in favor of standard models that are readily available. By doing so, it is easier to obtain repair parts, and there may even be an aftermarket for disposing of the asset when the company no longer needs it.
- *Asset features*. Managers have a habit of wanting to buy new assets with all of the latest features. Are all of these features really needed? If an asset is being replaced, then it is useful to compare the characteristics of the old and new assets, and examine any differences between the two to see if they are really needed. If the asset is the only model offered by the supplier, would the supplier be willing to strip away some features and offer it at a lower price?
- *Asset standardization*. If a company needs a particular asset in large quantities, then adopt a policy of always buying from the same manufacturer, and preferably only buying the same asset every time. By doing so, the maintenance staff becomes extremely familiar with maintenance requirements, and only has to stock replacement parts for one model.
- *Bottleneck analysis*. As noted earlier in this chapter, assets that improve the amount of throughput in a production operation are usually well worth the investment, while those not impacting the bottleneck require substantially more justification, usually in the direction of reducing operating expenses.
- *Duration of need*. It is possible that a capital purchase is being contemplated because of what may be a short-term spike in demand. If so, a reasonable question is whether that demand will extend over a sufficiently long period to justify the purchase of the asset. If not, it could make more sense to pay overtime for a short period of time during extra shifts, or

outsource the work. If the heightened demand eventually becomes more consistent, that could be a better time to make a capital investment.

- *Extended useful life.* A manager may be applying for an asset replacement simply because the original asset has reached the end of its recommended useful life. But is it really necessary to replace the asset? Consider conducting a formal review of these assets to see if they can still be used for some additional period of time. There may be additional maintenance costs involved, but this will almost certainly be lower than the cost of replacing the asset.

- *Facility analysis.* If a capital proposal involves the acquisition of additional facility space, consider reviewing any existing space to see if it can be compressed, thereby eliminating the need for more space. For example, shift storage items to less expensive warehouse space, shift from offices to more space-efficient cubicles, and encourage employees to work from home or on a later shift. If none of these ideas work, then at least consider acquiring new facilities through a sublease, which tends to require shorter lease terms than a lease arranged with the primary landlord.

- *Monument elimination.* A company may have a large, fixed asset around which the rest of the production area is configured; this is called a monument. If there is a monument, consider adopting a policy of using a larger number of lower-capacity assets. By doing so, you avoid the risk of having a single monument asset go out of service and stopping all production, in favor of having multiple units, among which work can be shifted if one unit fails.

The sponsors of capital proposals frequently do *not* appreciate this additional review of their proposals, since it implies that they did not consider these issues themselves. Nonetheless, the savings can be substantial, and so are well worth the aggravation of dealing with annoyed managers.

The Outsourcing Decision

It may be possible to avoid a capital purchase entirely by outsourcing the work to which it is related. By doing so, the company may be able to eliminate all assets related to the area (rather than acquiring more assets), while the burden of maintaining a sufficient asset base now shifts to the supplier. The supplier may even buy the company's assets related to the area being outsourced. This situation is a well-established alternative for high technology manufacturing, as well as for information technology services, but is likely not viable outside of these areas.

If you are in a situation where outsourcing is a possibility, then the likely cash flows resulting from doing so will be highly favorable for the first few years, as capital expenditures vanish. However, the supplier must also earn a profit and pay for its own infrastructure, so the cost over the long term will probably not vary dramatically from what a company would have experienced if it had kept a functional area in-house. There are three exceptions that can bring about a long-term cost reduction. They are:

- *Excess capacity*. A supplier may have such a large amount of excess capacity already that it does not need to invest further for some time, thereby potentially depressing the costs that it would otherwise pass through to its customers. However, this excess capacity pool will eventually dry up, so it tends to be a short-term anomaly.
- *High volume*. There are some outsourcing situations where the supplier is handling such a massive volume of activity from multiple customers that its costs on a per-unit basis decline below the costs that a company could ever achieve on its own. This situation can yield long-term savings to a company.
- *Low costs*. A supplier may locate its facility and work force in low-cost countries or regions within countries. This can yield significant cost reductions in the short term, but as many suppliers use the same technique, it is driving up costs in all parts of the world. Thus, this cost disparity is useful for a period of time, but is gradually declining as a long-term option.

There are also risks involved in shifting functions to suppliers. First, a supplier may go out of business, leaving the company scrambling to shift work to a new supplier. Second, a supplier may gradually ramp up prices to the point where the company is substantially worse off than if it had kept the function in-house. Third, the company may have so completely purged the outsourced function from its own operations that it is now completely dependent on the supplier, and has no ability to take it back in-house. Fourth, the supplier's service level may decline to the point where it is impairing the ability of the company to operate. And finally, the company may have entered into a multi-year deal, and cannot escape from the arrangement if the business arrangement does not work out. These are significant issues, and must be weighed as part of the outsourcing decision.

The cautions noted here about outsourcing do not mean that it should be avoided as an option. On the contrary, a rapidly growing company that has minimal access to funds may cheerfully hand off multiple operations to suppliers in order to avoid the up-front costs associated with those operations. Outsourcing is less attractive to stable, well-established companies that have better access to capital.

In summary, outsourcing is an attractive option for rapidly growing companies that do not have sufficient cash to pay for capital expenditures, but also carries with it a variety of risks involving shifting key functions to a supplier over which a company may not have a great deal of control.

The Post Installation Review

It is very important to conduct a post installation review of any capital expenditure project, to see if the initial expectations for it were realized. If not, then the results of this review can be used to modify the capital budgeting process to include better information.

Another reason for having a post installation review is that it provides a control over those managers who fill out the initial capital budgeting proposals. If they know there is no post installation review, then they can wildly overstate the projected results of their projects with impunity, just to have them approved. Of course, this control is only useful if it is conducted relatively soon after a project is completed. Otherwise, the responsible manager may have moved on in his career, and can no longer be tied back to the results of his work.

It is even better to begin a post installation review while a project is still being implemented, and especially when the implementation period is expected to be long. This initial review gives senior management a good idea of whether the cost of a project is staying close to its initial expectations. If not, management may need to authorize more vigorous management of the project, scale it back, or even cancel it outright.

If the post implementation review results in the suspicion that a project proposal was unduly optimistic, this brings up the question of how to deal with the responsible manager. At a minimum, the proposal reviews can flag any future proposals by this reviewer as suspect, and worthy of especially close attention. Another option is to tie long-term compensation to the results of these projects. A third possibility is to include the results of these project reviews in personnel reviews, which may lead to a reduction in employee compensation. A really catastrophic result may even be grounds for the termination of the responsible party.

EXAMPLE

Milford Sound has just completed a one-year project to increase the amount of production capacity at its speaker production work center. The original capital budgeting proposal was for an initial expenditure of $290,000, resulting in additional annual throughput of $100,000 per year. The actual result is somewhat different. The analyst's report includes the following text:

> **Findings:** The proposal only contained the purchase price of the equipment. However, since the machinery was delivered from Germany, Milford also incurred $22,000 of freight charges and $3,000 in customs fees. Further, the project required the installation of a new concrete pad, a breaker box, and electrical wiring that cost an additional $10,000. Finally, the equipment proved to be difficult to configure, and required $20,000 of consulting fees from the manufacturer, as well as $5,000 for materials scrapped during testing. Thus, the actual cost of the project was $350,000.

> Subsequent operation of the equipment reveals that it cannot operate without an average of 20% downtime for maintenance, as opposed to the 5% downtime that

was advertised by the manufacturer. This reduces throughput by 15%, which equates to a drop of $15,000 in throughput per year, to $85,000.

Recommendations: To incorporate a more comprehensive set of instructions into the capital budgeting proposal process to account for transportation, setup, and testing costs. Also, given the wide difference between the performance claims of the manufacturer and actual results, to hire a consultant to see if the problem is caused by our installation of the equipment; if not, we recommend not buying from this supplier in the future.

The Lease or Buy Decision

Once the asset acquisition decision has been made, management still needs to decide if it should buy the asset outright or lease it. In a leasing situation, a lessor buys the asset and then allows the lessee to use it in exchange for a monthly fee. The decision to use a lease may be based on management's unwillingness to use its line of credit or other available sources of financing to buy an asset. Leases can be easier to obtain than a line of credit, since the lease agreement always designates the asset as collateral.

There are a multitude of factors that a lessor includes in the formulation of the monthly rate that it charges, such as the down payment, the residual value of the asset at the end of the lease, and the interest rate, which makes it difficult to break out and examine each element of the lease. Instead, it is much easier to create separate net present value tables for the lease and buy alternatives, and then compare the results of the two tables to see which alternative is better.

EXAMPLE

Milford Sound is contemplating the purchase of an asset for $500,000. It can buy the asset outright, or do so with a lease. Its cost of capital is 8%, and its incremental income tax rate is 35%. The following two tables show the net present values of both options.

Buy Option

Year	Depreciation	Income Tax Savings (35%)	Discount Factor (8%)	Net Present Value
0				-$500,000
1	$100,000	$35,000	0.9259	32,407
2	100,000	35,000	0.8573	30,006
3	100,000	35,000	0.7938	27,783
4	100,000	35,000	0.7350	25,725
5	100,000	35,000	0.6806	23,821
Totals	$500,000	$175,000		$360,258

Lease Option

Year	Pretax Lease Payments	Income Tax Savings (35%)	After-Tax Lease Cost	Discount Factor (8%)	Net Present Value
1	$135,000	$47,250	$87,750	0.9259	$81,248
2	135,000	47,250	87,750	0.8573	75,228
3	135,000	47,250	87,750	0.7938	69,656
4	135,000	47,250	87,750	0.7350	64,496
5	135,000	47,250	87,750	0.6806	59,723
Totals	$675,000	$236,250	$438,750		$350,351

Thus, the net purchase cost of the buy option is $360,258, while the net purchase cost of the lease option is $350,351. The lease option involves the lowest cash outflow for Milford, and so is the better option.

Summary

This chapter addressed a variety of issues to consider when deciding whether to purchase a fixed asset. We put less emphasis on net present value analysis, which has been the primary capital budgeting tool in industry for years, because it does not take into consideration the impact on throughput of a company's bottleneck operation. The best capital budgeting analysis process is to give top priority to project proposals that have a strong favorable impact on throughput, and then use net present value to evaluate the impact of any remaining projects on cost reduction.

Chapter 22
Cost Management Reports

Introduction

Any system of cost management requires a detailed reporting system to assist with the identification of cost opportunities, and to give feedback to management regarding its progress in tackling cost issues. In this chapter, we address a number of report formats that can be used to aggregate cost information in such areas as general expenses, payroll, margins, and spend analysis. We also note the concept of responsibility reporting, and provide an introduction to the reporting of a cost reduction matrix.

Related Podcast Episodes: Episodes 65, 148, and 257 of the Accounting Best Practices Podcast discuss responsibility accounting, best practices for accounting reports, and how to present cost control information, respectively. They are available at: **accountingtools.com/podcasts** or **iTunes**

Expense Reporting

The most common cost management report is one concerning expenses incurred in various parts of a business. When issuing this report, do not simply state the expense incurred in the previous period (which is the usual request), since it provides little useful information. Another option is to provide the information in comparison to the budgeted expense for the period, but the budgeted amount could be unrealistic, so the resulting comparison may not be useful. A better approach is to present the information alongside the same expenses incurred in previous periods. Doing so provides a solid basis of comparison, and reveals whether the most recent expenses are in accordance with historical trends. The following sample report shows the concept.

Sample Expense Report Format

	September	October	November	December
Wages	$45,000	$46,500	$47,250	$53,000
Payroll taxes	3,150	3,250	3,300	3,700
Rent	3,500	3,500	3,750	3,750
Office expenses	1,200	1,350	1,400	1,650
Travel and entertainment	800	950	800	4,000
Utilities	620	600	700	750
Other expenses	450	425	470	510
Totals	$54,720	$56,575	$57,670	$67,360

The sample shows the expenses incurred by a typical department. Wage expense is listed at the top of the report, since this expense is frequently the largest one incurred by many departments; other expenses are listed in declining order by the amounts usually incurred. Thus, the reader's attention is drawn to the top of the report, where most of the expenses are located. Also, the presentation of side-by-side results by month makes it easy for the report recipient to skim through the report and make note of anything that rises above or falls below the long-term average.

A possible approach to reporting is to only report expenses by exception. Thus, the preceding sample expense report might trigger an accompanying explanation that the change in office rent in November was triggered by a new lease, while the surge in the travel and entertainment expense in December was caused by the company's Christmas party. This additional level of reporting centers the attention of management on the key expense exceptions, while ignoring all expenses that do not change.

Better yet, go one step further and make recommendations regarding how to make changes to expenses. Here are examples of such commentary:

- "The rent expense is 20% above the rents for similar buildings within one mile of the company facility; recommend negotiating with the landlord to drop the lease rate in exchange for extending the term of the lease."
- "Telephone expenses can be reduced by 15% if the company adopts a single cell phone carrier for all employees."
- "Travel expenses can be reduced by 5% if the company adopts a common travel agent for all company travel."

Payroll Reporting

There are two principle types of payroll reports from a cost management perspective, which are trend reports and annualized cost reports. A trend report targets sudden bumps in pay, which may call for investigation to see if overtime was authorized. The following report focuses on overtime pay in each time period.

Sample Overtime Trend Report

Name	Jan. 7	Jan. 14	Jan. 21	Jan. 28	Feb. 4
			Week of		
Brett, J.	$0	$30	$0	$312	$0
Horton, M.	23	19	41	230	22
Indie, J.	0	0	30	185	0
Masters, K.	7	12	0	214	0
Totals	$30	$61	$71	$941	$22

The sample report indicates two issues. First, the company is spending an inordinate amount during the last week of the month on overtime, which may indicate a variety of problems with jamming shipments into the final week of each month. Second, there is an employee (Mr. Horton) who is consistently taking a small amount of overtime every week; this amount is so small that it may be escaping the attention of his supervisor, but the amount can add up over time.

The other type of payroll report is concerned with the total cost of an employee and incorporates all expenditures related to a person. This report is more difficult to compile, and so is usually assembled only on an annual basis. The report can reveal that certain employees are much more expensive than their base pay might initially indicate. A sample employee total cost report follows.

Sample Employee Total Cost Report

Name	Base Pay	Overtime	Taxes	Pension	Medical	Phone	Total
Abrahams	$42,500	$16,000	$5,200	$4,000	$5,500	$0	$73,200
Duran	120,000	0	10,800	12,000	3,200	1,000	147,000
Neederly	29,000	0	2,600	500	0	0	32,100
Quintana	60,500	23,000	7,500	6,000	6,700	850	104,550
Totals	$252,000	$39,000	$26,100	$22,500	$15,400	$1,850	$356,850

The preceding total cost report is designed to show a typical mix of expenditure levels. In the report, there are several employees who are clearly being paid hourly wages, and who heavily supplement these wages with overtime, resulting in a much higher total compensation level than their base pay would initially indicate. There are also large differences in the expenditure level for medical insurance, ranging from zero for those not taking this option to very high expenditures for what are presumably the company-paid portions of family medical insurance.

Margin Reporting

Management will likely make inquiries about the earnings that the company is achieving in such areas as customers, products, product lines, stores, and operating units. If the chart of accounts has been constructed to accumulate information for any of these categories, it should be possible to provide the requested information. However, here are several issues to consider regarding the construction of margin reports:

- *Cost allocations.* It is rarely advisable to allocate overhead costs in a margin report. By doing so, the reported margin on every line item in the report is being artificially reduced, which may lead to management shutting down products, product lines, stores, or divisions that actually have adequate profit margins. See the Cost Object Analysis chapter for more information.
- *Automation.* If a margin report proves to be valuable, take all possible steps to automate it. For example, if management wants to see a margin report by product, create standard costs for the direct costs associated with each product, include those standard costs in the margin report, and set up a process for routinely reviewing how closely the standard costs match actual costs.

Perhaps the most common of all margin reports is one that details the margin for individual products during a particular time period. When creating this report, only include those costs that vary directly with changes in unit volume; this usually means that only the cost of materials is included in the report, since manufacturing overhead and direct labor costs do not vary at the unit level. A sample product margin report is shown next.

Sample Product Margin Report

	Revenue	Units Sold	×	Standard Cost of Materials	=	Total Cost of Materials	Margin $
French press	$180,000	900		$90.00		$81,000	$99,000
Moka pot	62,000	380		73.25		27,835	34,165
Percolator pro	220,000	1,500		66.00		99,000	121,000
Roaster home edition	470,000	3,760		56.50		212,440	257,560
Roaster junior	100,000	1,100		40.90		44,990	55,010
Roaster pro	250,000	800		140.00		112,000	138,000
Vacuum coffee maker	123,000	300		184.50		55,350	67,650
Totals	$1,405,000	8,740				$632,615	$772,385

Another possible addition to the product margin report is the cost of commissions (if any), since they usually vary directly with unit sales. See the Cost Object Analysis chapter for other discussions of relevant product costs.

If a company has a number of similar products that are aggregated into a product line, there may be a request to determine the margin associated with the entire product line. When constructing this report, more expenses can be included than just the cost of materials, since other expense types may be directly associated with the product line. The following expenses might be included:

- *Advertising.* This is the cost of any advertising or other marketing expenses related to the product line in question.
- *Engineering.* There may be a dedicated team of engineers involved with the design of only those products included in the product line. Only include those engineering compensation and other costs that would disappear if the product line were to be cancelled.
- *Manufacturing overhead.* There may be a large amount of overhead cost associated with a product line, such as a production manager, equipment maintenance, and utilities. Only include those costs that would disappear if the product line were to be cancelled.
- *Selling expenses.* There may be a dedicated sales force that only sells the product line. Their compensation, payroll taxes, and travel and entertainment expenses should be included.

Again, see the Cost Object Analysis chapter for more information. A sample product line margin report that includes the preceding expense elements is shown below.

Sample Product Line Margin Report

Product Line	Revenue	Direct Materials	Engineering	Overhead	Sales and Marketing	Margin
Home products	$800,000	$320,000	$65,000	$165,000	$130,000	$120,000
Restaurant products	390,000	156,000	82,000	80,000	40,000	32,000
School products	640,000	320,000	39,000	128,000	90,000	63,000
Totals	$1,830,000	$796,000	$186,000	$373,000	$260,000	$215,000

The same format just shown for a product line works well for a margin report constructed for a retail location, though you should replace the engineering, overhead, and sales and marketing costs with expenses that would terminate if the store were closed, such as:

- *Wages and payroll taxes.* This is the compensation and related payroll taxes that would disappear if the store were closed. Thus, you would not include an apportionment of the cost of a regional store manager.
- *Advertising.* There may be advertising expenses related to a specific location. Do not include advertising if the expenditures are for a group of stores.

- *Rent.* This is the rent that would be eliminated if a store were closed. Do not include it if the company must still pay rent even if the store closes.
- *Utilities.* There are usually some electrical and heating costs that would be eliminated as a result of a store closure.

A sample store margin report that includes the preceding expense elements appears in the following exhibit.

Sample Store Margin Report

Store Location	Revenue	Direct Materials	Wages	Advertising	Other Expenses	Margin
Evanston	$900,000	$360,000	$270,000	$25,000	$200,000	$45,000
Freeport	1,050,000	420,000	270,000	25,000	230,000	105,000
Muncie	820,000	328,000	270,000	20,000	190,000	12,000
Totals	$2,770,000	$1,108,000	$810,000	$70,000	$620,000	$162,000

If you are asked to create a margin report for customers, be extremely careful about adding any expenses to the report. The reason is that most expenses related to the servicing of customers are incurred for *many* customers, not just one. For example, it would be unwise to include in a margin report the labor cost associated with the customer service or field service calls related to a specific customer, because those costs are likely to still exist even if the customer were to be terminated. However, it is acceptable to include other costs in a customer margin analysis, such as:

- *Commissions.* Include salesperson commissions related to a specific customer.
- *Deductions.* Include deductions taken by customers when paying their invoices.

Again, see the Cost Object Analysis chapter for more information about costs relating to specific customers. A sample customer margin report that includes the preceding expense elements is shown next.

Sample Customer Margin Report

Customer Name	Revenue	Direct Materials	Commissions	Deductions	Margin
Gadzooks Coffee	$95,000	$48,000	$4,000	$13,000	$30,000
Kona Distributors	130,000	70,000	5,000	32,000	23,000
Marlowe Coffee	247,000	136,000	10,000	20,000	81,000
Peaberry Coffee	86,000	41,000	3,000	1,000	41,000
Totals	$558,000	$295,000	$22,000	$66,000	$175,000

The preceding customer margin report reveals a common issue that triggers the request to develop the report – there are substantial differences in the amount of payment deductions taken by customers. In the sample, the second-largest customer, Kona Distributors, takes such large deductions that it is the least profitable of the customers listed in the report.

As can be seen from the various sample margin reports presented here, be careful to *only* include those expenses in the analysis that would be eliminated if the subject of the report were to be terminated. All other expenses are irrelevant, and so should not be included.

Spend Reporting

When the purchasing department decides to aggregate its spending with a smaller number of suppliers, it needs several reports that give feedback on its progress in driving down costs. One of these reports measures the amount actually paid for parts in comparison to contract prices. The report only highlights negative variances, and ideally includes supplier contact information, so that the purchasing staff can contact suppliers immediately to point out the problem. A sample report of this type follows.

Sample Contract Compliance Report

Supplier	Invoice Number	Invoice Date	Item Billed	Billed Price	Contract Price	Extended Variance
A.C. Bolton, Inc.	32879	1/04/X1	Green widgets	$13.50	$13.00	$1,412
Barlow Inc.	4801	1/07/X1	Square holes	42.10	39.95	815
Orton Ltd.	11589	1/02/X1	Smoke shifters	23.25	19.95	3,045
Smith Brothers	8824	1/12/X1	Snipe detectors	81.95	75.45	209
					Total	$5,481

When the purchasing manager is engaged in the rollout of a spend management program, it is useful to review spend results from a high level, to see how much of the total corporate spend is being directed toward preferred suppliers. The following report achieves this by itemizing all spend by commodity code, and noting for each commodity the amount of total spend and the amount of spend already directed to preferred suppliers. There could be an additional report layer that identifies the amount of spend sent to *each* preferred supplier, as well as the types of spend that are not currently being sourced with preferred suppliers.

Sample Spend Distribution Report

NAICS Code	Commodity Description	Total YTD Spend	Preferred Supplier Spend	Percent of Total Spend
322212	Folding paperboard box	$1,440,000	$950,000	66%
323113	Commercial screen printing	685,000	420,000	61%
325520	Adhesives	320,000	100,000	31%
325910	Printing ink	1,850,000	1,200,000	65%
333316	Photographic equipment	295,000	60,000	20%
	Totals	$4,590,000	$2,730,000	59%

A selection of the information in the spend distribution report can also be stated on a trend line, to show progress toward a greater concentration of spending with preferred suppliers. If so, there could be an additional report layer that identifies the amount of spend with each supplier in a commodity category. A sample trend line report follows.

Sample Spend Trend Line Report

		Percent of Spend with Preferred Suppliers			
NAICS Code	Commodity Description	First Quarter	Second Quarter	Third Quarter	Fourth Quarter
322212	Folding paperboard box	55%	60%	63%	66%
323113	Commercial screen printing	72%	71%	67%	61%
325520	Adhesives	0%	0%	15%	31%
325910	Printing ink	22%	31%	48%	65%
333316	Photographic equipment	5%	8%	19%	20%

The sample report reveals a general improvement in the concentration of spend over time, with the notable exception of the commercial screen printing commodity, where the concentration of spending has declined, and which therefore should receive a detailed review.

Responsibility Reporting

Responsibility reporting is based on the assumption that every cost incurred must be the responsibility of one person somewhere in the company. For example, the cost of rent can be assigned to the person who negotiates and signs the lease, while the cost of an employee's salary is the responsibility of that person's direct manager. This concept also applies to the cost of products, for each component part has a standard cost, which it is the responsibility of the purchasing manager to obtain at the correct price. Similarly, scrap costs incurred at a machine are the responsibility of the shift manager.

Ideally, responsibility reports should only contain information about controllable costs. These are the costs that the recipient of a report can take action to adjust. Thus, a responsibility report should not include a cost allocation, on the grounds that any such allocation is out of the control of the recipient. If management insists on including non-controllable costs in a responsibility report, they should at least be separated from the other costs and clearly labeled as non-controllable.

As you move upward through the organizational structure, it is common to find fewer responsibility reports being used. This is because there is a natural progression of reports that aggregate the information going to higher levels of authority. The aggregation is based on the following concepts:

1. *Cost center.* A cost center only has control over the costs incurred, and not revenues, profitability, or invested funds. There can be many cost centers, such as for a specific machine, an administrative task, or a building lease. Cost center reports can be sent to a large proportion of employees.

2. *Profit center.* A profit center is responsible for both a set of costs and the revenue that those costs generate. This report tends to encompass a number of cost centers. There are far fewer profit centers than cost centers, and there are correspondingly fewer profit center reports issued.

3. *Investment center.* An investment center is a profit center whose manager is also responsible for investing funds back into the business. One investment center can incorporate several profit centers, so very few of these reports are issued.

By using this approach, cost reports can be tailored for each recipient. For example, the manager of a work cell will receive a financial statement that only itemizes the costs incurred by that specific cell, whereas the production manager will receive a different one that itemizes the costs of the entire production department, and the president will receive one that summarizes the results of the entire organization.

Cost Reduction Opportunity Reporting

All of the preceding reports have been related to a rehashing of costs that have already been incurred, and which are merely being sliced and diced to arrive at the most palatable form of consumption. But what if the intent is to itemize actions that will reduce costs in the future? If so, one of the better presentations of this information is a simple grid on which cost management activities can be categorized as either having a high or low cost impact, and the level of difficulty required to implement them. The concept is noted in the following example.

Sample Cost Reduction Matrix

	High Cost Impact	Low Cost Impact
Easy Implementation	Cancel endorsement contract Close Iowa facility Outsource IT Savings = $1.8 million	Cut travel budget Freeze pay Outsource payroll Savings = $200,000
Difficult Implementation	Revise product designs Consolidate foreign operations Change to new facility Savings = $1.2 million	Alter production layout Move programmers offshore Savings = $300,000

It is easiest to maintain this matrix manually, rather than as a formal report, since potential projects will move around on the report with great frequency.

Summary

The nature of the cost reports used will likely change over time. For example, management may initially decide to "dive deep" on compensation costs, and will request a number of detailed reports in this area, which may result in the imposition of multiple cost controls. After that project is complete, management no longer needs such comprehensive reporting in the payroll area, and instead opts for a simple payroll exception report to highlight cost spikes, while turning its attention to a more detailed analysis of another part of the business. Consequently, do not expect to develop and then lock in a set of standard cost management reports that will be essentially unchanged. Or, if this *is* the case, it probably indicates that management is no longer committing significant time to probing company operations in search of cost reductions.

An additional tool for cost management is the use of ratios and other forms of measurement; these concepts are addressed in the next chapter, *Cost Management Measurements*.

Chapter 23
Cost Management Measurements

Introduction

One of the better ways to manage costs is to constantly monitor them through a group of performance measurements. By regularly reporting this information to management, it is much more likely that active interest will be taken in costs – especially if these measurements are also tied to employee bonuses.

We have provided a set of measurements that relate to the cost topics in most of the preceding chapters for specific functional areas and asset types. There are a large number of possible measurements that could be suggested, so we have limited the measurements to a maximum of three per category, in order to focus attention on the most effective measurements.

Related Podcast Episode: Episodes 222, 234, and 250 of the Accounting Best Practices Podcast discuss the best way to report performance measurements, how to find the right metrics, and the burn rate, respectively. They are available at: **accountingtools.com/podcasts** or **iTunes**

Compensation Measurements

Compensation expense is one of the largest costs, and so is worthy of a significant amount of measurement. In this section, we propose the use of profitability per person, which is particularly useful in an organization with a high ratio of headcount to sales. Also, we suggest tracking the proportion of pay at risk, with the intent of having more compensation coming from company results. Doing so should create a notable amount of employee interest in the performance of the business. Finally, in cases where the cost of employee turnover is high, consider the use of employee turnover as a percentage of total headcount as yet another key metric.

Profit per Person

Measuring the amount of profit per person is a substantially better alternative than sales per person, since the sales per person figure does not incorporate the expense portion of the income statement. Profit per person, on the other hand, measures both the ability to generate sales and the ability to convert those sales into profits.

The main failing of the profit per person measurement is that it can be skewed by shifting work to outside contractors or by outsourcing tasks to third parties. The first issue can be corrected by adding the contractor headcount back into the calculation. However, the use of outsourcing completely shifts work outside of the company and cannot be tracked. Thus, if someone wanted to increase the profit per person metric, perhaps to earn a bonus, one option would be to outsource, even if the outcome were not favorable to the business. Consequently, this measure is useful for tracking the effectiveness of an organization, but should not be used as the basis for a bonus payment.

The calculation of profit per person is profits divided by the full-time equivalent headcount for both in-house employees and contractors. The formula is:

$$\frac{\text{Net after-tax profit}}{\text{Full-time equivalent employees + Full-time equivalent contractors}}$$

EXAMPLE

Jonathan Lucre is the president of Nefarious Industries. The board of directors is concerned that the company's headcount appears to be too high, and so offers him a bonus if he can improve the company's current profitability from $5,000 per employee to $10,000 per employee. The company currently has 50 people on staff. Mr. Lucre decides to outsource the company's entire production department despite the higher cost of doing so, which yields the following outcome:

	Before	After
Total additional production expense	--	$100,000
Total profitability	$250,000	$150,000
Total headcount	50	15
Profit per person	$5,000	$10,000

In short, Mr. Lucre earns his bonus by manipulating the numbers to arrive at a lower net profit for the business, rather than by improving the overall efficiency of the organization.

Proportion of Pay at Risk

There are many cases where the entire workforce is receiving a flat compensation package that does not give employees an interest in business performance. Also, a flat compensation package is frequently increased based on inflation every year, whereas a performance-based compensation component is not. Accordingly, consider measuring the proportion of pay at risk for employees.

This measure can be subdivided in a number of ways. One option is by department, since management may decide that some areas (such as administration) have less impact on profits, and so should share in only a small amount of it. Another variation is to measure it only by job classification, for the same reason. A third measurement possibility is to measure based on projected outcome, such as compensation being based on high, medium, and low estimates of variable pay outcomes. And finally, the measurement could simply be on a historical basis, showing the proportion of variable pay that was actually paid out. The basic calculation for all of these variations is:

$$\frac{\text{Variable compensation}}{\text{Variable compensation} + \text{Wage and salary compensation}}$$

EXAMPLE

The new president of Currency Bank wants all members of the bank to participate in company profits, in order to turn the focus of the organization toward selling high-profit services to customers, and improving customer service. The profit sharing pool is 20% of company profits, and is paid out to everyone based on their base pay. Full profits for the year were $1,000,000, of which $200,000 was therefore paid out in profits. The total wage and salary compensation paid during the year was $3,800,000, resulting in the following proportion of pay at risk calculation:

$$\frac{\$200,000 \text{ Variable compensation}}{\$200,000 \text{ Variable compensation} + \$3,800,000 \text{ Wage and salary compensation}} = 5\% \text{ Proportion of pay at risk}$$

Employee Turnover

A high level of employee turnover is usually considered harmful to a business, since institutional knowledge and experience are lost when large numbers of employees leave. Also, their replacements require extra training time, and so are not as efficient as their predecessors for their first few months on the job. Thus, employee turnover is one of the higher-rated metrics that managers want to examine.

It may be useful to focus the employee turnover measurement on those parts of the business where employee replacement costs are extremely high, such as in the engineering department, rather than merely adopting a company-wide measure. Doing so more tightly focuses management attention on areas where there is a demonstrable profit decline associated with high turnover.

The calculation of employee turnover is to divide the number of departed full-time equivalents in the measurement period by the average number of full-time equivalent personnel on staff during that period. The formula is:

$$\frac{\text{Number of departed full-time equivalents}}{\text{Average number of full-time equivalents on staff}}$$

EXAMPLE

Oberlin Acoustics suffers from a 15% employee turnover rate in its production department. While some of the staff in this area can be readily replaced with minimal training, other areas call for lengthy training periods that can last for more than a year. The human resources manager of Oberlin develops the following employee turnover calculation for the past year for each part of the production process:

	Wood Stamping	Wood Curing	Body Construction	Wood Inlay	Seal and Varnish
Employee departures	8	4	6	5	5
Total headcount	32	16	65	43	12
Turnover percentage	25%	25%	9%	12%	42%
Months of training	2	3	24	30	3

The table reveals that by far the most critical areas in which to monitor employee turnover are in the body construction and wood inlay areas, where the months of training required for a new employee are massively higher than for the other production areas. Thus, Oberlin should concentrate its retention activities and expenditures in these two areas.

This measurement can be manipulated by shifting work to outsourcing firms and contractors, which reduces the headcount that would otherwise be included in the calculation.

Benefits Measurements

The cost of benefits can be quite high, and yet there are not many effective measurements to track this cost. We suggest the ratio of benefits to base pay as the primary measurement, to give management a general feel for the extent of benefit expenditures. Also, consider tracking the extent of employee cost sharing as a proportion of their base pay, which can be a cause of increased employee turnover. In addition, we have included a non-financial metric, which is days away from work. This last measure could be important if employee sicknesses keep they away from work for extended periods of time, which results in significant amounts of lost productivity.

Benefits to Base Pay Ratio

If management is intent upon achieving a reduction in the benefits expense, it should track the progress of this project with the benefits to base pay ratio. The measurement should be reviewed on a trend line, to see if there are any expense spikes that require additional attention from management.

The basic calculation is to divide the net benefits expenditure in each reporting period by the base pay for the same period. The benefits expenditure in the numerator should be net of any deductions from employee pay for benefits. Also, the denominator should not include any one-time payments, such as bonuses, profit sharing, or stock grants that might unexpectedly water down the effect of the ratio. The formula is:

$$\frac{\text{Benefits expenditures} - \text{Deductions from employee pay}}{\text{Wage and salary expense}}$$

What this ratio does not show is the effect of any tweaking of the benefit package to redirect benefits to those areas of greatest interest to employees. Thus, it is possible to have the ratio decline or remain steady over time, while employee satisfaction with the plan *increases*. For the same reason, it is dangerous to compare this ratio with the same measurement for a competing firm, since the other business may not be doing such a good job of applying funds spent to the benefits that employees want the most.

EXAMPLE

Finchley Fireworks currently spends 22% of employee base pay on benefits. The benefits package is a mix of pension, disability, vision, medical, and life insurance benefits. The work force is young and largely unmarried, and when surveyed, it turns out that they attach no value to the life insurance and pension components of the benefits. The CEO has mandated a 2% decline in the cost of benefits. The human resources manager elects to manage the situation by terminating the pension plan, making life insurance 100% payable by employees, and increasing medical benefits – all while reducing the expense from 22% to 20% of base pay. The result appears in the following table, net of all deductions from employee pay:

(annualized information)	Before	After
Pension cost	$130,000	--
Disability cost	80,000	$80,000
Vision cost	20,000	20,000
Medical cost	620,000	700,000
Life insurance cost	30,000	--
Total benefits expense	$880,000	$800,000
Base pay	$4,000,000	$4,000,000
Benefits to base pay ratio	22%	20%

Employee Cost Sharing as Percent of Pay

One option for reducing the benefits cost for a business is to shift some of the burden to employees by making deductions from their paychecks. However, it is of some importance to understand the full amount of these deductions, which at some point may drive employees away, either increasing employee turnover or dissatisfaction.

The basic calculation for employee cost sharing as a percent of pay is as the name implies. It may make sense to further subdivide the measurement for those employees taking each of the classifications of benefits, such as family benefits or single benefits. Typically, those taking family benefits will have a much higher cost sharing percentage than those taking single benefits, depending on how the company apportions benefit costs to employees. Accordingly, it may make sense to track this measurement *and* employee turnover by benefits classification, to see if those paying for higher family cost sharing are more likely to leave the company.

The formula for employee cost sharing as a percent of pay is:

$$\frac{\text{Annualized deductions from employee pay for benefits}}{\text{Annualized base pay}}$$

EXAMPLE

Suture Corporation has a highly-trained staff that engages in the electronic remediation of cancer. Many of these employees are married, and a number of them are starting families. The company currently pays for 80% of all *employee* benefits and half of the incremental additional cost for other family members, which results in significantly higher cost sharing by married employees. The human resources director of Suture derives the following table that shows the cost sharing percentage for each group of employees, as well as the turnover rate for each group.

	Single	Married	Single Parent with Children	Married with Children
Cost sharing as percent of pay	8%	12%	14%	21%
Employee turnover	5%	7%	9%	15%

The combination of high cost sharing for those employees with children and their turnover rates might cause management to rethink its cost sharing formula.

Days Away from Work

When employees are away from work due to sickness, there can be a significant decline in productivity within the firm. By measuring days away from work over a long period of time, one can discern how well the company's preventive care activities and its chosen healthcare providers are reducing time away from the office. A large organization with many employees could use this metric as the basis for working with healthcare providers to give its employees same-day access to care, as well as to judge how well employee conditions are being resolved.

It is difficult to turn the concept of days away from work into a single useful number, since it is excessively aggregated. Instead, days away from work can be tracked at a more detailed level. For example, a company might offer on-site flu shots, and then tracks how this service impacts days away from work that are specifically caused by flu-related illnesses. This means it will be necessary to track more information than simply the number of employee days away due to sickness; it will also be necessary to track the specific cause of sickness, the amount of time required for the employee to be treated, and the name of the provider (if this is allowed under the applicable patient privacy laws).

Sales Measurements

The traditional focus in the sales area is on the ability of a salesperson to generate sales dollars. However, since this is a top-line item in the income statement that does not necessarily relate to profitability, we instead suggest that sales productivity be the key measure, along with the ancillary sales effectiveness measurement. Sales productivity is best derived at the department level, and compares profitability to selling expenditures. Finally, we suggest the more specialized quote to close metric, which is only used in more complex sales environments where formal quotes are issued to customers.

Sales Productivity

Sales productivity is the ability of the sales staff to generate profitable sales. A profitable sale is considered to be one that has a high throughput, where throughput is sales minus all totally variable expenses. We do not measure the sales generated by the sales staff, since there may be little throughput associated with those sales.

To calculate sales productivity, divide the total estimated throughput booked by the sales staff by the total sales department expense incurred. The formula is:

$$\frac{\text{Total sales booked} - \text{All variable expenses associated with sales booked}}{\text{Total sales department expenses}}$$

EXAMPLE

The president of Armadillo Security Armor is concerned that the sales department is not being overly productive in booking new sales. He has the company controller accumulate the following information:

	January	February	March
Bookings	$4,200,000	$4,315,000	$4,520,000
Related variable expenses	$1,470,000	$1,726,000	$2,034,000
Throughput percentage	65%	60%	55%
Sales expenses	$250,000	$260,000	$265,000
Sales productivity	10.9x	10.0x	9.4x

The analysis reveals that the sales staff is increasing sales, but giving away margin in order to do so. The result is an ongoing decline in the department's sales productivity. It would be better to book fewer sales at higher margins, thereby generating more profit for the company.

Sales productivity should be judged over multiple periods, since some sales can take several reporting periods to finalize, and so might yield a measurement that spikes and slumps from month to month. Also, the measurement correlates with the experience level of the sales staff, so expect it to decline immediately after new sales employees are hired.

Sales Effectiveness

The preceding sales productivity measurement is useful for tracking the total amount of throughput generated, but does not track the amount of time required at the company's bottleneck operation to generate that throughput. If sales are made that require lots of processing time at the bottleneck, then a company will soon find itself unable to process additional orders. The sales effectiveness measurement is designed to monitor bottleneck usage in new orders. The measurement is used as feedback for the sales staff, which can be encouraged to have customers order those goods generating the largest amount of throughput per minute of bottleneck processing time.

To calculate sales effectiveness, divide the total throughput for all orders booked in a period by the total minutes of processing time required for these orders at the bottleneck operation. The formula is:

$$\frac{\text{Total sales booked} - \text{All variable expenses associated with sales booked}}{\text{Total minutes of bottleneck processing time required}}$$

EXAMPLE

Horton Corporation manufactures widgets. The CFO wants to focus more sales attention on the company's new olive widget, introduced in February, which generates $25.00 of throughput per minute of bottleneck processing time. This rate is significantly higher than the average throughput per minute of Horton's other widget products. The following table notes the effect of the new product on sales effectiveness, with a notable increase in the metric occurring in the final month.

	January	February	March
Throughput booked	$910,000	$868,500	$1,014,300
Bottleneck minutes	50,000	45,000	49,000
Average throughput/minute	$18.20	$19.30	$20.70

* Note that the amount *booked* in each month does not necessarily equate to the number of minutes of bottleneck processing time available in that month.

Quote to Close Ratio

In an environment where the sales process requires the issuance of a formal quote on a competitive basis, the quote to close ratio is valuable for determining the ability of the sales staff to convince a customer to accept a quote. A high performance ratio can indicate a combination of excellent quote writing ability, product quality, and product demonstration skill. Conversely, if few quotes are leading to customer orders, then the same factors must be investigated to see where the problem lies.

EXAMPLE

The sales manager of Milford Sound believes that the company's recent revamping of its quote-writing unit has improved sales. Accordingly, he asks the company's financial analyst to prepare a quote to close ratio for each of the last four quarters. The following results indicate that sales have indeed risen.

	1st Quarter	2nd Quarter	3rd Quarter	4th Quarter
Sales booked	$12,000,000	$12,500,000	$14,000,000	$17,000,000
Sales quoted	$54,500,000	$62,500,000	$56,000,000	$58,600,000
Quote to close ratio	22%	20%	25%	29%

An issue to be aware of is that the quote to close ratio only measures sales booked, not throughput booked. Thus, it is possible that an increase in the ratio could be caused by lower price points that give away profits.

Production and Maintenance Measurements

A massive number of production measurements have been developed, but tracking them all tends to divert attention from the constrained resource in the production area, which is the true source of profitability. Consequently, we strongly recommend manufacturing effectiveness as the primary metric for the production area, followed by the tracking of post-bottleneck scrap. Order cycle time is also noted as a key measurement in those companies where fast fulfillment is considered a strategic imperative. While other measurements can certainly be added, these items should form the core of a production measurement system.

Manufacturing Effectiveness

Ideally, the entire system of production should be configured so that the amount of throughput generated by the system is maximized for every hour that the bottleneck operation is used, which is called manufacturing effectiveness. Doing so results in the highest possible profit for the business as a whole, so this should be the key measurement for the production staff to monitor.

A continuing focus on manufacturing effectiveness could, for example, drive the manufacturing staff to engage in the following activities, all of which directly improve manufacturing effectiveness:

- Reduce the amount of out-of-specification raw materials fed into the bottleneck operation, since these items must eventually be scrapped, and therefore waste bottleneck time.

- Add maintenance staff to the bottleneck operation, in order to reduce the amount of time that the equipment is not operational.
- Hire a machine changeover consultant to shorten the time required to change over jobs at the bottleneck operation.

The calculation of manufacturing effectiveness is to divide the total throughput dollars shipped in the period by the number of bottleneck hours used. However, there are some issues to be aware of. For example, if an order is shipped from stock, rather than production, the throughput figure can be artificially elevated. Also, the mix of products scheduled for production can strongly impact the amount of throughput achieved, since jobs with unusually high or low throughput can skew the measurement.

EXAMPLE

The marketing manager of Rapunzel Hair Products runs a 25% off coupon for the company's patented hair straightener product, which results in a tripling of production for this item during July. Unfortunately, the size of the coupon seriously impacts the manufacturing efficiency of the company's production operations during that month, as noted in the following table.

	June	July	August
Throughput dollars shipped	$280,000	$240,000	$251,000
Bottleneck hours used	612	744	558
Manufacturing efficiency	$458/hr	$323/hr	$450/hr

In addition, the heavy demand for the bottleneck operation in July required the company to operate it at nearly 100% utilization, which results in a machine breakdown in August that requires extensive repairs, and an attendant drop in efficiency in that month.

Based on the sharp decline in manufacturing efficiency in July and the consequences in August, the president of Rapunzel orders the marketing manager to clear all coupon deals through her in advance of offering them to the public.

Throughput of Post-Bottleneck Scrap

One of the better ways to improve profitability in a production environment is to impose an intensive focus on the reduction of scrap after the bottleneck operation. The reason is that these scrap items have already used up valuable time at the bottleneck operation, which can never be regained. If the constrained operation has a large amount of throughput passing through it, subsequent scrap can involve an enormous amount of foregone profits. Thus, monitoring the throughput in this scrap should drive management to great lengths to ensure that scrap levels are reduced.

To calculate the amount of post-bottleneck scrap, add up all the bottleneck processing time used by the scrap that was generated after the bottleneck, and multiply this amount by the average throughput per hour of the constrained operation. The formula is:

(Aggregate throughput time in scrapped goods) × (Throughput per hour)

Conversely, any scrap occurring before the bottleneck operation presents a much lower cost to the business, since it never uses any bottleneck time. Accordingly, management should only remediate the cost of this scrap *after* it has attended to all of the scrap issues after the bottleneck.

EXAMPLE

The Atlas Machining Company produces cobalt widgets for a variety of industrial applications. The company's bottleneck is the stamping machine, which generates an average of $1,000 of throughput per hour. In a search for greater profits, the management team institutes an examination of where scrap is located throughout the production process, and the cost of this scrap. The examination produces the following information for the past month of production activity:

Production Process	Material Cost	Throughput Time Used	Throughput Cost	Total Scrap Cost
Material prep	$7,000	0 hours	$0	$7,000
Tempering forge	5,000	0 hours	0	5,000
Polishing	2,000	15 hours	15,000	17,000

The analysis reveals that the operation resulting in the largest total cost to the company is the polishing operation, which is located after the bottleneck. The scrap incurred in the material prep stage does have a high cost in destroyed materials, but is still lower than the foregone profits arising from the polishing stage.

Order Cycle Time

A key competitive point in many business strategies is how quickly the business can fulfill customer orders. An unusually short cycle time for an order can lock in customers who value quick delivery. However, cycle time may not be an issue in cases where the company strategy is to offer a very low price in exchange for a longer wait to receive goods.

To calculate order cycle time, subtract the date of receipt of an order from the ship date of the order. However, this calculation does not factor in any orders that are late for delivery and have not yet been shipped, so also include in the calculation the estimated ship date for these late orders. The resulting formula is:

(Ship date or if late, best estimate of ship date) – order date

This measurement should be presented in two parts, as an aggregated order cycle time for all orders, and also as a detailed report that shows the measurement for each underlying order. This type of presentation allows management to drill down into the supporting information to determine which orders are causing problems, and correct whatever the related problems may be.

A variation on the order cycle time concept is to run it for each individual customer on a trend line, to see if any of the more important customers are suffering from below-standard fulfillment rates. The same approach can be used for product families, to see if certain types of products are more difficult to produce.

EXAMPLE

Sharper Designs is having trouble fulfilling some of its orders for an advanced form of ceramic knife that has achieved cult status among executive chefs. The trouble appears to be cracking in some of the blades, which can only be found through detailed inspection of every knife. Each of the knives scrapped must be replaced from current production, which throws off the shipping schedule.

The production manager calculates an aggregate order cycle time of 4.0 days to fill an order, but then subdivides the information by product family to derive much more troubling results, as noted in the following table.

Product Family	Order Cycle Time	Gross Margin
Steel knives	0.8 days	15%
Tungsten knives	1.2 days	24%
Titanium knives	1.1 days	18%
Ceramic knives	42.5 days	75%

The table shows a massive fulfillment problem for the ceramic knife product family. This is particularly troubling, seeing that the high prices charged for these knives could yield excellent profits for the company – if only the knives could be shipped. This information is the basis for a full-scale assault by management on the production processes used to manufacture ceramic knives.

Procurement Measurements

Cost management in the procurement area centers on the effective use of the purchasing staff to avoid picayune orders and focus on centralized purchasing with a core group of key suppliers. Tracking procurement card usage can assist in keeping the purchasing staff away from small orders, while the measurement of spend dollars managed and the proportion of spend directed to preferred suppliers can help to monitor how well the purchasing staff is being utilized.

Procurement Card Usage Percentage

The use of procurement cards drastically reduces the amount of time required by the purchasing department to create purchase orders, and so should be strongly encouraged for smaller purchases. To track the company's performance in using procurement cards, divide the total number of these transactions below the purchasing card threshold by the total number of purchasing transactions below the card threshold. The card usage threshold typically starts fairly low, at perhaps $250, and then tends to ratchet upward as an organization becomes more accustomed to this form of purchasing.

EXAMPLE

The purchasing manager at Milford Sound has been pleased with the reduced purchasing time spent by her staff since procurement cards were introduced a year ago, but suspects that additional time can be saved. Her particular focus is on shifting 100% of purchases under $500 to these cards. She conducts an analysis of card usage by department, and arrives at the following information:

	Purchases with Procurement Cards	Total Purchases Under $500 Limit	Card Usage Percentage
Accounting	40	43	93%
Engineering	208	212	98%
Maintenance	72	520	14%
Sales and marketing	190	202	94%

The information reveals that the best source of additional time reduction is purchases made by the maintenance department, where the person in charge of the procurement card is clearly not using it very much.

As illustrated in the example, the measure will typically reveal that a specific card user is not employing the card to its full effect. Once corrected, there tend to be only a few residual transactions for which procurement cards are not used.

Proportion of Spend Managed

An active procurement program should aggregate all purchasing information by type of commodity purchased, and gradually work through these commodities, concentrating purchases with a smaller number of suppliers to gain volume discounts. As the spending for each commodity is reviewed and improved upon, the company should create a monitoring infrastructure to ensure that the improvements made will continue, thereby ensuring continuing reduced costs. To monitor the amount of this active spend management, the procurement manager should receive a measurement for the proportion of spend managed. The calculation is to divide the total spend on commodities under active management by the total amount of company spend.

It is entirely possible that some portions of company spend are so minor or difficult to manage that the company will never achieve 100% spend management. At some point below the 100% level, the procurement manager will likely find that assigning more staff to spend management is not a cost-effective proposition, and will cease further efforts in this area.

EXAMPLE

The purchasing manager of Armadillo Industries initiated a spend management program several months ago, and wants to start tracking his progress toward a higher level of active spend management. The company is in the business of manufacturing body armor, protective shielding, and high-pressure containers (such as submarine hulls). This complex business contains many commodity types, so the manager has been focusing on the top commodities on which the company spends money. His analysis of spend being actively managed so far is as follows:

NAICS Code	Commodity Area	(000s) Spend	Percent of Total Spend	Cumulative Spend Percentage
332111	Iron and steel forging	$90,000	18.0%	18.0%
331523	Nonferrous metal die-casting	12,000	2.4%	20.4%
332114	Custom roll forming	42,000	8.4%	29.2%
332119	Metal stamping	4,500	0.9%	30.1%
332313	Plate work manufacturing	7,800	1.6%	31.7%
332912	Fluid power valves	3,900	0.8%	32.5%
332613	Spring manufacturing	1,800	0.4%	**32.9%**

The table reveals clear progress toward a high level of active spend management, with nearly a third of all spend now being closely monitored.

Proportion of Spend with Preferred Suppliers

The use of preferred suppliers is the best way not only to obtain volume purchase discounts, but also to buy from those suppliers proven to have the best product quality, delivery times, and other services and terms considered important to the buyer. There are several ways to measure the amount of total spend going to preferred suppliers. Consider the following alternatives:

- Do so in aggregate, as a single percentage. This is most useful when reporting high-level performance information to management.
- Do so by commodity type. This approach shows where commodities are actively being managed, since close observation of a commodity tends to lead to significant supplier concentration.

- Do so by business unit. This approach shows the commitment to purchasing management, and can lead to the revamping of purchasing departments where the use of preferred suppliers is negligible.

EXAMPLE

The vice president of procurement at Electronic Inference Corporation is pushing for the redirection of spend to a small group of preferred suppliers. He elects to aggregate preferred supplier information at the business unit level, which results in the following information:

(000s)	Spend with Preferred Suppliers	Total Spend	Proportion of Spend with Preferred Suppliers
Atomic computing division	$17,890	$21,200	84%
Calculators division	5,230	38,100	14%
Memory chip fabrication division	81,000	96,500	84%
National security computing division	58,280	60,800	96%
Totals	$162,400	$216,600	75%

The vice president finds that, despite an overall excellent 75% spend rate with preferred suppliers, the calculators division is far behind the other business units, which presents a large opportunity for further improvement.

Administration Measurements

The administration area is generally viewed as a cost center, not a profit center. If management follows this view, then the first two measurements in this section will support their cost control efforts, comparing administration costs to the general level of corporate activity. The third measurement is designed to track errors, which consumes a notable part of the total administration expense.

Administration FTEs per $1,000,000 Revenue

Administration inherently requires a considerable amount of headcount. Since employee compensation tends to increase faster than the rate of inflation, headcount is clearly an area of concern to anyone managing costs. Comparing revenue to headcount is a reasonable way to determine the adequacy of a company's investment in this area. The comparison should reveal an initial spike in headcount when a business is starting up, since a minimum amount of staffing will be required.

A key element in the calculation is the full-time equivalent (FTE) concept, which is the equivalent number of employees who are working full-time (that is, a 40-hour week). For example, if two employees each work 20 hours per week, that is considered one full-time equivalent. If a business has a large proportion of part-time staff, the FTE concept can make a substantial difference in the calculation of administrative staff to revenue.

The calculation of administrative FTEs per $1,000,000 of revenue is described in the following example.

EXAMPLE

Milagro Corporation employs 44 staff in its corporate, accounting, and treasury departments, many working on a part-time basis. In January, this group worked 3,360 hours. Since there were 168 working hours in January, the calculation of FTEs for this period is:

$$3,360 \text{ hours worked} \div 168 \text{ hours} = 20 \text{ FTEs}$$

Milagro had annualized sales of $20,000,000 in January, so the calculation of administration FTEs per $1,000,000 of revenue is:

$$\frac{\$20,000,000 \text{ Sales}}{20 \text{ FTEs}} = 1 \text{ FTE per } \$1,000,000 \text{ revenue}$$

Administration Cost as Percent of Revenue

A reasonable way to evaluate the administrative cost of a business is to compile all administrative costs and calculate their percentage of net revenues, and then compare this percentage to the same information for competitors and best-in-class organizations. A further step after making this comparison is to drill down into the reasons for any significant variance between the company's percentage and the comparison entities, and then take action to adjust the administration expenses.

EXAMPLE

Lethal Sushi caters to the high-risk crowd that wants to sample the more dangerous types of fish. The company charges a high price to customers in exchange for the extra effort required to obtain these more toxic fish, and is also on the receiving end of lawsuits by a few next of kin, who are suing on behalf of those who encountered some poison in their plates. The CFO of Lethal wants to compare the administrative costs of the business to those of its competitors, but must first strip away the outsized legal costs of the business, which are skewing the results. The calculation is:

Revenues	$12,000,000
Accounting expenses	180,000
Corporate expenses	340,000
Facility expenses	420,000
Legal expenses	Not applicable
Total administration expenses	$940,000

The administration cost as a percent of revenue is 7.8%, which is calculated as $940,000 of administration costs, divided by revenues of $12,000,000.

A danger in using this measurement is to assume that the company's use of administrative activities is similar to how they are used by other businesses, when in fact the company's strategy may mandate either a bare bones, low-cost administrative function or the reverse.

The administration cost as a percent of revenues should decline as revenues increase, since a business should be able to take advantage of efficiencies as it grows. However, this may not be the case if administrative activities are not centralized, as happens when there are many retail locations, or a company grows by acquiring other businesses.

Transaction Error Rate

It is critical to avoid transaction errors, since the cost of correcting them is several multiples of the cost of initially completing them correctly. Consequently, one of the better metrics is to monitor the transaction error rate. The error rate should be reviewed in conjunction with the total number of transactions processed by each person, in order to ascertain whether certain individuals cause more errors.

To formulate the transaction error rate, add up all transaction-related errors in a reporting period and divide them by the total number of transactions completed within the same reporting period. This calculation should match transactional errors to the pool of the same types of transactions completed, which will result in a separate error rate for each general type of transaction.

EXAMPLE

The senior accounting clerk of the Divine Gelato Company wants to reduce the amount of staff time spent correcting transactional errors. She has derived the following information for the last reporting period:

Processes	No. of Errors	No. of Total Transactions	Transaction Error Rate
Billing transactions	175	1,390	12.6%
Cash receipt transactions	28	3,010	0.9%
Payable transactions	200	1,720	11.6%

The most egregious error rate is in the billing transactions area, with payable transactions coming in a close second. The senior clerk realizes that the effort needed to correct errors in the payables area is much greater than in the billing area, so she elects to focus her process improvement efforts in the payables area in order to most rapidly reduce the total amount of staff time spent on error corrections.

Facilities Measurements

Our focus in this section is on the utilization and cost of facilities. The first recommended metric is square feet per person, which is most effective in high-headcount environments, while the following cost per square foot measurement is applicable to all facilities.

Square Feet per Person

The measurement of square feet per person places an emphasis on arranging a work space to maximize space utilization, especially during the initial layout phase for a facility. Likely outcomes of using this measurement are shifting storage space offsite, increased use of cubicles, and the reduction of "dead space" that serves no useful purpose. The following issues can impact this measurement:

- *Hoteling.* If a company transitions some staff to common-usage areas that they are assigned upon arrival, there is an open question regarding how to incorporate what may be quite a large number of hoteling employees into the calculation.
- *Part time staff.* A part-time staff person still fills a cubicle, so unless several people are using the same office space in sequence, it is probably best to consider a part-time person a full-time employee for the purposes of calculating square feet per person.
- *Work at home part time.* Many employees work from home for a portion of the week, but still retain their office space. If so, continue to count anyone as a full-time, on-site employee if he or she retains exclusive use of a work space.

Based on these issues, we suggest the following measurement for square feet per person:

$$\frac{\text{Total facility square footage} - \text{Hoteling square footage}}{\text{Total number of employees} - \text{Hoteling employees}}$$

In essence, that portion of the facility used for hoteling is stripped away from the calculation, leaving only that portion of the facility that is regularly used by non-hoteling employees.

EXAMPLE

New Centurion Corporation translates Latin texts for its university clients. There is an on-site staff of translators that work primarily from cubicles, while a number of visiting scholars are assigned space in a common area under a hoteling arrangement. There are also part-time translators that are assigned their own office space on a permanent basis. Management wants to understand the space utilization of the facility, and so compiles the following information:

Total square footage	20,000
Square footage of hoteling common area	5,000
Number of on-site full-time staff	38
Number of on-site part-time staff	12

Based on this information, square feet per person is calculated as:

$$\frac{20{,}000 \text{ Total square footage} - 5{,}000 \text{ Hoteling square footage}}{38 \text{ Full-time staff} + 12 \text{ Part-time staff}}$$

$$= 300 \text{ Square feet per person}$$

This measurement is most useful in an employee-intensive environment, and much less so where most of the square footage is taken up by retail, production, training, or storage space.

Cost per Square Foot

An excellent way to measure the cost of any facility is to aggregate all rent, maintenance, and utility costs for it and then divide by the square footage of the facility to derive the cost per square foot. This information can be used to compare the cost of the facility to alternative forms of housing elsewhere in the area. The result may be a switch to a facility with a lower aggregate cost per square foot.

This measurement does not track the usage level of a facility, only its total cost. Thus, even an inexpensive facility could be shut down if its usage level is minimal.

EXAMPLE

Kelvin Corporation's CFO is reviewing information regarding the possible lease of replacement office space for the company. The company's current facility contains 20,000 square feet, and the company pays its share of utility and maintenance costs, as well as for the rental of parking spaces for employees. The proposed replacement facility contains 25,000 square feet and has the same cost sharing arrangement, except that parking is free. The relevant information is noted in the following table.

	Current Facility	Proposed Facility
Square footage	20,000	25,000
Total rent	$340,000	$400,000
Utilities and maintenance cost	52,000	60,000
Parking fees	28,000	0
Total cost	$420,000	$460,000
Cost per square foot	$21.00	$18.40

Based on the total cost of these facilities, it initially appears that the company should retain the current facility. However, the lower cost per square foot of the larger facility could make it more attractive if the company expects to add staff during the lease term, or can sublease the excess space.

This measurement does not factor in the duration of a lease agreement, which could be a critical factor. For example, if there is a choice between a long-term lease at a very low rate per square foot and a short-term lease at a much higher rate, it may still make sense to enter into the short-term lease, to give the company the option in the near term to shift its operations elsewhere.

Finance Measurements

Finance is one of the more difficult areas to measure, because the wrong metric can lead to the wrong behavior, such as investing in high-risk securities in pursuit of higher earnings on invested income. Instead, we simply propose that the amount of cash being invested be tracked, rather than the return on investment. Also, we suggest tracking the relative rate of interest on debt, to encourage behavior that may drive down the cost of debt.

Proportion of Cash Invested

When a business' cash is stored in a variety of bank accounts, there should be a measurement that tracks the proportion of this cash that is routinely shifted into some form of investment instrument. The emphasis is less on the interest rate achieved, and more on ensuring that some type of investment activity is occurring. If a return on investment metric were to be used, this might trigger an inappropriate action to place excess cash in riskier investments. Thus, we advise de-emphasizing return on investment, or at least not tying it to a bonus plan.

EXAMPLE

Hegemony Toy Company operates a chain of retail stores, each of which has its own operating account with a branch of the First United Bank. The CFO finds that none of these accounts have been set up for cash sweeping or notional pooling, which would allow for the centralized management of cash. Accordingly, he arranges with First United to set up a cash sweeping arrangement, which will automatically move all funds over $5,000 in all of the retail accounts into a central investment account. He sets up the following measurement to track the rollout of the cash sweeping system by geographic region:

| | Number of Accounts Not Yet in Cash Sweeping Arrangement | | | |
	Quarter 1	Quarter 2	Quarter 3	Quarter 4
Northeast	42	36	14	2
Southeast	57	41	23	8
Central	95	60	35	18
Mountain West	83	84	88	93

The table shows that First United is working its way through the company's retail bank accounts, setting up the cash sweep arrangement on the east coast first and working its way west. The Mountain West region's cash sweep has not yet been implemented, as evidenced by the increasing number of accounts not affected by the arrangement (and reflecting the opening of new stores in that region).

The preceding example emphasized the number of bank accounts not under active cash management, which is the easiest way to address the measurement. A more complex approach is to aggregate the cash in these accounts to determine the amount of cash currently not being managed; doing so gives a better idea of the amount of investment income being lost.

Average Interest Rate Paid in Excess of Prime Rate

When it is necessary to incur debt, tracking the interest rate paid makes little sense, since the rate is largely dependent on the market interest rate, rather than anything under the control of the business. However, it may make more sense to track the difference between the rate paid and the prime rate, since this difference is an indicator of two items:

- The lender's perceived risk of the company in comparison to the lender's prime customers; and
- The concentration of lending business with a single lender

Both of these issues are at least somewhat under the control of the company, particularly the latter item. Thus, it would be reasonable for a business to use this measurement as the basis for a drive to concentrate its borrowings with a single lender in order to drive down the interest rate charged.

EXAMPLE

Albatross Flight Systems currently borrows from five different lenders in order to pay for the commuter planes that it flies. Albatross pays an average of 3% over the prime rate with this group, as noted in the following table.

Lender Name	Loan Outstanding	Rate over Prime
First Bank	$13,000,000	3.3%
Flight Bank	6,500,000	3.1%
Federal United Bank	3,900,000	2.8%
Commercial United	4,750,000	3.0%
Commercial Industrial	9,200,000	2.9%
Total	$37,350,000	

Albatross' CFO is interested in consolidating these loans in exchange for a reduced interest rate, and finds that Federal United Bank is interested in taking on all the debt at the current rate it charges, which is 2.8% over prime. This represents a $74,700 interest expense reduction per year.

Asset Measurements

The management of assets is all about how intensively they are used, which means that all three of our recommended assets involve turnover – of receivables, inventory, and fixed assets. The fixed asset turnover metric is not commonly used, but we recommend it in order to focus attention on one of the largest expenditure line items that many businesses must deal with.

Receivables Turnover

Accounts receivable turnover measures the ability of a company to efficiently issue credit to its customers and collect it back in a timely manner. A high turnover ratio indicates a combination of a conservative credit policy and an aggressive collections department, while a low turnover ratio represents an opportunity to collect excessively old accounts receivable that are unnecessarily tying up working capital. Low receivable turnover may be caused by a loose or nonexistent credit policy, or an inadequate collections function.

To calculate receivables turnover, divide average receivables into the total amount of net annual credit sales. The formula is:

$$\frac{\text{Net annual credit sales}}{\text{Average receivables}}$$

The result of this calculation can be divided into 365 days to arrive at days of receivables on hand, which may be a more understandable figure. Thus, a turnover rate of 8.0 becomes 46 days of receivables.

EXAMPLE

The controller of Hammer Industries wants to determine the company's accounts receivable turnover for the past year. In the beginning of this period, the accounts receivable balance was $316,000, and the ending balance was $384,000, for an average receivable balance of $350,000. Net credit sales for the last 12 months were $3,500,000. Based on this information, the controller calculates the accounts receivable turnover as:

$$\frac{\$3,500,000 \text{ Net credit sales}}{\$350,000 \text{ Average receivables}} = 10 \text{ Turns per year}$$

The 10 turns figure is then divided into 365 days to arrive at 36.5 days of receivables.

Inventory Turnover

The inventory turnover ratio is defined as the rate at which inventory is used over a measurement period. This ratio is used to judge the relative amount of the inventory asset that a company is maintaining. Inventory turnover is typically measured on a trend line or in comparison to the industry average to judge performance.

When there is a low rate of inventory turnover, this implies that a business may have a flawed purchasing system that bought too many goods, or that stocks were increased in anticipation of sales that did not occur. In both cases, there is a high risk of inventory aging. When there is a high rate of inventory turnover, this implies that the purchasing function is tightly managed. However, it may also mean that a business does not have the cash reserves to maintain normal inventory levels, and so is turning away prospective sales.

To calculate inventory turnover, divide the ending inventory figure into the annualized cost of sales. If the ending inventory figure is not a representative number, then use an average figure instead. The formula is:

$$\frac{\text{Annual cost of goods sold}}{\text{Inventory}}$$

The result of this calculation can be divided into 365 days to arrive at days of inventory on hand, which may be a more understandable figure. Thus, a turnover rate of 4.0 becomes 91 days of inventory.

EXAMPLE

The Hegemony Toy Company is reviewing its inventory levels. The related information is $8,150,000 of cost of goods sold in the past year, and ending inventory of $1,630,000. Total inventory turnover is calculated as:

$$\frac{\$8,150,000 \text{ Cost of goods sold}}{\$1,630,000 \text{ Inventory}} = 5 \text{ Turns per year}$$

The five turns figure is then divided into 365 days to arrive at 73 days of inventory on hand.

Fixed Asset Turnover

The fixed asset turnover ratio is the ratio of net sales to net fixed assets. A high ratio indicates that a company is doing an effective job of generating sales with a relatively small amount of fixed assets. Conversely, if the ratio is declining over time, the company has either overinvested in fixed assets or it needs to issue new products to revive its sales. Another possible effect is for a company to make a large investment in fixed assets, with a time delay before the new assets start generating revenues.

EXAMPLE

Subtract accumulated depreciation from gross fixed assets, and divide into net annual sales. It may be necessary to obtain an average fixed asset figure, if the amount varies significantly over time. Do not include intangible assets in the denominator, since it can skew the results. The formula is:

$$\frac{\text{Net annual sales}}{\text{Gross fixed assets} - \text{Accumulated depreciation}}$$

Grubstake Brothers has gross fixed assets of $5,000,000 and accumulated depreciation of $2,000,000. Sales over the last 12 months totaled $9,000,000. The calculation of Grubstake's fixed asset turnover ratio is:

$$\frac{\$9,000,000 \text{ Net sales}}{\$5,000,000 \text{ Gross fixed assets} - \$2,000,000 \text{ Accumulated depreciation}}$$

$$= 3.0 \text{ Fixed asset turnover}$$

The fixed asset turnover ratio is most useful in "heavy industry," such as automobile manufacturing, where a large capital investment is required in order to do business. In other industries, such as software development, the fixed asset investment is so meager that the ratio is not of much use.

A potential problem with this ratio may arise if a company uses accelerated depreciation, since this artificially reduces the amount of net fixed assets in the denominator of the calculation, and makes turnover appear higher than it should be. Also, ongoing depreciation of any kind will inevitably reduce the amount of the denominator, so the turnover ratio will rise over time unless the company is investing an equivalent amount in new fixed assets to replace older ones.

Summary

The measurements presented in this chapter are by no means the only ones that a management team may want to review, but they can be considered among the core metrics to be used in any organization that wishes to closely manage its costs. However, it will likely be necessary to enhance the set of measurements used over time, as continual attention to the results of these measurements will likely lead to a stopping point at which no further cost management progress can be made. At that point, additional metrics will probably need to be added that are used to monitor other aspects of the business. Thus, the appropriate set of measurements will vary over time, depending on the objectives of management.

Glossary

A

A-B testing. A method for altering messages to customers to see which version maximizes customer response.

B

Bill of materials. A record of the materials used to construct a product.

Bottleneck. An operation that impedes the ability of a process to generate goods or services.

Breakeven point. The sales level at which a business earns a zero profit.

Budgetary slack. When managers deliberately under-estimate the revenues that will be generated, or over-estimate the amount of expenses that will be incurred during a budget period.

C

Capital expenditure. A payment made to acquire or upgrade an asset. A capital expenditure is recorded as an asset, not an expense.

Capitalization limit. The threshold beyond which expenditures may be classified as fixed assets.

Cash sweeping. The process of automatically moving excess cash from one bank account and into a central deposit account.

Check sheet. A method for quickly recording observed results in a grid format.

Co-pay. A requirement to pay a specific dollar amount when obtaining health-related services or drugs.

Collateral. An asset that a borrower has pledged as security for a loan. The lender has the legal right to seize and sell the asset if the borrower is unable to pay back the loan by an agreed date.

Collection agency. A third party hired by a seller or lender to recover funds that are past due.

Committed cost. An obligation or investment that has already been made, and which cannot be undone.

Conditional budgeting. When expenditures are made only after certain targeted revenue levels are attained.

Constraint. A bottleneck that caps the amount of output that can be generated.

Contribution margin. Sales minus all variable costs associated with those sales.

Cost object. An item for which a cost is compiled, such as a product service, project, customer, or activity.

Credit insurance. A guarantee by a third party against non-payment of an invoice by a customer.

Cross docking. The process of shifting goods from an incoming truck to an outgoing truck for delivery to the customer.

Cycle counting. The process of counting a small portion of the inventory on an ongoing basis to detect and correct errors.

D

Differential cost. The difference between the cost of two alternative decisions, or of a change in output levels.

Direct costing. A costing methodology that only assigns direct labor and material costs to a product or other cost object; it does not assign any indirect costs to a product or other cost object.

Discount rate. The interest rate used to discount a stream of future cash flows to their present value. Depending upon the application, typical rates used as the discount rate are a firm's cost of capital or the current market rate.

Discretionary cost. A cost that can be curtailed or eliminated in the short term without having an immediate impact on short-term output.

Drop shipping. The practice of having a supplier ship goods directly to a customer.

Dunning letter. A letter sent to a debtor, requesting payment of a receivable.

E

Early payment discount. A discount allowed to customers if they pay an invoice within a certain period of time.

Engineering change order. A document authorizing design changes that affect the structure of a product.

Evaluated receipts. The payment of suppliers based on production volumes, rather than invoices.

F

Factoring. An arrangement where a financing company takes over a company's accounts receivable in exchange for an immediate cash payment.

Fixed cost. A cost that does not vary in the short term, irrespective of changes in activity levels.

Full-time equivalent. The hours worked by a full-time employee, even if those hours are actually worked by several part-time employees.

G

Garnishment. A court order that requires a third party to remit funds normally payable to an individual to a creditor of the individual.

H

Health maintenance organization. An organization that provides health services to the employees of a contracting entity.

Hedging. A risk reduction technique whereby an entity uses a derivative or similar instrument to offset future changes in the fair value or cash flows of an asset or liability.

High-low method. A method used to identify the fixed and variable components of a mixed cost.

Hoteling. The concept of assigning open seating to employees as needed.

I

Incremental cost. The extra cost associated with manufacturing one additional unit of production, or the cost that will change as the result of a decision.

K

Kaizen costing. The process of continual cost reduction that occurs after a product design has been completed and is now in production.

Kanban. An authorization to produce more goods.

L

Lockbox. A mailbox operated by a bank, which opens mail sent by a company's customers and deposits the contents into the account of the company.

M

Margin of safety. The reduction in sales that can occur before the breakeven point of a business is reached.

Marginal cost. The cost of one additional unit of output.

Maverick spending. Unauthorized spending by employees, usually to unauthorized suppliers.

Mixed cost. A cost that contains both fixed and variable cost components.

N

NAICS. An acronym for the North American Industry Classification System, which classifies a wide range of industries by a unique code, and which is commonly used for spend analysis.

Negative approval. The concept of paying all supplier invoices unless an invoice is specifically disapproved.

Notional pooling. To concentrate cash in a bank on a notional basis for investment purposes, without actually shifting any cash between accounts.

O

Overtime. A multiplier that is added to an employee's base wage for hours worked over 40 hours in a work week.

P

Payroll cycle. The length of time between payrolls.

Perpetual inventory system. The continual updating of inventory records to account for additions to and subtractions from inventory.

Pro forma. Financial statements that incorporate assumptions or hypothetical conditions regarding either past or future events.

Procurement card. A credit card used by employees to purchase goods and services on behalf of the business that pays for the card.

Production cell. A cluster of machines used to process a part.

Purchase order. An authorization from a buyer, for a supplier to deliver specified goods or services at the price, quality level, delivery date, and other terms specified in the agreement.

Purchase requisition. A form on which an employee requests that specific goods or services be ordered from a third party.

R

Real property. Land and any property attached to land, such as buildings.

Remote deposit capture. The process of digitizing a check and sending the digitized image to a bank as an electronic deposit transaction.

Root cause analysis. A method for examining and correcting the reasons for an error or other undesirable condition.

Run chart. A table on which is plotted the observed results of a process.

S

Safety stock. Excess inventory that acts as a buffer between forecasted and actual demand levels.

Sales channel. A method for selling goods and services to customers, such as through retail stores, catalogues, and Internet stores.

Sales mix variance. The difference between actual and planned sales.

Spend management. The aggregation of purchasing information to determine the commodity classifications in which a company is expending funds, and using the information to concentrate purchases with a preferred group of suppliers.

Step cost. A cost that changes at discrete points, rather than in direct proportion to changes in activity levels.

Stock option. The right to purchase a certain number of shares at a specific price not later than a designated date.

Sublease. The lease of a property where the lessor has a primary lease obligation on the property.

Sunk cost. A cost that has been incurred, and which can no longer be recovered by any means.

T

Target costing. A system under which a business plans in advance for the product price points, product costs, and margins that it wants to achieve.

Three-way matching. The comparison of a supplier invoice, purchase order, and receiving documents to ensure that the prices and quantities billed are correct.

Throughput. Revenues minus totally variable costs.

V

Vacation carryover. The right to carry forward unused accrued vacation for use in a future period.

Value stream map. A method used to document the flow of information in a process.

Variable cost. A cost that varies in relation to changes in production or other activity volume.

W

Workers' compensation insurance. An insurance policy purchased by a business that provides coverage for payments to employees who become ill or are injured while working for the company.

Working capital. The amount of an entity's current assets minus its current liabilities. It is considered a prime measure of the liquidity of a business.

Z

Zero-base budgeting. A budgeting process where a complete analysis is made of the need for expenditures in a budget period.

Index

304

www.ingramcontent.com/pod-product-compliance
Lightning Source LLC
Chambersburg PA
CBHW080512220326
41599CB00032B/6058